IN TREES

An Exploration

ROBERT MOOR

SIMON & SCHUSTER
New York   Amsterdam/Antwerp   London
Toronto   Sydney/Melbourne   New Delhi

Simon & Schuster
1230 Avenue of the Americas
New York, NY 10020

For more than 100 years, Simon & Schuster has championed authors and the stories they create. By respecting the copyright of an author's intellectual property, you enable Simon & Schuster and the author to continue publishing exceptional books for years to come. We thank you for supporting the author's copyright by purchasing an authorized edition of this book.

No amount of this book may be reproduced or stored in any format, nor may it be uploaded to any website, database, language-learning model, or other repository, retrieval, or artificial intelligence system without express permission. All rights reserved. Inquiries may be directed to Simon & Schuster, 1230 Avenue of the Americas, New York, NY 10020 or permissions@simonandschuster.com.

Copyright © 2026 by Robert Moor

All rights reserved, including the right to reproduce this book or portions thereof in any form whatsoever. For information, address Simon & Schuster Subsidiary Rights Department, 1230 Avenue of the Americas, New York, NY 10020.

First Simon & Schuster hardcover edition April 2026

SIMON & SCHUSTER and colophon are registered trademarks of Simon & Schuster, LLC

Simon & Schuster strongly believes in freedom of expression and stands against censorship in all its forms. For more information, visit BooksBelong.com.

For information about special discounts for bulk purchases, please contact Simon & Schuster Special Sales at 1-866-506-1949 or business@simonandschuster.com.

The Simon & Schuster Speakers Bureau can bring authors to your live event. For more information or to book an event, contact the Simon & Schuster Speakers Bureau at 1-866-248-3049 or visit our website at www.simonspeakers.com.

Manufactured in the United States of America

1 3 5 7 9 10 8 6 4 2

Library of Congress Cataloging-in-Publication Data is available.

ISBN 978-1-4767-3925-0
ISBN 978-1-4767-3928-1 (ebook)

*"Cosimo looked at the world from the tree:
everything was different seen from up there..."*

—Italo Calvino

T.O.C.
(Tree of Contents)

PROLOGUE: SKY
1

1. BRANCHING   2. PRUNING   3. ASCENDING   4. GNARLING
19   47   85   128

5. SHADOWING   6. STEMMING
172   218

7. RESISTING
262

8. ROOTING
309

EPILOGUE: SOIL
365

IN TREES

PROLOGUE: SKY

Think of a tree.

Now, let your thoughts expand.

First, consider all of the trees that are not "trees." Consider your family tree. Consider the evolutionary tree of life. Consider a branch of science, its sub-branches and sub-sub-branches. Consider a lightning bolt, a river system, the blue veins in your forearms, the red threads in the whites of your eyes. Consider the billions of neurons strung through the pink-gray meat of your own brain, a tangled forest of cells flickering with electricity even as you read this sentence.

A tree is not just a thing made up of bark and leaves and sap and wood. At its core, a tree is not even really a noun. It is more like a verb. A tree is what a tree does. It is hard for us to perceive this fact, however, because most of the time, a tree does what it does so slowly. A mature oak tree, which might live for one thousand years, appears to be as unchanging as a mountain. But if we could watch the full life cycle of an oak play out in a few seconds, it would look as violent as a fireworks display: A single green tendril slithers up from the shell of an acorn and thrusts itself through the soil; it unfurls tiny leaves, then it sprouts branches; and then those branches branch, and branch, and branch again. Some branches starve away or are torn off—pruned by wind, rain, ice, fire, pests, disease, and the gravitational pull of the earth itself—while others thicken and strengthen. Upward this thing (this process) erupts, until, in its final days, just before it comes crashing back down to earth, a keen botanist would be able to read it like a book, gleaning its entire history from its shape alone.

A tree, in other words, is not only a living being. It is also a *way of being*. Put very simply, that way of being—what philosophers call arborescence—consists of three simultaneous processes: branching, pruning, and gnarling. The result is something inventive, exacting, and long-lasting. Something wise.

+

I began writing this book not long after moving to the woods. In 2013, the man who would later become my husband and I relocated from an apartment in New York City to a cabin in a provincial forest in British Columbia. Our new home was surrounded by trees, like a toy castle submerged in an aquarium—a swaying green mass of cedars, Douglas firs, maples, alders, and yews. In New York, trees had resided in the blurry periphery of my daily life, mere ornamentation for the cityscape, but in the forest, they suddenly leapt into focus. There was one tree in particular, a monstrous big-leaf maple growing stubbornly on the side of a cliff that I once spent the better part of an hour lying beneath, gazing up into its branches in a state of soft, lucent awe.

It reminded me a bit of another grand tree I'd once known. In my early twenties, I had lived for a few months in a monastery that was a short walk from the Bodhi tree, beneath which the Buddha is said to have attained enlightenment. The tree—in truth, a descendant of the original Bodhi tree, which died millennia ago—was a huge ficus with low crooked pale arms propped up by metal crutches, like some kind of decrepit extraterrestrial. Each day dozens, sometimes hundreds, of pilgrims gathered around it. I loved to sit and watch them perform their various rituals of respect. When approaching, some pilgrims got down on their knees and touched their foreheads to the ground three times. Others laid offerings of marigolds and buffalo milk at its base. A few performed a grueling ritual known in Tibetan as *chag-tsel*—stretching themselves out face down on the hot marble paving stones, rising to their feet, and then lying flat again, repeating this act for days or even weeks on end. The Buddha apparently wanted it this way. *Don't worship a statue of me*, he'd told his followers. *If you must worship anything, worship a tree.*

Trees seem to naturally absorb devotion, just as they draw water from the soil. Holy trees, fiercely guarded from harm, can be found on every continent except Antarctica. The authors of the Bible and the Quran portrayed trees as celestial symbols, as have Hindus, Jains, and the thousands of diverse cultures we rather crudely lump together as "animist." In Cambodia, during the nightmarish rule of the Khmer Rouge, religious practices of any kind were banned, under pain of death. Nevertheless, one man who grew up outside Siem Reap told me that his parents would regularly sneak out to the forest behind their home and pray to the ancestral spirits that were believed to dwell in certain old trees. This form of animist worship has been taking place there for an unfathomably long time. It survived the arrival of Hinduism, and then Buddhism, and then communism, and it persists to this day.

Even nonbelievers sacralize trees. My mother, a lapsed Episcopalian, never forced me to go to church, but she took me for long Sunday walks through the patches of relict forest in our "leafy" little suburb in Illinois, and she packed me off to a summer camp called Pine Island each June. Nearly all the kids I knew were raised like this. The explosion of nature worship in the late 1960s had diffused over the decades into a kind of cosmic background radiation. Instead of illustrated copies of the Bible, our parents read us *The Lorax* and *The Giving Tree*. In this new natural theology, trees were our saints: We were taught that they selflessly sucked up the poisons we pumped into the sky and gave us back food and lumber and shade and sweet air to breathe. To my young mind, the felling of an old-growth forest was a greater tragedy than the destruction of a cathedral. (A church, after all, can be rebuilt, whereas, per the old poem, "only God can make a tree.")

Why, I wondered, do trees maintain this mythic hold over our collective imagination? Where, ultimately, does their power lie? It's odd, when one stops to think about it. In one sense, they are nothing more than very big plants. And yet they affect us as no other plant does.

After a few years living in the forest, I set out to write a book about our cultural entanglement with trees. Much had already been published about how humans have altered trees over the millennia, transforming them into houses and food, battleships and books, medicines and poisons. Instead, what I wanted to write about was *how trees transform us*: how they have shaped our sense of nature and time, self and other, life and nonlife. This relationship predates the very dawn of our species. Our apelike ancestors once spent their entire lives scampering around in the canopy; they were fed by trees, housed by trees, and, occasionally—with the slip of a hand or the shedding of a branch—killed by trees. Perhaps, I thought, this is why from time to time we still find ourselves regarding these vast, silent beings in our midst with a curious mix of awe and confusion, as if gazing up at ancient gods whose names we'd long ago forgotten.

As I delved deeper into the history and biology of trees, an odd thing happened: The halo around them gradually faded, and something more complicated emerged. Some trees share food and messages beneath the soil, but others emit poison to kill off their neighbors. One species in the Panamanian rainforest, known as the choibá, appears to have evolved an unusually tall crown so it can attract lightning bolts, which it absorbs and then channels to other nearby trees; in the aftermath of a thunderstorm, the surrounding trees eventually die off, but the choibá thrives. The Bodhi tree, that great symbol of peace, is especially murderous: Ficuses begin their lives as parasitic seeds in the crowns of other trees, then they send their roots downward, slowly ripping their host apart. The Quran speaks of an Edenic tree of life, but also of the tree of Zaqqum, which stands at the center of hell. In the Deep South, where generation after generation of my ancestors lived and died, an old oak provides cool summer shade, but it also recalls a sinister history of lynchings.

One day in the course of my research I ran across a study showing that Canada's trees—especially the fast-growing conifer plantations that had largely replaced diverse old-growth forests—had taken a cruel turn. As they burned in wildfires and rotted due to pest outbreaks, they were releasing more carbon into the atmosphere than they absorbed. A few years later, it was found that large swathes of the Amazon basin, due to increasing wildfires and deforestation, had become a net carbon source, rather than a carbon sink. We had transformed the "lungs of the earth" into smokestacks.

The human world, too, seemed to be poised on the brink of catastrophic change. While I read book after book about trees, my attention was pulled away from my work by news of the pandemic, of wars, of political upheavals. In the summer and fall, as ever larger wildfires swept through the forests of Canada and tear gas filled the streets of far-off cities, I would occasionally glance up from my desk to take in the weird Venusian atmosphere—the clouds a nicotine yellow, the sun a droplet of fresh blood—and think: *What the hell am I even doing?*

Before the Second World War, the German playwright Bertolt Brecht wrote that, when one is living through a turbulent moment in history, it is "almost a crime" to "talk about trees" for in doing so "we maintain our silence about so much wrongdoing." As I wrote this book—as bombs fell and delusions spread and the fires continued to grow—I felt the acid truth of these words eating away at my resolve. Spending all day thinking about trees, secluded in my quiet little patch of forest, sometimes felt like averting my gaze from a world I'd rather not see. As Brecht knew all too well, it is far easier to go for a walk in the woods than it is to stop monsters from marching to power.

Eventually, the book I thought I was writing crumbled to loam. Then, in one of those quiet miracles common to the creative process, it regrew in a new form. I came to see trees as something more than plants; I recognized them as a source of wisdom, a pattern of flourishing, an answer to chaos, which extends from mossy glades to the hard corners of the metropolis.

Brecht was right: In times like these, we should not just talk about trees. We should listen to them.

+

My first inkling that a tree might be wiser than it seems began with a single crooked neuron—a mysterious little squiggle no more than a few thousandths of an inch long.

It was a spring afternoon, and I was in the office of a neuroscientist named Jeff Lichtman at Harvard. He was renowned for creating finely detailed maps of the brain's "connectome"—the way that one brain cell links to the next, and the next, and the next, and how that all joins up to form the human intellect.

One of the most surprising findings of his research, Lichtman told me, was how inelegant the mammalian brain is, structurally speaking. Scientists had assumed that, for the sake of efficiency, neurons would find the shortest distance between two points. However, when Lichtman began measuring the length of the axons in the brain of a mouse, he found that some were as much as 25 percent longer than they needed to be—a startling waste of precious space.

He tilted his computer monitor toward me and pulled up a digital image of one tiny sector of a mouse brain. With his finger, he traced the course of a neural branch as it took a wide, loopy detour on the way to its destination.

I wondered: *Does my brain also look like that?*

Lichtman assured me it did. Indeed, in scanning human brains, he would later discover even more inefficient brain cells—called "whorls"—that circle back on themselves, growing in tangled knots.

"But why would a neuron take a *less* efficient route?" I asked.

He explained that it was a product of pure chance. When the brain is forming, neurons grow blindly, seeking to connect to other neurons, and then over time, the connections that aren't used wither away. "There's a survival of some branches and a loss of others," he said. "And the ones that survive are not necessarily the most direct route." Once the brain has finished growing, the neurons are locked in place by the other brain cells that have grown around them.

I stared at the crooked neuron on his screen. I found myself feeling repulsed by the sight of it. Back then I was working on a book about trails, and I pointed out to Lichtman that if that neural pathway were a footpath, by walking it, we would gradually shave away and straighten out that curve.

With an air of detached amusement, Lichtman acknowledged

that the shape of the brain was "a little irrational." It was important to remember, he said, that a "neural pathway" is not really a pathway. It's a living thing. And life, as a rule, doesn't need to be perfect. It only needs to be good enough to survive.

Part of me knew that the meandering shape of our neural pathways was a problem so tiny that it was almost beneath consideration. But it disturbed me nonetheless, because it gestured to something much larger. I had always assumed that life has a tendency to self-optimize, a will to elegance. Raised in that golden lull after the thawing of the Cold War and before the melting of the ice caps, I had taken it on faith that the arc of the moral universe bent toward justice, that technology naturally grew sleeker and quicker, that the world's rough edges would be steadily sanded away until everything fit smoothly into place. These axioms helped shape my (generally, optimistic) worldview. So it was a shock to find—here, in the most powerful organ the earth has ever produced—something so stubbornly inelegant. Life, I was beginning to realize, contains something ugly, something hard and arthritic and irremediably flawed, in its very nature.

The memory of that crooked neuron returned, terrifyingly, years later, when one December morning, my husband, Remi, awoke to find he was unable to get out of bed. In his sleep, a blood clot had slipped through a hole in his heart and into the branching network of vessels in his brain, blocking one up. Starved of fresh blood, millions of neurons had died off. We rushed him to the hospital, but by the time we arrived, scans showed that the clot had already dissolved. It was as if a ghost had lightly traced a finger across the surface of his sleeping brain, withering everything it touched, and then vanished into the gray morning light.

The results were surreal. The whole right side of his body, from his shoulder down to his toes, was completely numb. As he dozed in the hospital bed, waiting for test after test, he would occasionally wake up in alarm because he felt a stranger's hand brushing against his face, only to realize that it was his own. Language, too, had become phantasmal. Words would recede from his grasp, or else they would leap to mind, only to magically change shape; when asked what month it was, he said, with total certainty, "Tomato." Thoughts, atomized and evanescent, floated tracelessly through his head, less a stream of consciousness than a wave of photons.

Each time we spoke with the doctors, we found reasons for hope and reasons for despair. The brain, they explained, is a wonderfully flexible organ, capable of reprogramming itself endlessly, but it has its limitations. One of these limitations is that, past a relatively young age, damaged neurons never grow back. This thought is what vexed Remi most. An injury is ultimately harmless so long as it is temporary; pain, no matter how intense, soon fades into hazy memory. But a wound that refuses to heal threatens to become a little piece of death that dwells forever within one's life.

Thankfully, in Remi's case, this fear was largely misplaced. His brain started to rewire itself, using its remaining neurons, and slowly, the abilities he'd lost began to return. It has now been more than five years since the stroke, and Remi has made what the doctors say is a miraculous recovery. To me, he seems no different than he was before that awful night. But he still suffers from a haunting sense that something has been taken from him that he can never get back. Once, while clearing a plot of forest in order to build us a vegetable garden, Remi held up a dense brown clump of rootlets and fungal threads and said to me, "This is exactly the way it feels. Like someone has reached in and ripped out a bunch of the roots in my brain."

+

As part of our new garden, Remi planted five wild blueberry bushes, and then he fenced them off with nylon netting to keep out pests. One day we discovered a small bird, a dark-eyed junco, tangled up in the netting. In its attempt to escape, it was thrashing around, ensnaring itself further. Remi gently held it down while I used a pair of scissors to cut away the netting, first from its feet, then from its wings. But when I peered closer, I discovered that beneath the bird's feathers, the black threads had bitten into its flesh. After an agonizing few minutes, we finally managed to free the junco, but we weren't able to extract all of the cord. The bird hobbled off into the underbrush, fluttering its wings ineffectively. We guiltily assumed it would soon meet its death at the claws of an owl.[*]

A week later, to our surprise, we saw the junco again. It had somehow regained its power of flight (and resumed raiding our garden) with a length of black string dangling from behind its wings. It appeared to be unharmed, even though it now had a piece of polyester fiber woven into its being.

Looking at it, I began to think about how what maims us also makes us: Our wounds, rather than healing entirely and disappearing with time, tend to leave behind traces, contorting our growth. I had often noticed this in the people closest to me: a neighbor, walking funny to accommodate a back injury he suffered in his twenties; a close friend, left forever wary of dark alleys. People all over the world seemed to be coming to a similar realization all at once. "Trauma," a word I seldom heard growing up outside of televised medical dramas, was suddenly on everyone's mind. A wave of previously straightlaced people had begun turning to psychedelics in an attempt to loosen up mental scar tissue. At the same time, the public seemed to be awakening en masse to the ways that history intrudes upon the present. In the shadow play of politics, sinister echoes of ideas and events from prior centuries kept reverberating. Efforts were made to rectify the past—statues were taken down, places renamed, his-

---

[*] We ultimately decided to surround the berry patch with steel chicken wire, which succeeded in preventing any more birds from falling prey to the sad fate of that junco.

tory books updated—but the underlying systems proved stubbornly (even violently) resistant to reform. Power, over time, produces its own architectures, as rigidly unchanging and snugly self-serving as an oyster shell, within which the powerless, human and nonhuman alike, are required to spend our lives.

Looming above it all was the grim intractability of climate change. As affluent countries continued to fuel their growth by burning the corpses of long-dead plants and animals, the earth began locking itself into deadly new thermal patterns. The ice caps melted, and then the seas absorbed more heat, melting more ice. Time bombs, made of methane, began detonating in the permafrost of the Russian snow forests. Farther south, forest fires burned hotter each year, releasing more greenhouse gases, which fueled even bigger, hotter fires. The architects of this world-historic shift were the executives of fossil fuel companies, men who were now well on their way to being fossils themselves. But in the meantime, the world had hardened around ideas they once jotted down on monogrammed notepads. By the time I began writing this book, most people had come to understand that we needed to quickly replace oil and coal with sun and wind and water. The trouble was that, by then, carbon capitalism had already insinuated itself into every aspect of our lives. A black nylon thread running through our flesh: It seemed impossible to cut out.

In studying trees, I finally found language to make sense of this phenomenon. What I was seeing was life's tendency to *grow gnarled*. Though "gnarls" originally referred to "knurls," or large bumps on a tree trunk, I tend to think of the word in its broader sense. A gnarl is part deformation, part adaptation. It is formed when a tree experiences some calamity—when it loses a branch, or suffers an injury, or gets an infection, or develops a genetic mutation—and then it grows around that old wound, which deforms the otherwise smooth flow of its grain. A tree's refusal to let go of its past might seem like a flaw, and in some cases it is; arborists warn that gnarled maples and willows are often more brittle than uninjured ones. But gnarling is also vital to the beauty and brilliance of very old trees. It is striking—and, to me, moving—that the oldest trees on earth, the bristlecone pines, are also among the world's most contorted.

This is hard wisdom, the kind we don't usually want to hear. Brains, bodies, branches, the winding course of our lives, the arc of our collective histories: all are forced to hold on to their gnarls. These things aren't perfect, but they don't need to be. They only need to find a bit of light, hold it, and pass it along.

+

Over the course of my research, I eventually came to understand that there are many reasons why trees inspire such powerful feelings of reverence in us. Trees outlive us, expanding our sense of time; they tower over us, putting our lives into perspective; they provide for us, inspiring a sense of gratitude; and they trouble us, challenging us to embrace what John Fowles calls the "green chaos" of the more-than-human world. But there is something else, which, in our tendency to focus solely on the sunny side of arborescence, we too often overlook: A tree is a way of persisting in a world of wounds.

Each tree begins its life with a number of limitations: It is born rooted to one spot, its flesh is hard, and its insides are mostly dead. All day long the sun moves through the sky, and the rain falls in a diffuse scattering across the soil. If trees were animals, they would simply turn their heads to eat the sunlight and wriggle around their roots to suck up the rainwater wherever they could find it. They would duck lightning bolts, crush pests, and flee from fires. But they cannot. They must stay put. With all of these innate weaknesses, it seems incredible that trees have managed to survive at all. And yet, certain old trees have remained standing for millennia, while empires crest and crash in their shade.

A tree overcomes its limitations by doing what trees do: It arboresces. It begins by branching outward in all directions, growing upward to explore the bright, dry air and downward into the dark, wet soil. It eventually prunes back the limbs that snag too much wind or fail to reach the light. What remains grows stronger over time, as each new layer of wood wraps around the old, locking those curves into place. Branch, prune, gnarl. In this way, a tree learns to live with, and then outgrow, its imperfections.

Our brains work in much the same way. As an infant's brain is developing, it forms a lush profusion of neural connections, far in excess of what it needs. Then, as we age, we begin deleting the neural links we don't use. Neuroscientists have a lovely term for this process: "blossoming and pruning." Though it should more accurately be called a process of "blossoming, pruning, and gnarling," since what is retained is gradually strengthened, crooked though it may be.

This strategy repeats itself in every realm of life, through the mechanism of Darwinian evolution. Species evolve by gradually branching apart from one another, but certain traits tend to become fixed in place. Many land-dwelling animals, for example, are descended from a slimy, four-legged, fishlike creature, informally known as a fishapod, that crawled out of the sea some 375 million years ago. Clumsy as it may have been, the fishapod eventually gave rise to a vast array of new body types. Its blunt arms and legs hardened into the hooves of horses; they sharpened into the claws of iguanas; they swelled into the legs of elephants; they splayed into the wings of birds; and they tightened to form the precision grip of the human hand. However, as Charles Darwin once noted, if you examine the skeletons of these various species, you'll tend to find a remarkably similar structure lying hidden within all their fins and wings and hands: four (or more) long digits, often with a shorter thumb-like digit at the end—just like the ancient fishapod once had. My head swims just thinking about it. When I was prying that junco loose from its netting, one hand of our primordial ancestor was, in effect, freeing the other.

It is little wonder that, when the time came for Darwin to select an overarching metaphor for his model of evolution, he chose a tree. Life arboresces: Death pares us back, and vestigial flaws persist, but new growth continually blossoms atop the old.

+

When Darwin returned home from his voyage around the globe on board the HMS *Beagle*, having just seen the world's prismatic diversity of animals and plants and human cultures, a family member remarked that the shape of his skull appeared to have changed. "If it wasn't true phrenologically, it was apt as metaphor," notes the science writer David Quammen. "The shape of his thinking had changed."

The standard worldview of Darwin's intellectual milieu was linear, reductive, and hierarchical: All species were believed to be arranged one atop the next, like bureaucrats in a vast universal office tower, with wealthy white men occupying the floor just beneath the angels. But on his voyage aboard the *Beagle*, Darwin began to understand how mushrooms and beetles and elephants and sparrows and bacteria and bare-chested Patagonian fishermen and bald-headed Oxford dons were all just the outer tips of branches on a single, planetary process of growth. The shape of his mind *had* started to change.

Darwin's grand theory—what he called the evolutionary "Tree of Life"—unsettled, and then reshaped, the world. It remains so disturbing that many people still either fail to or refuse to properly understand it. This, argues the evolutionary biologist Robert J. O'Hara, is because it demands what he calls "tree thinking." Many people are still beholden to what might be called "tower thinking," which assumes that we humans are the natural apex of evolution. But tree thinking forces us to reject that comforting belief. There is no one pinnacle of evolution; there is a broad crown, and every living being is a part of it. Thinking in this arborescent manner also helped scholars pry themselves away from the oppressive belief that people are arranged in a strict racial hierarchy; instead, all humans are now widely understood to be part of a single (very complicated) family tree. Much of the social progress of the past century has been founded upon this basic shift in thought—from kinds to kin, from a tower to a tree.

Tree thinking begins when you learn to see the world as the result of an ongoing pattern of growth. This perceptual shift is somewhat hard to make. But, I've found, it is worth the effort, because, when it takes place, a cosmos of cold objects and abstract ideas is suddenly revealed to be a forest: entangled, ever-evolving, and eternally wild.

Life, in short, is fundamentally arborescent. In order to make sense of it, it helps to think in trees.

+

In the decade it took me to write this book, I, too, felt the shape of my mind change. It was a slow but thrilling (even, at times, terrifying) process. I began by reading everything I could get my hands on about the science, history, and philosophy of trees. Then I put down the books and went outside. I fell in with a clan of tree-climbing arborists and scientists; eventually, I made my way all the way to the top of a giant sequoia, the largest species of tree on earth. In addition to the very largest, I studied the very smallest: While in Japan, I became enchanted with bonsai, the magical art of growing "nature in miniature." I traveled to Papua so I could spend time learning from a tribe of people who live in treehouses high above the jungle floor, and I traveled to East Africa so that I could study our arboreal cousins, the great apes, in the wild. I traced my family tree to haunting places, and I traced my evolutionary tree to wondrous ones. In the end, I found myself sitting in a treetop blockade with a stockpile of canned food, staring down at a tactical team of police intent on dragging me away in handcuffs. On each of these journeys, I explored a range of intellectual mysteries, but no matter where these various explorations brought me, I found myself returning to a central question, one so ancient and all-encompassing that it felt hubristic to even consider it: *How should we*—as individuals, as communities, as denizens and stewards of the earth—*live?*

"Learn good sense from a tree, O mind." This line is taken from a Hindi *bhajan*, or hymn, that Mahatma Gandhi and his followers used to sing. When I ask myself how a person should live, this is the advice I now turn to: Learn to branch out like a tree, to let go like a tree, to weather hardship like a tree, to rise above like a tree, to set down roots like a tree. In a scarred and storm-battered world, we couldn't hope to find wiser teachers.

Before we embark on this exploration, I have one last gnomic piece of wisdom to pass along. "A tree is a tree," writes Roland Barthes. This phrase, simple as it may seem, is surprisingly powerful. A tree differs from a human in profound ways; by eliding these differences, we diminish our understanding of what trees are and we impoverish our own imagination of what they might be. In looking to trees for wisdom, my aim has never been to anthropomorphize them. Quite the opposite: I hope to arborize humanity.

1. BRANCHING

ONCE A week or so I step out the back door of my cabin and walk into the forest, and then I keep walking until I reach the sea. Where the forest meets the sea, there's a rocky outcropping padded with moss and wildflowers, an area the locals call "the Grassy Knoll." Atop it stands a tall Douglas fir in whose shade I often sit on hot days. A bald eagle once floated down from the sky and alit on the topmost branch of that tree. It sat there for the better part of an hour, stone-still, gazing imperiously out over its domain. I craned my neck and squinted, watching the eagle watch the world. The view from up there, I imagined, must be sublime: the swaying forest on one side, the heaving ocean on the other, and above only vacant sky.

One summer morning, I was seized by an urge to climb that old Doug fir beside the sea. I hadn't climbed a tree in ages, but this one seemed particularly amenable; I noticed that, unlike most Doug firs, which shed their lowest limbs, this one had a regular array of branches growing on its seaward side, a sort of broken ladder, which offered a clear route from the base all the way to the top. I traced that route with my eyes, imagining each move I'd have to take. It seemed straightforward enough.

I strolled over to the base of the tree and, with a quick anticipatory breath, jumped up and caught hold of the lowest branch. I hooked my leg over it, rolled upright, straddled it, and—after an awkward, ball-crunching moment—managed to stand up. This was a maneuver I knew well; I'd performed it hundreds of times as a kid. I was a bit less fluid (and considerably heavier) than I'd been in my youth, but I was happy to find I hadn't totally lost the knack.

The next branch was just above my head. Again I grabbed hold of it and pulled myself up. But this time, as I squirmed over it, solar plexus pressed against scaly bark, legs dangling, I suddenly had a clear view of just how far I already was off the ground. Before me was fifteen feet of open air, and then a snarl of sharp rocks. My vision wobbled—an aqueous, nauseous sensation—and I felt my heart thrashing in my rib cage. My body mutinied. Before I even consciously decided to, I found I was retreating back toward the ground.

But now, another problem arose. When my foot reached for the lower branch, it seemed farther away than it had mere moments before. Quivering, I extended my toes farther, farther, into the empty air. I envisioned myself slipping and crashing down onto the rocks below. Then I imagined my husband finding my pathetic, crumpled body, hours or days later. My friends, hearing the news and thinking: *What a tragedy.* But also: *What an idiot.*

I knew that being scared would make me more likely to fall, but that likelihood only made me more scared, which made me more likely to fall. I was caught in a kind of mental doom loop. In these moments, the last wisps of adolescent bravado in one's soul evaporate, and the full, brutal solidity of life presses down upon you with terrible force.

Time gelatinized.

When I finally made it back down to solid ground a few minutes later, still a bit twitchy from the residual adrenaline, I reflected on what the hell just happened. Where had this suffocating feeling of fear come from? I didn't have it as a kid. I hadn't noticed it growing larger with age. It had simply appeared, unannounced and unwelcome, like a tumor.

+

Growing up, I loved to climb trees. My favorite was a Norway spruce that stood beside my friend Andy's house, which had big, low-hanging branches that we could easily grab hold of, without needing an adult to hoist us up. As we ascended, the branches closed tighter and tighter together, until we were forced to wriggle between them like eels. We could spend hours up there, navigating the strange logic of the tree's inner architecture.

Children are born tree creatures. A study in 1891 showed that babies less than a month old are able to hang by their hands from a horizontal bar for at least ten seconds, while one tenacious three-week-old held on for two and a half minutes. As babies grow, they attempt to climb things (stairs, chairs, adults' legs, sleeping dogs' gently heaving backs) before they learn to walk. Once they have become ambulatory, without any parental encouragement—in fact, often despite active scolding—kids begin attempting to climb trees. This is true everywhere in the world. My niece, when she was only five years old, would regularly climb a spindly mulberry in her backyard in Houston, with her feet pressed flat against the trunk and her hands wrapped around its far side, precisely the way coconut harvesters in the tropics do. By the age of ten, children are typically nimble enough to clamber up high into the crowns of trees and stubborn enough to refuse to come back down.

Many people believe that kids climb trees because they are following an atavistic urge inherited from our apelike ancestors. There is no doubt some truth to this; our shoulder sockets, our fabled opposable thumbs, even the whorls of our fingerprints are modified remnants of adaptations we acquired as tree-climbing apes. But Jeff Lichtman—the Harvard neuroscientist who, in showing me the brain's gnarled nature, in an oblique way kicked off the writing of this book—has a more parsimonious theory. Children, he argues, have an irrepressible urge to try *all sorts of things*. They are continually, unconsciously widening what he calls their "behavioral repertoire." This is why children act so crazy so much of the time. They are chaos embodied: They run and jump and splash in the bath and dig huge pointless holes in the sand. They *explore*.

This is true even down to the neuronal level. The brains of children are far branchier than those of adults. As children play, their brains are stress-testing that superabundance of neural connections. The behaviors that are rewarded with positive feedback become stronger over time, and the others gradually weaken and then vanish. If I had needed to gather fruit or honey in order to survive, I would have received a sweet reward each time I climbed a tree, and I would have continued doing it throughout my life. This is why the Mbuti people living in the Congo basin and the Korowai people of Papua can still climb trees with ease, even well into old age, but most adults living in Cleveland cannot. Tree climbing is just one of a thousand other potential skills that we lose as we get older.

What worried me most, though, was not that I had lost the *ability* to climb up a tree. It went deeper than that. I was beginning to realize that, at some invisible point in my life, I had lost the *spirit* of a tree climber, that irrepressible force that compels the young to keep trying new things. I was growing ever more bracketed, ever more linear, ever more specialized to the task of my work. That unconscious narrowing, it seemed to me, was a harbinger of terminal decline.

Talking with Lichtman, I had begun to envision the shape of a human life in arboreal terms. Young people are masters of ramification and experimentation: We sprout upward and outward, learning to crawl, to walk, to climb; we try out new skills and acquire new talents; we rise from one grade to the next, into the heights of our chosen careers. Middle age is a time of gnarling: Our strengths amplify, our skin toughens, our flexibility diminishes, and our midsections thicken. Our final years, by contrast, are marked by deletion, followed by decay: We retire; we shed burdens; we slough off obligations; we forget names; we gradually lose our vision and our hearing and our hair and our teeth; we slouch, then we hunch, until we finally collapse into the soil. Looking at a human life in this way reveals our species to be somewhat weedy—short-lived, fast-growing, and physically unimpressive. A tree, by contrast, grows slowly, but it never stops growing throughout its long life.

Our species' innate tendency to narrow with age is exacerbated by the structure of the modern world. The market pressures us to specialize, maximizing the profit our minds and bodies can produce, sharpening us to its needs. Then, when we are worn down to a nub, it tosses us away. The old person who chooses to grow in a tree-wise manner—to continue trying new things, shedding bad habits and false beliefs, and strengthening what works best—throughout life, even until the very end, stands in defiant opposition to all that. Truly *growing* old, as opposed to merely *getting* old, is a guerrilla war waged against the overwhelming forces of gravity, entropy, and social convention.

That day on the Grassy Knoll, I was thirty-three years old. Until then, I had never needed to consciously decide how to age. After all, I still had my hair, my teeth, most of my strength, at least some of my wits. But what Lichtman's research makes painfully clear is that by the time you feel yourself starting to "get old," it might already be too late. The mind must be kept branchy, or else it will become ever more narrow. The goal of tree-wise aging is not to stay forever young, which is both impossible and, ultimately, undesirable. The aim is to stay forever wild.

After my failed ascent of the old Doug fir by the sea, I stewed for a few weeks. I consoled myself with the knowledge that I'd done the prudent thing by retreating, rather than recklessly endangering my life. I told myself that climbing trees was an activity best left for kids, who are blissfully unburdened by the weight of time and the fear of death. I should just do my best to age gracefully, down here on earth. I could still gaze up at the treetops, even if I would never again touch them. Wasn't that enough?

Then a certain defiance, almost an anger, welled up in me. I was still young, goddamn it! (Or at least young*ish*!) I didn't want to passively streamline toward the quietude of old age and the nullity of death. I wanted to remain curious and venturesome, even if it meant accepting a certain measure of pain and risk. Trees keep growing throughout their lives. Why shouldn't I?

Groping around for a means to accomplish this new, admittedly diffuse life goal, I decided to begin by taking on the most natural challenge I could think of, one that was still fresh in my mind. To internalize the wisdom of a tree, perhaps I just needed to relearn how to climb one.

I began casting about for a teacher. Eventually, I ran across a British man named Ben Atkinson, who had posted a short film on Vimeo showing himself climbing a gorgeous old beech tree. What caught my attention was how he transformed climbing into an aesthetic act, almost a spiritual practice. He did not simply climb up the trunk and then back down, as most people do. Instead, he made what he called "circuits" around the branches, exploring the tree in all directions, trying to find his "edge." He swung apelike along boughs using only his hands; he walked along the branches as if they were balance beams; he even jumped from one limb to another, à la parkour. "There's something very zen about the balance," he says in the film. "I'm just *there*, in the reliance of my own hands."

I eventually managed to track him down and get him on the phone. He lived in England's Lake District, where he worked as an arborist and firefighter. On the side, he ran a business renting out yurts and huts to tourists. He said he viewed tree climbing as part of a larger societal return to "natural" forms of exercise, pulled directly from our evolutionary past, like barefoot running and wild swimming. At the end of our short conversation, Ben invited me to come stay in one of his yurts for a few days so that he could show me how to properly climb a tree. The timing was perfect; I already had a trip to London planned in the fall, which I could easily extend by a week.

I asked him if there was anything in particular I needed to bring.

I didn't need to bring anything at all, he said. That was the beauty of it.

+

The following October, I caught a train north from London to Windermere, a gray stone town surrounded by nuclear-green hills.

Ben Atkinson, stubble-cheeked and shorn-headed, was waiting for me when I arrived. He was wearing a tweed jacket but no shoes, a combination you don't often see. He took my duffel and set off through town at a quick pace, his calloused feet treading lightly on the concrete. With each step, his toes spread out wide, like cat paws. He told me he never wore shoes, except when he went rock climbing.

Once we'd settled in Ben's rattly old Land Rover and set off for his house, I was free to inspect him more closely out of the corner of my eye. It was hard to place his age. His glacial-blue eyes were shadowed in dark circles and the stubble on his cheeks was frost white, but his smile, with its gap between the two front teeth, was youthful, even impish.

The sky grayed, then blackened, and began to rain. We drove

back through the deepening gloom to Ben's home, a sprawling stone building called the Hermitage, which he rented, he said, from a family with roots stretching back to William the Conqueror.

Inside, we sat down at a wooden table in the kitchen. Ben served me a plate of sautéed wild hedgehog mushrooms, a side of pickled wild garlic, and a bowl of French onion soup. He had a philosophy about food, as he did about most things. His practice was to gather as much wild fare as he could (including roadkill, so long as it was fresh) and then go to the grocery store and buy whatever produce was on the verge of expiring; this, he judged, saved him money and prevented food from going to waste. He had recently purchased a ten-pound bag of onions, which meant he'd been eating a lot of French onion soup.

Over mugs of herbal tea, Ben told me about how he fell in love with climbing trees. At the age of thirteen, his family had moved from a small village in the south of England to the city of Nottingham, where, as a quiet kid with a strange accent, he felt out of place. To get away from bullies and find some peace, he took to climbing trees in a nearby park, and then, for reasons he couldn't fully explain, he just never really stopped.

+

The following morning, after a late breakfast, my tree-climbing course officially began. Our classroom was a large estate with a number of huge, broad-armed trees, which sat just across the road from Ben's house. He said he had been given permission to climb them from the owner of the property, but he'd only asked to be polite. "Otherwise he'd have to put up with a complete anarchic stranger walking across his land, climbing all his trees," he said.

It was a cool morning, with pale rain clouds blobbing through the aquamarine sky. We hopped over a barbed wire fence, crossed a shallow stream, and hiked across a sheep field. Ben had convinced me to make the trip barefoot. I enjoyed the fresh sensation of the cold, wet grass crushing icily between my toes, though the novelty soon wore off, and then my feet started to go numb. He warned me to look out for piles of sheep shit, which were slippery, and milk thistles, which were sharp. By necessity, I walked a little more mindfully.

We eventually made our way to the base of an enormous old sycamore tree, Ben's favorite for teaching newcomers. Its thick, evenly spaced branches reached in all directions. One of them even curved all the way to the ground, as if reaching down to gently pluck a beetle from the grass. It was, at first glance, the Platonic ideal of a tree-climbing tree.

Then I inspected the branches more closely. I noticed they were covered in fine green moss, which flaked off with the lightest touch. When, moments later, the sky began misting down a sugary rain, the branches became slipperier still. The thought of climbing out on those branches, ten or twenty or thirty feet above the ground, gave me a heliated feeling in my belly and a swelling sensation in my throat.

"Let's start with this one here," Ben said, pointing to one of the branches that touched the ground. He demonstrated what he wanted me to do: He stood up on the branch; heel-toed along it, following its upward slant until he could touch the trunk; then turned and walked back. Now it was my turn. I stood on it and took a few wobbly steps, then turned and successfully made it back to where I started.

"See?" Ben said. "Dead easy!"

Next he had me walk along a slightly higher branch. Climbing a tree in this way, with only one's feet, forces the climber to acquire an intimate knowledge of every inch of a given branch. ("Pay attention to microfeatures," Ben said. "This isn't just a blanket of bark. You've got a little ledge there, you've got a little ledge there . . .") Cramming my toes into various crevices, I followed that branch until I stood about six feet off the ground, high enough up to hurt myself but not to die. Ben followed, with annoying ease, until we were standing chest to chest. He noticed that my knees were shaky.

"I can see you're a little nervous. Let's play a game," Ben said. "Focus on trying to touch my chest." I reached out and tried to poke the center of his sternum, and he gently swatted my hand away. I tried with a different hand, and at different speeds, but each time he blocked me. "You see," he said, pointing down to my knees, which had stopped shaking. "You're a lot more stable. Now you're not overthinking it. Give up control and let your body do it. Because it does it all the fucking time!"

The key to tree climbing, Ben said, was to find a way to get off what he called the "neurotic merry-go-round." It helped to have companions along, because social pressure can push you to embody a boldness you may not feel, a posture of confidence that, in turn, breeds real confidence.

Next, Ben had me climb higher up the tree, ducking under branches and stepping up onto others. As we moved upward, I occasionally reached areas where I thought I couldn't go any farther; at these points, Ben instructed me to just sit with that emotion for a little while and allow it to subside. It worked: I paused, breathed, allowed the feeling to dissipate somewhat, and kept moving.

Fear, I was learning, is a poison. A little bit is fine—it can be medicinal, even—but in high enough doses, it stiffens your movements and scatters your thoughts. I yearned to be cleansed of it entirely, a kind of chelation of the soul. But once you know fear, you can never fully unknow it. (Katharine Hepburn, in her autobiography, recounts climbing a hemlock tree on the edge of her family's property. Her neighbors spied her there in the branches and called her mother to alert her. "Yes, I know," Hepburn's mother replied. "Don't scare her. She doesn't know that it's dangerous.")

Eventually, we were about twenty-five feet off the ground.

"You're now entering incredibly dangerous territory," Ben said.

"Thanks for reminding me," I said.

We were both sitting on a long branch, near the trunk. He told me to walk as far out as I felt comfortable. After my first few steps, something shifted inside my brain; I slipped into a state of hyperfocus, my mind's aperture blown wide open, taking in the sensations of the scaly branch beneath my toes, the light breeze on my face, the tiny, woozy, sealike shifts in balance. One thing I did not feel was fear. The anthropologist Alfred Kroeber once argued that the optimum headspace for an individual was not one of "bovine placidity"; rather, the ideal was "the highest state of tension that the organism can bear creatively." I suspect this quivering, zen state of mind I was experiencing was what he had meant. Anyway, it only lasted for two or three seconds: As soon as I consciously noticed my own calmness, it vanished.

I made it about three-quarters of the way out on the branch, until I felt it beginning to flex beneath my weight, and then my nerve failed me. I sat down in a little cradle of three branches, my legs crisscrossed. I looked down over the green fields. Above them, a pale sun carved a snowy tunnel through the clouds.

The branch bobbed gently in the wind. I felt the comforting but humbling sensation, one I hadn't felt since I was a young child, of being held by a creature much larger than myself. My life, I realized, was entirely in the tree's hands.

"Now I want to show you where my comfort zone is," Ben said. I returned to the trunk, and then he walked out onto the same branch. But he went far past where I had sat down, at least another fifteen feet, until the branch, which was only about as thick as my thigh bone, started to bow under his weight. He then reached up and grabbed a higher tree limb, swung his body up onto it, and paced calmly back toward the trunk. He noted that the tree had recently lost "a beautiful moss-covered branch," which he used to love to heel-toe along. "Especially when it was dry, it was like walking a garden path," he said. This is one of the downsides of tree climbing, which rock climbers do not often need to worry about. "The tree is not a certain thing," he said. "It is a living thing."

+

Over the next two days, I watched as Ben climbed a number of other trees, some tall, some broad. He shinned up trunks; he walked on thin branches, or dead branches, like a tightrope walker; he leapt from branch to branch, sometimes many stories above the forest floor, landing each time with the graceful certainty of a lemur. I never saw him fall, or even come close. On one occasion, he compelled me to climb a tall tree beside his home, a Norway spruce, and then, when we were at the tippy top, he grabbed the trunk and began rocking from side to side, which set the tree to teetering wildly. "It's a great feeling doing this in the wind!" he cried.

Ben urged me to approach tree climbing not as an athletic activity, like rock climbing, or as a form of childish play. Instead, I came to see it as being much closer to certain forms of long-distance walking, which verge on religious pilgrimage. There is no goal to it, no glory. But one comes away from it feeling, in some way, mentally (one might even say spiritually) enlarged.

The fact that this particular act of pilgrimage takes place in the branches of a living being is significant. What we choose to do with our time, and where we choose to do it, matters. The world rubs off on us, bleeds over, seeps in. Science has shown conclusively that our perceptual environment shapes our brains. We know, for example, that being around trees makes us feel calmer and happier; psychological studies have shown that as few as ten minutes spent in a forest lowers a person's blood pressure, reduces stress hormones, and increases serotonin. But what struck me, climbing with Ben, was that being in the branches of a tree, high up off the ground, feels completely different from being at the base. Up there, I did not feel calm, exactly. I felt alert, almost painfully so. I felt the emptiness beneath my feet. I felt that if the branch I was standing on should drop, I would drop with it. I suspect this is how our arboreal ancestors felt much of the time: precarious, grateful, and, most of all, alive. From just a few days of tree climbing, I thought I could feel my brain subtly rewiring—or, rather, rewilding.

I wondered: Did Ben feel that climbing trees shaped his brain as well? Or was he simply born with a brain suited to tree climbing?

He said he didn't know. Indeed, since he had been climbing trees continually since his childhood, how could he possibly disentangle the two?

What he could say for certain is that trees had saved his life on multiple occasions. In college, he had lost faith in Christianity and tumbled headlong into an existential crisis, so he dropped out and went to live on a kibbutz, tending to an orchard of persimmons and kumquats. Next, wanting to cultivate a sense of inner strength, he chose to enroll at Sandhurst, the prestigious military school that Prince Harry and Prince William attended, but was "chucked out," he says, for his failure to conform; he was, among other things, an out bisexual and an avowed pacifist. Again, he took refuge in trees, this time by finding work as an arborist. He eventually got married and had a son. He moved to the Lake District and began his yurt-rental business. Then, his wife left him. Broke and overwhelmed by the demands of solo parenting, he fell into a deep depression; at his lowest points, he said, he looked to suicide "in the middle distance" as an escape. He attributed his recovery to two things that forced him to get out of his own head: cold-water swimming and tree climbing. Both, he said, made him feel like a "happy naked ape."

One thing he knows for certain *did* change his brain was his choice to work as an arborist. He told me that he had initially been drawn to the career because of his love of climbing trees, but he quickly grew disillusioned by it. Being a "tree doctor" very often (about 80 percent of the time, in his experience) involves euthanizing the patient, because people tend to call an arborist only after the tree is too far gone to save. In a bitterly ironic turn, he realized he was now, on a near-daily basis, killing the very beings that had saved his life. "When you take down a really big beech tree, it feels a bit like harpooning a whale," he said. "It was emotionally traumatic to me. And it affected the way I looked at trees. Now I wasn't looking at them in terms of *How can I climb this?* or *How beautiful is it to be up here?* I was thinking: *How can I cut this down?* It really upset me for a while." Over time, he learned to make his peace with the profession. He strove, whenever possible, to convince landowners to nurse their trees back to health—through deft pruning, watering, soil management, and a sparing application of fungicides and pesticides—rather than felling them. He even came to relish the new view of trees his profession afforded him. "The upside is that you kind of become an anatomist of trees," he said. "You get to see them beneath the surface, in ways that, if I'd only just remained a recreational tree climber, I never would have seen."

+

One afternoon, Ben took me on a hike up the valley, to visit one of his favorite swimming holes, at a place called Buckstones Jump. His two sheepdogs, Kali and Bosun, followed along. Barefoot but moving briskly, we traced an old bridle path up the green valley, past orange-brown bracken ferns and volcanic rocks tinged purple with rust.

Along the way, Ben pointed out some of his favorite trees: a wide, tentacular sycamore, which he called the Octopus Tree; a horse chestnut with smooth gray bark, which he called the Elephant Tree; and an ancient alder, tall and symmetrical, in whose crown he liked to meditate.

At the top of the hill, the river kinked up and formed a small swimming hole. We both stripped off our clothes, waded in, ducked under the gelid water, and came up gasping. We stood on the riverbank, air-drying ourselves in the hard wind, every inch of skin pricklingly alive.

The sun fell behind the hills, but the sky remained lit for a long time. We walked home in that weird bright shade. It occurred to me that I was passing through a kind of ur-landscape, something I had often visited in my mind even though I was just seeing it now for the first time. This soft green ground, these clouds the color of pulped cantaloupe, these mercury streams, these happy dogs: This was the landscape where English Romanticism—and with it, much of the modern environmental spirit—was born.*

Two hundred years earlier, this path was likely trodden by William Wordsworth, who spent most of his life in the Lake District. He was said to go for long hikes each afternoon, sometimes covering as many as twenty miles in a day, during which he would mentally compose his poems. Those sparkling verses often described a growing sense of alienation from "this green earth," which he deemed "the anchor of my purest thoughts, the nurse, / The guide, the guardian of my heart"—a somewhat shocking sentiment for its time. Not surprisingly, Wordsworth also became one of the first people to publicly suggest preserving wild tracts of land for public enjoyment. He campaigned against the construction of a railway into the area, and he fought to save certain old trees from being hacked down by shortsighted landowners. "It may legitimately be claimed that all who hike or simply gaze in the wild places are legatees of Wordsworth's poetry . . . and his way of seeing," writes the scholar Jonathan Bate in *Radical Wordsworth*.

One of the recurring themes of Wordsworth's early work is the freshness with which children view the world, and how that dims

---

*In her book *Magnificent Rebels*, the historian Andrea Wulf argues that English Romanticism was shaped in turn by the writing of a slightly earlier cadre of German Romantics, most notably the brilliant, tempestuous, and botanically obsessed polymath Johann Wolfgang von Goethe, who, Wulf writes, passed his young adulthood in a torrent of passion, including "drunken brawls, theatrical declarations of love, naked swimming and nightly tree climbing."

over time. In "Ode: Intimations of Immortality," he describes how the weight of life had settled like a heavy frost upon his soul, slowly robbing him of the radiant clarity he had as a child, when everything held "the glory and the freshness of a dream." He was thirty-four when he wrote these lines. He would live another forty-six years, but his vision continued to steadily dim. His politics, progressive in his youth, became cautious, and his poems grew dull—he became, in the words of Rebecca Solnit, "increasingly conservative and decreasingly inspired." Indeed, Bate rather coldly points out that, had Wordsworth died at the age of thirty-six, as Lord Byron did, only one of his best poems would have gone unwritten, and his reputation may have been all the brighter.

In the summer of 1833, a young Ralph Waldo Emerson, then an unpublished writer and lapsed pastor, traveled to the Lake District to meet Wordsworth, who was one of his intellectual heroes. He found "a plain, elderly, white-haired man," with a broken tooth (he had recently fallen down while out on a walk), wearing green-tinted glasses to protect his failing eyes. Wordsworth greeted the young stranger cordially, took him for a stroll through his garden, and recited a few poems. Emerson came away unimpressed. He judged Wordsworth "a narrow and very English mind," someone who "paid rare elevation by general tameness and conformity." Wordsworth was then only in his early sixties; he would go on to live to the age of eighty. His life, ultimately, fulfilled the words he had written in his thirties: "The good die first, / And they whose hearts are dry as summer dust / Burn to the socket."

As we walked, I found myself mulling over the quintessential difference between a man like Ben Atkinson and a man like William Wordsworth. It did not interest me much that one was a genius and the other was merely smart, that the one was a canonized poet while the other was an obscure tree surgeon. What interested me more was the shape of their lives.

Wordsworth was born with a mind of enormous curiosity, sensitivity, and eloquence, but he refracted it into a lone point of monomaniacal focus; his work described the intersection of nature and the human soul, and little else. Over time, it was as if, along with his gray sideburns, he grew a pair of blinders on either side of his eyes. "He sees nothing but himself and the universe," quipped the essayist William Hazlitt, who knew him personally. "He hates all science and all art; he hates chemistry, he hates conchology; he hates Sir Isaac Newton. . . . He hates all poetry but his own." The word Emerson chose to describe Wordsworth was apt: He had grown *narrow*.

By contrast, Ben spread his attention across a huge number of fields—too many, probably. In one of his notebooks, which he showed me, he had copied down a quote by the author and polymath Robert Heinlein, proclaiming that "a human being should be able to change a diaper, plan an invasion, butcher a hog, conn a ship, design a building, write a sonnet, balance accounts, build a wall, set a bone, comfort the dying, take orders, give orders, cooperate, act alone, solve equations, analyze a new problem, pitch manure, program a computer, cook a tasty meal, fight efficiently, die gallantly." (Ben said that, to complete this list, he only needed to learn how to program a computer, set a bone, and write a sonnet. "And of course, I haven't yet died gallantly," he added.) He was, in some sense, the Romantics' ideal man: a perpetual climber of, in Byron's words, "life's strange tree."

This eternally curious outlook, and this willingness to remain a permanent neophyte, had kept Ben youthful even into his fifties. But the cost, Ben told me, was a nagging feeling that his life lacked a sense of direction. "I avoid choosing," he said. "I'm not a tree surgeon or a firefighter; it's just shit I've done. Whereas I know people who really identify with stuff; they become a photographer. That's their whole thing. I've never done that, and actually I kind of feel like I'm missing out." Rainer Maria Rilke, in a letter written in his twenties, captured this sense of aimless diffusion beautifully. "I keep dividing and flowing off in all directions,—and would like so much to course through one riverbed and become great," he wrote. "Aren't we to hold ourselves together and surge on?"

Psychologists sometimes distinguish between two types of happiness: *hedonic* happiness, born of sensual delight, and *eudaemonic* happiness, which is rooted to a strong sense of personal and communal flourishing. In short: Should we pursue pleasure, or should we try to find a purpose in life? Research suggests that people with a strong sense of purpose have stronger friendships, have healthier habits, sleep deeper, and are less prone to dementia. According to the psychologists Andrew Steptoe and Daisy Fancourt, this pattern becomes especially pronounced later in life, "when social and emotional ties often fragment, social engagement is reduced, and health problems may limit personal options."

Within a capitalist system, our sense of purpose tends to come from our jobs. The danger is that our jobs will cause us to mistake *purpose* for *usefulness*, and to forsake all but the shallowest forms of hedonic pleasure to maximize profits (and, by extension, pleasure) for someone else. In pursuit of purpose, we end up becoming instrumentalized. But Ben faced the opposite problem; having never pursued any one job with a sense of personal attachment, he fretted that his purpose—to be a full human being, as well as a good dad—was too diffuse to clearly pursue.

I wondered if there wasn't some healthy synthesis to be found between Wordsworth's one-track mind and Ben's omnidirectional sprawl. Was it possible to lead a life that both branches out and prunes back? A life with a single trunk—a single directional thrust—but also a wide-open crown?

The essayist Stefan Zweig describes precisely this when he writes about the life of the great Russian author Leo Tolstoy. He describes Tolstoy as an oak tree "spreading its branches wide . . . firmly rooted in the earth from which it springs." Tolstoy's arborescent mind allowed him to write novels that were somehow both vast and concise, books that moved forward like a swift river fed by a thousand tributaries. He read widely, soaking up works of history, science, philosophy, poetry, and esoteric religion, and then he rendered all of that down into lithe prose, speaking to the basic concerns of everyday life. During each waking moment, he was physically and mentally active, to an almost astounding degree. His brother once remarked that he always wanted to "embrace everything all at once, without leaving anything out, even gymnastics." He forged an unusual, even paradoxical, relationship with the basic problem of living: whether to specialize and excel or whether to generalize and expand. He somehow chose to do both.

There also seems to be something about the arborescent mind that, like an old tree, resists the deleterious effects of time. Most writers, Zweig notes, have a tendency to shrink with age, just as Wordsworth had. In a wonderful chapter entitled "Vitality and Its Counterpart," he describes how even the greatest geniuses can grow small and timid: In his later years, Goethe was paranoically hiding from cold breezes; Voltaire had come to resemble a "plucked fowl"; and Kant was a "mechanical mummy." Tolstoy, by contrast, never stopped growing. He taught himself to ride a bicycle at the age of sixty-five, and even into his eighties, he was still playing ferocious games of tennis, swinging a scythe alongside the peasants on his estate, and swimming in the icy sea. "His mind shows the imprint of the years as little as his body," Zweig writes. "His conversation outsparkles that of all others; an alarmingly efficient memory enables him to reconstruct every detail of the past. Nothing is lost, nothing has been obliterated by the friction of time. . . . The topmost boughs of this giant Russian oak, which is turgid with sap flowing into its finest ramifications, have grown up into the sky of the patriarchal years, without as yet any withering of the roots."

I wondered what science had to say about the art of growing a quercine mind like Tolstoy's. Seeking an answer, I called up Lichtman, the neuroscientist. It had been a decade since we last spoke, but he remained one of the world's foremost experts on how brains grow. He had begun his career by tracing a single nerve within the body of a bullfrog, which he dyed black with an extract made from horseradish. Forty years later, his work has evolved to where his team can dye individual neurons in neon hues using genetic material extracted from coral, jellyfish, and bacteria, which causes the neurons to glow in a random array of colors, like the swept-up snarl of threads in the corner of a dressmaker's workshop. They then shave the brain into micron-thick slices and scan those slices into a computer, which they use to trace each glowing nerve cell as it wends its way through the brain. The result is a three-dimensional map of the mammalian mind.

Through this work, Lichtman has helped pioneer our understanding of the branching-pruning mechanism of brain development. It doesn't work how most people imagine it does, nor, indeed, as they would probably like it to. The human brain does not continue steadily branching and pruning throughout its existence, as a tree does. Rather, when the brain is first forming, it branches out all at once, and then, for the most part, it spends the rest of its life paring those branches back. Between the ages of two and ten, about 50 percent of the brain's synapses—the nerve junctions where one neuron links to another—are snipped away.

This pattern of pruning and gnarling, Lichtman explained to me, is not just some unfortunate by-product of the process of learning; it is *how* the brain learns. "As in a tree, pruning one branch is often a way of getting robust growth in another branch," he explained. Strengthening one neural connection means weakening another; learning to play a piano concerto properly means unlearning the thousands of ways to do it improperly. Pruning is also how the brain removes the extraneous connections that slow down its functioning and introduce "noise" into the system. Indeed, it has been shown, through scanning the brains of teenagers, that the least synaptically pruned brains are the most prone to depression, various phobias, and ADHD. If branching is akin to writing, then pruning is editing. Ideally, over time, a sense of clarity and concision emerges.

However, the act of pruning, too, has its costs. Except in a few small regions of the brain, new neurons are not being formed, and deleted synapses do not tend to grow back. This continual neuronal winnowing is what leaves us, in old age, less able to learn new languages, master new skills, or generate new ideas. I asked Lichtman, who is now in his seventies, whether he could feel this process taking place in his own brain. "My children certainly see it when they talk to me," Lichtman said. "They feel that I've become much less open to other ideas than the particular ideas I believe in. They don't ask me questions anymore, because they know what I'm going to say. There's no point in talking to me, because I've become such a hardwired creature." He paused, then added, "Now *I* don't think that's true. But I remember feeling exactly the same way about my parents!"

What may seem like a genetic flaw, Lichtman explained, is in fact a rational evolutionary by-product. The human brain evolved to "master" a given set of skills necessary for its survival; there is no clear evolutionary advantage to being able to learn to play the piano at the age of eighty. He asked me to imagine the life of an elder in a hunter-gatherer clan living one hundred thousand years ago. That person would have already learned all of the necessary ecological information for their given area, mastered the skills necessary to harvest food, and (ideally) refined the kinds of social skills that minimize conflict. Their nervous system would have grown to fit the niche of their lives, just like everything else in the forest in which they live.

Lichtman believes the modern desire for an eternally youthful brain is largely a result of us having become evolutionarily maladapted to our own cultural landscape. "The problem with modern old people is that the world is changing far more quickly than our nervous system was designed to adapt," he said. "Our brains were not designed for a world that was changing when we were adults. We were supposed to be really wise by the time we're old. Now, old people are not only *not* wise, we feel stupid!"

I continued pressing Lichtman for advice. Did brain-training apps work? What about psychedelics—was it true that ayahuasca had been shown to spur the growth of new brain cells? He seemed lukewarm on these suggestions. I asked him about the ever-growing field of research in what is known as "neuroplasticity"—the ability of the brain to continually reprogram itself. In the past two decades, I'd skimmed dozens of articles touting the glories of our miraculously malleable brains. One such story is recounted in *The Brain That Changes Itself*, by the psychiatrist Norman Doidge, perhaps my favorite of a slew of books that I devoured back when I was trying to make sense of my husband's stroke. Doidge tells the story of one remarkable patient, a poet and scholar named Pedro Bach-y-Rita, who suffered a devastating stroke in his sixties, which left him paralyzed on one side of his body. Over the course of a year of physical therapy, he gradually regained the ability to crawl, then to walk. He eventually made a full recovery and resumed his old job teaching at a college. Seven years later, he died at the age of seventy-two, while climbing a mountain in Colombia. When his body was autopsied, the doctors were astonished to find that the stroke had destroyed 97 percent of the neurons running from his cerebral cortex to his spine. Looking at the wreckage of his nervous system, most neuroscientists would have assumed that Bach-y-Rita was paralyzed. And yet, he had managed to recover virtually all of the powers he'd lost, simply by rerouting the necessary neural pathways through a comparatively tiny number of remaining neurons.

Stories like these are inspiring, especially to those of us who have suffered (or know someone who has suffered) a catastrophic brain injury. But Lichtman made it clear to me that, strictly speaking, neuroplasticity is a form of *change*, not of growth. This is something that biohackers and wellness hucksters tend to gloss over: As we age, our powers of plasticity tend to continually decrease, because there are fewer redundant neural connections to choose from. We are like musicians attempting to play new melodies on a piano that, every passing year, has one or two fewer keys. We can still master "Frère Jaques," and perhaps even "Für Elise," but Liszt's Hungarian Rhapsody will remain forever out of reach.

"Pruning is a one-way street, unfortunately," Lichtman told me. I could tell, by the tone of his voice, that he had spoken this particular sentence a thousand times before. Through his decades of research, he had pruned away all other ways of seeing the brain and strengthened this one branch of thought until it dominated all others.

But then he paused and thought for a moment. He noted one thing that had recently surprised him. Just one month earlier, he had been promoted to a new position, as the dean of science at Harvard. In his new administrative role, he was forced to familiarize himself with numerous areas of research—physics, earth sciences, statistics, and so on—that were outside his realm of expertise. "Because I'm a scientist, I'm not just letting it go in one ear and out the other—I'm struggling to make sense of this. And I've noticed just over this past month, a lot of new ideas have sprung into my head," he said. "Even in my seventies, new ideas are popping up, and I'm pissing everyone off with these new ideas, and I feel very invigorated by it!"

Here, amid what was otherwise a fairly grim picture of the workings of our gray matter, I managed to find an ember of hope. Brains are gnarled organs, yes. But new information can give rise to new ideas, new ideas can shape a new ethos, a new ethos can guide new actions, and new actions can create entirely new lives.

Among the people I know and love, I have frequently seen a single new idea spur mental growth spurts, even late in life. Often, these new ideas sprout up in the aftermath of a crisis, like saplings taking root in newly exposed soil after a forest fire. After Remi's stroke, the doctors told him that the best way to heal was simply for him to do as many things as he could. "Use it or lose it" was the phrase they kept repeating, a cliché that, in his raw state, struck him as profound. With the fresh urgency of a man who has felt the wing of death pass over him, he began living. He started a new, more creative, more financially risky line of work. He spent more time reading Russian novels, swimming in the sea, and hunting for wild mushrooms in the forest. He began taking chances, knowing for certain that life—as we had always been told but never fully believed—is all too brief. The same is overwhelmingly true of the close family members I've watched struggle with, and then recover from, addictions to alcohol and opioids. They managed to take some of the world's most blindingly simple truths—"one day at a time," "progress, not perfection," "nothing changes if nothing changes"—and use those words, like artificial sunlamps, to sprout new life atop the gnarled timber of the past.

Let your mind grow like a tree. This was the simple mantra I had chosen to guide my midlife growth spurt. I was learning that this kind of growth is not automatic; it is a choice, a risk. In those few days I spent with Ben, I had taken my first, tentative steps out over the void. But back down on earth, the challenge became less clearly defined. How do we go about living our lives with a tree climber's spirit—with a fearless playfulness welded to a fearsome urgency? How do we keep growing when it's easier to shrink?

+

My thoughts returned to Wordsworth and Tolstoy: the one whose mind withered, while the other never so much as wilted. One fact that distinguished Tolstoy, I noticed, was a quality he possessed, something like boldness, which we don't quite have a word for in

English. According to his biographer Rosamund Bartlett, he had an "astonishing fearlessness" and an "untiring zest for life." She describes how while out hunting as a young man, Tolstoy once startled a sleeping bear; the two wrestled for a time, and Tolstoy, bloodied, managed to escape. "Tolstoy was left with a permanent scar on his forehead and an anecdote to dine out on for the rest of his life," she writes. The Russians, unsurprisingly, have a word for the quality of almost savage vitality that Tolstoy embodied. They call it *dikost*. "*Dikost* literally means 'wildness,' but it can also convey unsociableness or shyness," Bartlett notes. "In other contexts it can mean weirdness, eccentricity, or absurdity." Tolstoy liked to define it as "the quality of possessing passion and daring."

Dikost can take many forms, and some are healthier than others. A fierce hunger for life, after all, can result in a feeling of disappointment when life fails to serve up ever-greater feasts. Tolstoy, in his forties, having already achieved the pinnacle of his professional career (as the internationally beloved author of *War and Peace* and *Anna Karenina*), found himself in a state of nihilistic anhedonia, where all his victories felt meaningless. He became despondent, and then suicidal; he picked out a tree in his garden where, should the time come, he would hang himself, and he stopped hunting entirely, out of fear that he would turn the gun on himself. But then, moved by his time scything hay alongside the peasants who labored on his estate, he experienced a slow spiritual awakening. Inspired by their humble religiosity, he vowed to rein in his ego and simplify his life, while also expanding his consciousness, his curiosity, and his compassion. This was the great adventure of the second half of his life. Feeling that his existence as a nobleman had been "parasitic" and "false," he began to buck social convention. He became a pacifist, gave away much of his wealth, adopted a vegetarian diet, and campaigned on behalf of the rights of the peasantry. He opened soup kitchens and funded schools. He devoted himself to an eccentric study of the Bible—reading fearlessly, separating "what is true and what is false"—as well as the works of Socrates, Schopenhauer, and the Buddha, eventually completing what Bartlett calls a "root-and-branch study of all the major world religions." However, the heart of his complicated personal philosophy was quite simple: an ever-growing sense of brotherly love. His adventurous spirit became directed toward improving the lives of others, rather than merely challenging himself.

People tend to become increasingly insular as they age. Indeed, it seems to be what the modern world wants from us: to cocoon us further within our homes, surrounded by apparently comforting but ultimately alienating technology. We are fundamentally ecological beings, hopelessly tangled up in one another's lives, and yet we are continually pulled (or, perhaps, pushed) to retreat into lonely and even bitter isolation. Numerous studies have shown that one of the greatest predictors of health late in life is not the size of one's bank account, but the number of friends one has. And yet, the publishing industry continues producing reams of "self-help books," and social media teems with hacks to maximize one's beauty and wealth and mental sharpness, while our sense of connection to one another grows thinner and thinner. What Tolstoy learned is that any attempt to perfect the self, without also attempting to improve the lives of others, will result in a hermetic, stale, narrow existence. The remedy to this condition, it turns out, is surprisingly simple: As Tolstoy writes, life cannot be "lived for myself alone." Our salvation, like his, lies in other people and other species.

Trees are excellent teachers in this regard. To climb a tree is, necessarily, to care about its survival; your life and the tree's life become knitted together. This sense of interdependence becomes yet more profound when, as Ben often does, you climb a tree in order to nurse it back to health. It seems no accident that Tolstoy, too, spent a great amount of time around trees, tending to the forests on his estate and studying botany. (He even once wrote a story from the perspective of a tree.) Caring for trees, recognizing one's reliance on them, grappling with the complexity of their alien lives—their gnarls, their absurdities, their endlessly variable beauty—forces one's sense of self-concern to branch out.

Ben had evidently learned this lesson well. What I came to admire most about him was that his love of adventure, much like Tolstoy's, pushed him out of the forest and into the messier realm of human politics. He had begun getting involved with activism in the early days of the Occupy movement, and then joined the climate movement Extinction Rebellion. He was arrested once for blocking the entrance to the Parliament building. Years later, he was arrested again, for a much more daring protest: dressed in an oil-spattered Boris Johnson costume (then the country's conservative prime minister), he climbed a scaffold on the outside of Big Ben, the historic clock tower, and unfurled a rainbow banner reading "NO PRIDE ON A DEAD PLANET." He sat down on some construction netting and clipped in his climbing harness; once he was safely positioned, he later told me, he took a single tab of acid, to experience this moment in its full intensity. When the police began pursuing him, Ben unclipped his harness and tiptoed out onto a steel girder and stood at the very end, where they couldn't reach him. He remained there for a time, posing for newspaper photographers, whose images would be reprinted around the world. Up there, he was the very embodiment of dikost.

He lasted three hours before police arrested him, using a crane, and hauled him off to jail, where he spent the night lightly tripping, but feeling no great anxiety. In a passionate speech before a judge, Ben explained that he had done what he had done because he felt a "duty of care" to other living things. The judge sentenced him to 250 hours of community service. He was assigned to tend to a small grove of ancient trees—yews, sycamores, oaks, spruces, and cypresses—growing in a churchyard. He spent most of his time up in the treetops, pruning branches and healing wounds, high above a field of weathered gravestones. Then, when his work was done and no one was looking, he would climb them once more, this time just for the hell of it.

2. PRUNING

THE NOVELIST Italo Calvino once traveled to see the largest tree in Mexico, a two-thousand-year-old Montezuma cypress known as El Árbol del Tule. Calvino—a lifelong tree lover, raised by a pair of professional botanists in a house full of exotic plants—was horrified by it. He judged it a botanical freak, "a monster." The tree's trunk, which was as wide around as a house, appeared to be made up of a small forest of lesser trunks, all grotesquely fused together. Its crown was massive and messy, a kind of "vegetal cloud." He had long assumed that the best things in life, the things that last, would be clear and elegant, "focused on one single end." But this tree, which had survived so long, was the opposite of simple. Then again, Calvino thought, aren't all trees profligate, blindly sending forth extraneous branches that are destined to one day be pruned away? "Does that mean that the secret of survival is redundancy?" Calvino mused. "Is it through a chaotic waste of matter and forms that the tree manages to give itself a shape and maintain it?"

+

One year into writing this book, I was beginning to feel similarly bewildered. I had decided to let my mind grow like a tree, but the more I learned about trees, the less I seemed to know. Trees were often wondrous, but they could also be villainous. Every summer, they filled the sky above my home with acrid smoke, stealing the breath from our lungs and suffusing our blood with deadly particulates. Some old trees had created forests so lovely they made me want to weep, while others formed such dense, low, spiny thickets that trying to hike through them became a living hell. Meanwhile, people kept telling me about strange new "trees" that I really must include in my book: 350-million-year-old fossils that looked like giant mops; bracket-shaped graphs charting the branching evolution of languages; the ever-ramifying strings of digital code that allow computers to beat Russian grand masters at chess. Everything I saw began to look vaguely tree-shaped. Is a palm tree a tree? Is a "decision tree"? Is a branching fissure in the surface of a frozen lake? There were nearly infinite avenues I might explore. But a book, like a brain, cannot ramify infinitely, lest it devolve into nonsense.

 I needed some clarity. So I decided to pare everything back and ask the simplest question of all: What *is* a tree?

+

I began to mull this question one spring day in 2017 while visiting a garden not far from my home. The garden's entrance is marked only with a discreet sign reading, simply: "BONSAI." I had driven past this garden dozens of times without giving it a second glance, but on this day, I decided to pull over and check it out.

 I parked my car and wandered up the gravel driveway. No one greeted me except two barking dogs. The place appeared to be empty. Feeling a bit like a trespasser, I wandered through the open gate. Near the entrance were rows of tiny trees arranged on long wooden tables. Many of them were small enough to fit into a shoebox, though a few were almost half my height. I peered closely at each. One striking and slightly surreal tree, a pine, was raised up on its own slender, exposed roots, like a cartoon squid trying to peek over a fence. I checked the little paper price tags affixed to some of their branches. One read $450. Another read $1,200. At first glance, they looked like little more than expensive curiosities to me, somewhere between a paperweight and a shrunken head. Still, they possessed an otherworldly beauty—an air of, if not quite the impossible, then at least the astronomically unlikely.

+

The history of bonsai, I would later learn, begins in magic. Before bonsai was brought to Japan, it was invented in China, where it was known as *penjing* (literally "tray landscape"). In *The World in Miniature*, the sinologist Rolf Stein writes that the practice of dwarfing trees was part of a range of Taoist rituals focused on the magical manipulation of the minuscule. Taoist hermits, as well as Buddhist monks, began creating shrunken gardens as objects of contemplation: toy-sized trees, rock-sized mountains, lakes no larger than soup bowls. "Hermits, although confined to the narrow world of their retreat, still had access to the entire universe in all its variety," Stein writes. It was said that even the smallest objects—a strand of hair, a grain of rice—contained entire galaxies. The larger lesson was that the very nature of the universe itself, in all its immensity, was accessible through everyday objects. "If reality and consciousness do not stray from each other," writes the Taoist sage Chang Po-Tuan, "creation is always in the palm of your hand."

+

Centuries later, with the advent of ever more powerful microscopes, modern scientists developed an understanding of small things that was not far off from that of the Taoist sages. A single grain of rice, we now know, contains millions of bacteria and trillions of molecules, each of which contains its own cosmos of spectral particles, residing on the outermost edge of what we can comprehend.

+

I ended up buying a bonsai, a dwarf garden juniper with a serpentine trunk, which I brought home and propped up on a boulder in my backyard, where it could receive sunlight all summer long and ample rain all winter. I chose the species for its low price and its considerable hardiness. Being absent-minded and often away from home, I tend to kill houseplants. The garden's owner assured me that if left outside, in normal weather, the tree would more or less take care of itself, requiring only a few sips of water every few days in the summertime. "See if you can manage to not kill that for a year or two, then come back and talk to me about getting a real tree," he said.

+

By a "real" tree, the garden owner did not mean a more expensive tree. He meant a tree that is a tree. The tree I had purchased, apparently, *resembled* a tree, but it was not one. The Japanese garden juniper is, technically, an evergreen woody shrub. In the wild, it does not grow upward, but instead sprawls out horizontally along the ground. (The plant's scientific name, *Juniperus procumbens*, comes from the Latin for "lying face down.") It turned out I could not even discern a tree from an impostor.

+

What makes a tree a tree? To better understand this question, I enrolled in an online course in tree biology through the University of Victoria. One of the first things my professor, Patrick von Aderkas, impressed upon us is that it is surprisingly difficult to define a tree. Biologically speaking, there is not much difference between the soaring Douglas fir trees in the forest behind my house and the tiny sprigs of rosemary growing in my garden. When plants really need to reach higher than their competitors, they tend to evolve into trees. This process of "treeification" has occurred at least nine times throughout history, as different types of plants (club mosses, horsetails, ferns, hazels) evolved to lift themselves higher than their competitors, a phenomenon known as "convergent evolution." "A tree is really just a growth form," von Aderkas said. The historian Jared Farmer takes this logic one step further. "Trees are plants that humans call trees—a term of dignity, not botany," he writes. An intriguingly postmodern idea, but not the most helpful definition. The biologist Colin Tudge came closer to a working definition when he defined a tree, cheekily, as "a big plant with a stick up the middle." An ecologist named Tom Langen once informed me that, while training to work in forestry for the Peace Corps, he was taught to define a tree as "a self-standing woody plant that a person can climb." This definition—specifically, the emphasis on the tree's entanglement with us—strikes me as truer than most.

+

One key trait all the differing definitions I've run across agree upon, though, is that a tree is a tree because, unlike other woody plants, a tree can grow tall.

+

What, then, is a miniature tree?

+

In a word, it is a paradox.

+

The bonsai garden where I bought my dwarf juniper was owned by an artist and landscape designer named Gerald Rainville. He was a goliath of a man, both tall and broad. When he shook my hand, he revealed a goofy grin and a jumbled set of teeth. (On later visits, these teeth would be wordlessly replaced with a straighter, whiter set.) His voice was deep, round. It resonated from somewhere far within him, as if his vocal cords resided just behind his belly button. Atop his large, bald head was a navy-blue ball cap bearing the orange logo of a baseball team in Tokyo called the Yomiuri Giants.

+

Trees begin their lives in miniature, as tiny embryos encased within seeds. Before the evolution of seeds, around 360 million years ago, all plants reproduced via spores, single cells packed with genetic information, light enough to float on the breeze. Seeds are like spores, only they are better equipped for survival. Encased in its hard shell and equipped with a tiny larder of sugar and water, a germinated seed can wait for weeks, even years for the proper conditions to sprout. Indeed, in some cases they can wait for millennia. A seed from a Judean date palm—another tree that is not technically a tree, but rather a "large woody herb"—sat for two thousand years in a clay jar, buried among the ruins of the palace of King Herod the Great, until, in 2005, a team of scientists decided to plant it in the ground. Miraculously, it sprouted to life. It is now a full-grown tree, putting out seeds of its own.

+

As he led me up the path to his house, Gerald told me about how, when he was a teenager, he had moved from Montreal to a small island in Japan to apprentice at a bonsai garden. This was in 1980. Among the Japanese he was freakishly large and socially alien, but a family of bonsai artisans accepted him into their fold. He lived there for three years, working eleven hours a day, seven days a week, before he felt he had sufficiently mastered his craft and moved back to Canada. In the ensuing decades he returned to Japan periodically to help out his master, fulfilling the lifelong obligation known as *giri*. When his master died recently, Gerald said he felt a deeper grief than when his own parents had died. "Everything I am is from that few years in Japan," he told me. "They took me in and gave me this gift."

+

A tree typically grows from a seed. But many don't. Some trees begin their lives as transplants, a single branch trimmed from another tree, which, when planted on a new patch of ground, sets down roots and develops into its own tree. This new tree is not the child of its parent, but a clone, an exact genetic replica. Willow trees perform this trick naturally, dropping their branches into rivers, where they float downstream, wash ashore, take root, and sprout up. I once visited a clone of the Bodhi tree in the city of Anuradhapura, Sri Lanka, which was brought over from India some two thousand years ago and had been growing larger ever since. People there worshipped it precisely as if it were the original Bodhi tree—which, in a sense, it was.

+

We entered a workshop, where two of Gerald's students were hunched over little trees propped up on plastic buckets. He handed me a foot-tall cypress tree, sat me down, and instructed me to pluck out all of the dead needles. I set it on the workbench in front of me. With my nose almost buried in the branches, I was able to focus on minute details. For a potted plant, the bonsai was surprisingly wild. A small insect—it was so quick that I wasn't able to identify it—flew out of the foliage and bounced off my glasses. I discovered a large brown moth nestled, almost invisibly, against the trunk. Around the base of the tree grew clovers and slender blades of grass. I noticed, however, that the scale of everything was slightly wonky; if these plants had been proportional to a full-grown tree, they would have been enormous, and the moth would have been the size of a pterosaur. I felt as if I had tumbled down into Wonderland.

+

How do you shrink a tree down until it can fit in the palm of your hand? Like the secret to most magic tricks, the answer is surprisingly simple: You just need to restrict the roots. This technique has been known since at least the Tang dynasty in China, circa 700 CE. One simple method is to plant a tree seedling in a dried orange peel and trim back the root tips when they begin to poke through. The resulting sapling will stay small, because each of its roots is connected by a bundle of tiny veinlike tubes to a corresponding branch up above, which it provides with water, allowing it to grow larger (which in turn allows the root to grow larger, and on and on).

It's tempting, therefore, to imagine that the roots of a tree are a mirror image of the branches: as above, so below. Henry David Thoreau suggested as much when he wrote that for every oak tree we could see, there was "a graceful ethereal and ideal tree" growing underground. This is false, however. Tree roots typically extend outward two to three times as far as the crown of the tree, with most of the roots growing near the surface. When trapped in a pot, like a bonsai, the roots will turn in on themselves, growing ever denser, until they attain a brain-like solidity. The roots must be exposed and carefully pruned back, once every few years. Otherwise, at a certain point, a tree becomes "root-bound" and stops growing, and then, starved of water, it begins to die. The real magic trick of bonsai, in other words, is managing to keep it alive.

+

I asked Gerald how he selected a new design for a bonsai. I was hoping to unlock the inscrutable logic of bonsai aesthetics. Why, for example, had he wrapped the branches of a juniper tree in copper wire and bent them as he had? How does he decide to trim this branch and not that one? "I don't," he said. "The tree decides." The goal of bonsai, he explained, was to reproduce the appearance of a wild, ancient tree, rendered down to its bare essence. He quoted a line by the renowned Japanese master Yuji Yoshimura. Bonsai, Yoshimura famously declared, "should remain a forest tree, seen through the wrong end of a telescope."

+

In wild settings, trees sometimes find their roots constricted by rocks or poor soil, and they naturally become dwarfed. The Japanese call these trees *yamadori*. The best ones, being rare, can fetch astronomically high prices. In previous centuries (when such trees were still numerous), certain brave individuals worked as professional yamadori hunters, lowering themselves down cliffsides with ropes to find the most stunted trees. Yoshimura notes that bonsai became popular in Japan in part because of the social cachet of these wild trees: After wealthy families began purchasing yamadori and displaying them in their homes around the sixteenth century, the lower classes emulated them by growing bonsai from seeds. "These could be produced in quantity and were often as beautiful as the older trees, with a naturalness out-rivaling nature," Yoshimura writes.

+

Consider the contradiction inherent in that statement: a *naturalness out-rivaling nature*. Therein lies the uncanny heart of bonsai: nature dissolving into a dreamlike image of itself.

+

This paradox makes a bit more sense when one considers the fact that the word "nature," in Japanese, does not have the same meaning it does in English. The word *shizen* does not refer to an objective thing or realm, wholly outside human influence. Rather, it refers to a *way of being*, which humans can attain as well. The word dates back to the Taoist concept of *ziran*, which refers to a kind of easy, unthinking spontaneity, the opposite of a methodical, premeditated, heavy-handed approach. The Taoist philosopher Zhuangzi once praised the life of a "deformed" man named Shu, whose body was twisted—"his chin buried down in his navel, his shoulders higher than the crown of his head." His life was hard, but his life was good, because he lived according to his abilities. Ever the provocateur, Zhuangzi then quips: "Imagine how much more he could have accomplished if he had deformed virtue, as well!"

+

Before I left his garden that first day, I mentioned to Gerald that I was heading to Japan in a few weeks with my husband, to see the blossoming of the cherry trees. Gerald's eyes widened to the size of gumballs. He informed me that the World Bonsai Convention would be going on while I was there. I asked him what that was. "Only the greatest bonsai convention in history!" he replied. The event was only held once every four years, in a different country. This year it was being hosted just outside Tokyo. Many of the older Japanese masters, who refused to travel to the other conventions, would be there to display their ancient, priceless bonsai. Since these artists would soon be dying off, this event promised to be something like the passing of a celestial comet. Before even leaving his garden, I'd already begun mentally rerouting my trip.

+

Much of what makes a tree a tree can be explained by the plain fact that a tree, unlike an animal, cannot travel. "A tree is stuck where its seed landed and sent down its original root, fixing its fate to a single spot," write David Suzuki and Wayne Grady in *Tree: A Life Story*, their imaginative account of the life of a single Douglas fir in the Pacific Northwest. Being rooted to the ground, a tree cannot outrun predators, so it must grow thick armor and deploy an arsenal of toxic chemical compounds to deter its attackers. It cannot seek out sexual partners, so it must release pollen and seeds in huge quantities, hoping the wind or animals will carry them to where they need to go. It cannot chase food, so it must put out as many branches and leaves as possible. It cannot seek out minerals, so it must send roots down, sucking its nutrients straight from the soil. It cannot hide from storms, so it must learn to endure them. It cannot be animate, so it must be arborescent.

+

A tree, in other words, is a tree because a tree stays in place. Bonsai mock this rule. A bonsai is a tree that can travel anywhere.

+

The World Bonsai Convention was held in an enormous arena on the outskirts of Tokyo. When I arrived, one warm spring day a few weeks later, a two-block-long line of people, predominantly older Japanese couples, were already patiently waiting outside. By wielding a press pass I had forged for myself, claiming to be on assignment for an ancient, beautiful, somewhat root-bound magazine based in New York, I was able to sneak in through a side door before the event officially opened. As I stepped inside the vast cool interior, I noticed a faint greenhouse odor: humid, vegetal, resinous. It smelled as if an entire forest had been uprooted and transported indoors.

+

Every breath a tree exhales contains a spritz of water molecules. This allows a tree to cool off its leaves, which prevents them from being scorched and dried out by the sun. (Von Aderkas calls a plant "essentially a water-cooled solar panel.") A single tree in the tropics can lift a thousand gallons of water from its roots to its leaves on a hot day. One might wonder how a being without muscles can find the strength to lift the equivalent of a liquified killer whale. The answer is that it doesn't need to. To exhale, trees open tiny pores on their leaves, allowing water to evaporate. Each molecule of water in the veins of a tree is chemically linked to nearby water molecules in a chain—a phenomenon known as "hydrogen bonding," familiar to anyone who's ever watched two adjacent water droplets on a tabletop merge into a single blob. So when one water molecule is exhaled, another is automatically pulled up to replace it. As Tudge writes, "Water is not pumped from below but dragged from above by the leaves... not in a crude and turbulent gush but in millions on millions of orderly threads." In other words, the tree does not lift water to the sky; the sky lifts water *through* the tree.

+

In the calm early preopening hours of the show, I explored the convention hall while a trio of young Japanese women wearing plastic headwear in the shape of bonsai practiced a choreographed dance on a nearby stage. The space was divided into a warren of corridors, partitioned by freestanding walls and long tables, and upon each table sat a row of meticulously groomed, dwarfed trees. I walked through row after row in silence. At first, the trees blurred together into an indistinguishable mass. My sleep-fogged mind still registered them as little more than curios. I felt a bit like a cranky old man staring at paintings of basic geometric shapes in a modern art museum. *Why all the fuss?* I wondered.

A handful of artists were still making last-minute adjustments to their trees. I watched as a man moved from one bonsai to another with a device resembling a giant dental irrigator, delicately watering the roots, careful not to disturb the surface of the soil. Another man, wielding a long pair of tweezers, reached into the branches of a beech tree, plucked out a leaf no larger than a weasel's tongue, then stepped back to survey his work, his head cocked to the side. I was impressed by the sharpness of their attention. As I moved on, I found that I now saw the trees in a new light. Every single leaf on every single tree, I realized, was the product of years of care, forethought, and hard work. As Calvino observed while touring gardens in Japan, "One can make the equivalent of a poem with the way one arranges trees."

+

Wild trees are masters at arranging themselves. Every tree faces a basic existential dilemma: It needs to eat sunlight and drink water, but the sun and rainwater are located in very different places (up in the sky and down in the soil). The solution trees have devised is to turn themselves into networks of tubes. A tree sucks up mineral-rich water from the ground via tubes called xylem, and it sucks a sugary solution down from the leaves to the roots via different tubes called phloem. How does the tree decide how to organize this complex plumbing system? Brilliantly—and brainlessly. Branches are covered in buds, which, when they receive enough sunlight, signal to nearby cells to begin growing some new tubes.* So while a tree grows upward from the tips of its branches, it also grows *downward* as well, adding layer upon layer of new tubes that reach all the way down to the root tips, deeper and deeper into the soil. In a large tree, these roots (including the hairlike structures called "fine roots"), if laid end to end, would extend for hundreds of miles.

+

---

*Bonsai artists know this trick well. Gerald told me that in order to thicken the trunk in a certain place, artists will often keep what's called a "sacrifice branch," even though it's unsightly; once the trunk, in its effort to feed that branch, has thickened sufficiently, the artist then prunes the branch away.

Bonsai artists, too, face a basic existential dilemma. The only way to make a decent living is to go big—caring for hundreds of trees at a time, teaching classes, training apprentices, managing the finances—but that creates the potential for spreading oneself too thin. Moreover, caring for the trees is a job that never ends; taking even a single day off during a heat wave or a cold snap could bring about the death of an entire garden. The result is that, though their lives appear serene and contemplative to outsiders, being a bonsai professional is a life of never-ending stress. "One day," a renowned Japanese bonsai artist told me, "my dream is to just lie down on the grass and see the sunshine."

+

A tree is a plant that has learned to grow vast without spreading itself too thin. The earliest plants had not yet mastered this skill. When plants made their way out of the sea and onto land more than 500 million years ago, they were little more than clumps of pond scum. Over time, they slowly grew taller and more complex, playing around with a variety of body types. Then they stumbled onto a useful architectural trick: By splitting themselves apart into multiple branches (and sub-branches (and so on)), they could gather more sunlight. By funneling those branches down to a single stem, they could conserve their building materials. And by fanning out once again into many roots, they could grip the soil and drink up more water. By the time the first trees appeared, about 400 million years ago, their ancestors had already mastered the art of branching. But now, with the use of sturdy wood, trees could grow even taller, reach out farther, and survive longer, casting larger and larger shadows on their competitors down below.

+

The most prized bonsai at the convention was located right by the front entrance. It was the first thing anyone entering with a normal ticket would see. But since I had entered through a side door and commenced through the show in reverse, I saw it last. I was glad I did, otherwise it may have ruined my expectations for the rest of the show. It was a Shimpaku juniper with a fantastically torsioned trunk, bearing two domes of dense green foliage. Its branches were mostly dead—bare, bleached, visibly disintegrating—but they were wrapped in thin brown ropes of live wood, which the artist had spared to keep the foliage nourished. It looked less like a tree than like some kind of enchanted skeleton, with raw veins bulging and tufts of new hair sprouting up while its bones sublimate to smoke. I stood before it for many minutes, tracing a single exposed vein of living wood as it made its journey up around the scoliotic spine of the tree, from the roots to the foliage. A small plaque beside the tree informed me that it was estimated to be one thousand years old.

+

A tree is a tree because a tree can grow ancient. Unlike us, trees are modular, which means that they can also shed their branches and regrow new ones. Certain species, like the 9,550-year-old Norway spruce in Sweden known as Old Tjikko, can even regrow a new trunk from their roots, a phenomenon that makes it almost impossible to declare which tree is actually the "oldest tree on earth."

What kills trees is not time, but the rest of the world: bad weather, hungry insects, harmful pathogens, chainsaw-wielding humans. Bonsai can be guarded from all these. As a result, writes the arborist and scholar Thomas Pakenham, "Bonsai experts believe that a bonsai might become virtually immortal—or at any rate live for thousands of years—if properly disciplined."

+

At nine o'clock sharp, the doors were opened, and a thick flow of visitors filled the aisles of the convention hall. The crowds soon became dense: solid bodies moving as liquid. (It was later estimated that a total of forty-five thousand people passed through over three days.) One would have expected a rising clamor to fill the hall, but the visitors uniformly spoke in a hush. The room, with its cathedral-high ceilings, had an almost sacramental air. I typically find crowds irritating, but here, among my fellow tree worshippers, I felt at peace. I was simply absorbed into their slow, laminar flow.

+

A tree in an open field is a picture of expansiveness, reaching out in all directions. But a tree in a dense forest—standing shoulder to shoulder with other trees, as it were—having only a narrow window of light up above to grow toward, will develop a long, straight, largely branchless trunk. This is possible because as it grows, a tree often sheds its lowest branches, using a form of self-amputation. Indeed, in some sense, trees are better surgeons than we could ever hope to be. When a branch no longer receives enough sunlight, the tree will begin to seal off its withered limb by growing layers of new tissues at its base, then dissolving some of the connective tissues, so that when the branch falls away, it does so cleanly. The wound heals before the wound is ever made.

+

As I walked around the convention hall, I noticed a cluster of Japanese men in black polo shirts bustling here and there. Everyone else stepped aside deferentially to let them pass. At their nucleus was an aged man in a gray suit, with an icily quiet presence. He wore a faint, forlorn, obliging smile, as if valiantly pushing through some indescribable pain. That man, a pair of Aussie bystanders told me, was Masahiko Kimura, the so-called magician of bonsai. I asked the Aussies if they thought he might be willing to talk with me. They were certain that he would not. This, of course, only made me want to talk to him all the more.

When a tree grows upward, it typically sends only one branch toward the sky—what's called the leader branch—while all of the other branches grow out laterally. Logically, it would seem that many branches would compete for the sunlight at the top of the tree. The reason why other branches tend not to challenge the leader's dominance is because, along with a trickle of nourishing sugars, the leader sends down special hormones, called auxins, which inhibit the vertical growth of the branches lower down on the tree. When the leader branch is broken off in a storm or nibbled down by pests, multiple branches will often compete to become the new leader. A kind of slow anarchy ensues, which can threaten the structural stability of the tree as a whole, until a new leader emerges.

+

By talking with my fellow convention-goers, I would soon learn that in the rigidly stratified world of elite bonsai, Kimura, then in his late seventies, was at the profession's apex. He was likely the world's highest-paid bonsai artist, as well as its most revered. At one point during the convention, Kunio Kobayashi, a bonsai celebrity who is one of Kimura's chief rivals, described him as "the kind of genius who comes along once every hundred years, or maybe more." Marco Invernizzi, one of Kimura's former apprentices, told me, simply, that in the world of modern bonsai, "he is God."

+

Trees worship no gods, only the sun. Their lives are an unending quest to be a little closer to it. This is true even when the sun is hidden by clouds, or a seedling is buried deep in soil. One might justly wonder how the tree knows which way is up. The answer is twofold. First, trees, like all living things, are affected by the pull of gravity; dense, starch-filled organelles are dragged downward, stimulating their roots to grow toward the earth's core and their shoots to grow away from it, even when they're in total darkness. Also, trees can sense the presence of light, via cells called photoreceptors. When a branch is exposed to sunlight, auxins are pumped away from the source of light, causing it to grow faster on the side with more auxins, which bends the branch toward the light. (In a brilliant twist, roots do precisely the opposite: There, the side with more hormones is genetically programmed to grow slower, which means it bends *away* from the light.) In the 1980s, NASA scientists proved this conclusively by growing a tiny forest of pine seedlings on board a space station, in a zero-gravity environment. They found that they grew more or less normally, with their branches reaching toward the light and their roots reaching down into the soil. As the farmer and author Gene Logsdon notes, "Sunlight seems like such a soft, passive, gentle kind of force, but it is strong enough to bend tree trunks."

+

Later that morning, I was able to observe Kimura's empyrean stature in the world of bonsai. At the center of the great hall was a large stage where bonsai artists from various countries would perform what were called "demonstrations." They would shape a single tree before a live audience, trimming, plucking, and bending the woolly trees into refined shapes, accomplishing in a couple of hours a process that would normally take days or even weeks.

That morning, a Malaysian man named Michael Siow Chee Long was shaping a wisteria. He set a bold course of action, tilting the tree to a perilous angle, then wrapping the branches with wire and bending them into every possible direction, like the waving arms of an anemone.

Midway through the demonstration, without warning, Kimura wandered onto the stage, inspected Siow's tree, frowned, and said something to the translator. A small gasp went up through the crowd.

Siow turned from his work and asked the translator, "What is Mr. Kimura's opinion, when he sees this tree?"

The translator paused. "I think that he's looking at it and he's thinking, 'I wouldn't have styled it that way, but that everyone has their own approach,'" he said.

The audience chuckled. Siow looked queasy. The translator attempted to console him. "The natural world has a million and one shapes," he said.

+

The term "arborescence," oddly enough, originated as something of a slur. It was coined by the postmodern philosophers Gilles Deleuze and Félix Guattari in their magnum opus, *A Thousand Plateaus*. Trees, they believed, were oppressive, even fascistic structures, with their multiple branches all flowing into a single trunk, like so many generals and governors reporting to a single dictator—forming what they called a "pseudo-multiplicity." (D&G preferred the anarchic model of the "rhizome," a truly decentralized tangle of roots that sends up multiple shoots, like ginger.) However, the contemporary philosopher Michael Marder has argued that D&G "got arborescence all wrong." "The physical verticality of trees does not mean that they are vertical in the way they live or grow," he writes. "Trees can branch out in quite unpredictable ways; they can accommodate the grafts of other species; they can give rise to shoots that can survive independently of them; they can change their sexes or become hermaphrodites for a limited stretch or for the rest of their lives; and the list continues." Arborescence, he insists, is far too weird—far too wild—to symbolize the spirit of totalitarianism. It is something else entirely.

+

After the convention, I toured the nation's great bonsai gardens. To reach them, I crisscrossed the country riding in bullet trains—long, white, plastic-skinned tubes with the elongated snouts of garfish. The landscape outside my windows was almost uncannily orderly. I looked out at man-made waterfalls plummeting in straight lines down stone walls. I noticed single-row vegetable gardens growing in the narrow gap between the railway and people's homes. I snapped a blurry photo of Mount Fuji rising pristinely above a soot-dark sea of houses and strip malls that stretched right up to its base. I walked down pathways where the branches of the flowering sakura trees had been trained to grow into an archway, as if a tunnel had been blasted through a hill of solid blossoms.

+

The best bonsai are meant to evoke a deep sense of place and time. Traditionally, bonsai are displayed in a special alcove of the house known as a *tokonoma*, alongside painted scrolls and small "accent plants." With the shifting seasons, a tree's leaves will change color; fruit trees will sprout forth flowers and fruits; and the scroll and accent plants will be regularly switched out for new ones—all of which reflects the ecological context in which that tree would have thrived in the wild. Moreover, in Japan there are not just four seasons; there are also seventy-two microseasons, or *kō*, labeled with ecologically specific names like "Peonies Bloom" and "Wild Geese Return." Bonsai, which looks to many outsiders like a perversion of wild nature, often functions as a window onto the city's local ecology, or a ghostly reminder of the ecology the city has displaced.

+

At a certain point in my travels, I began noticing that the forests in the countryside tended to be oddly uniform, segregated by species, with leafy trees on one side of the road and needled trees on another. During the "hermit kingdom" era in the 1600s known as the Tokugawa shogunate, when the Japanese could no longer import timber from neighboring countries, the ruling elite instituted one of the world's most rigorous silviculture plans, accounting for virtually every tree in every forest. Following the Second World War, this forestry system was industrialized with shocking, even surreal, efficiency. It is estimated that 40 percent of Japan's forests have been artificially planted, and some 40 percent of that reforested area is planted with a single species of fast-growing cedar known as *sugi*. These cedars have been planted in such huge numbers that when they begin to release their pollen in the spring, it descends on cities like a golden fog. The clouds of pollen often grow so thick, one allergy specialist told *The New York Times*, that people mistake it for forest fire smoke. Through their unceasing desire to prune the natural world, not only had the Japanese changed the composition of their forests; they had changed the very color of the sky.

+

Japanese bonsai artists divide forests in two: They refer to coniferous trees, like pines, as *shohaku* (needled trees), and they refer to broadleaf trees, like maples, as *zouki* (leafy trees). Leaves and needles employ two entirely different survival strategies. The deciduous leafy trees, like grizzly bears, have evolved for a life of feasts and famines. In the spring, they eat greedily, amassing a larder of energy in their roots, and then, when winter nears, they shed all of their leaves and enter a state of hibernation known as dormancy. Needled trees, by contrast, live more like polar bears, which gather food all winter long, since their narrow, waxy needles (and special drought-proof vascular tissues) have evolved to survive cold and stormy winters. As for the leafy trees in the tropics, they live like hummingbirds, or punk idols: They feast year-round, grow up quickly, and (typically) die young.[*]

---

[*] People who know a lot about trees continually correct me when I call a pine needle a "needle." They say that a pine needle is actually a leaf; it's just a harder, more narrow *kind* of leaf. *Sure,* I think. *But then, isn't every thing just another kind of thing?*

One by one, I toured the great bonsai gardens of Japan, starting with Mansai-en, a garden located not far from the convention center, which has been owned by the same family for five generations. At Shunka-en, the owner, Kunio Kobayashi, dramatically carved a tree with a chainsaw before my eyes. At Taisho-en, Taiga Urushibata showed me how he had invented special bonsai pots that could float atop water. (He coyly refused to divulge how he'd managed to create them.) The most impressive garden I visited belonged to Shinji Suzuki, a superhumanly meticulous man who had plucked and bent his trees into a state of unreal perfection. (In my notebook that day, I jotted the words "Nintendo trees.") However, my favorite garden was one called Fuyo-en, in Omiya, which specializes in leafy trees. One late afternoon, amid slanting light, as the day finally let go of its angry warmth, I found myself walking among a knee-high forest of flowering apricot trees. The aroma was overwhelming, like a delicately perfumed wrist pressed right to the nose. Oddly, though, it smelled nothing like apricots, but rather like cinnamon.

+

For most of my life, I have been bored by flowers. They always seemed to me to be frivolous, frilly, decorative, nonnutritive—merely beautiful. I was wrong. Flowers, it turns out, are one of the greatest innovations in the history of life on earth. Prior to roughly 140 million years ago, all trees on earth were gymnosperms, which means that they dispersed their pollen using the wind, in the hopes that their genetic information would float through the air and land on a female cone of the same species. By developing seeds hidden within flowers and fruit, a new class of trees—the angiosperms—found a way to reproduce more effectively. Rather than haphazardly releasing their pollen into the wind, the flowers of angiosperms could entice a wide array of animals (insects, birds, certain small mammals) to deliver their pollen to precisely where it needed to go. This tactic proved immensely successful; angiosperms soon spread around the planet, outcompeting their flowerless rivals. It had only one major downside. As the author Tristan Gooley notes, "Animal pollination is much more efficient than wind, but you have to make sure your flowers stand out. It's like the most ruthless horticultural competition imaginable: If you fail to get a gold medal, your family dies."

+

As my time in Japan was coming to a close, I had one last garden I wanted to see: Kimura's. He had repeatedly rebuffed my efforts to speak with him. Finally, by enlisting the help of a beautiful female translator (Kimura had a weakness for charming women, I had been told), I was able to get him to agree.

+

There are male trees (which produce pollen) and there are female trees (which produce fruit). But as with humans, the gender divide among trees is more complex than it initially seems. Some trees change sexes partway through their lives, like the hero of Woolf's *Orlando*. And a significant percentage (possibly as much as one-half) of all trees contain both male and female reproductive organs. Such trees are sometimes capable of impregnating themselves—a process called "selfing"—but the offspring, as one might imagine, tend to turn out a bit inbred.

+

Bonsai have genders too. In bonsai competitions, artists are sometimes penalized for gender-bending: A masculine tree should be paired with a masculine pot, and vice versa. Masculine trees are said to be heavier, with rougher bark and more forceful curves, while feminine trees are said to be graceful and smooth. But in the details, it can be hard to distinguish the boyish trees from the girlish ones. One person told me that Kimura's way of styling trees was the perfect balance of masculine and feminine, while another told me that it was "super-alpha masculine." Both seemed true.

+

On the appointed day, an apprentice greeted us at the gate of Kimura's compound and led us through the garden, past a pond haunted by albino carp, and into his sunny office. He sat on one side of a long table, and my translator and I sat on the other. His daughter brought us cups of green tea and cups of pale gelatin with a single piece of black mochi floating in the center. Kimura ate his quickly, set it aside, and lit a cigarette. Squinting contentedly, he took a small cloud into his chest and then, with puckered lips, transformed it into a stream.

Over the course of our interview, he smoked nine more cigarettes. He apparently enjoyed the ritual of lighting the cigarette as much, or more, than the experience of smoking it, because he often gently stubbed one out half-finished. Afterward he laid it in a neat row beside the others in a large crystal ashtray, like timber.

+

When you cut down a tree and peer at the concentric rings in its trunk, you travel back in time. Each year, a tree adds another thin layer of veiny flesh to its old bones, like a Matryoshka doll growing an ever-larger version of itself around the older versions. In colder climates, in the early spring the vessels in this new flesh grow larger to pipe water up to the tree's foliage, then as the summer turns to fall and the rain dwindles and the air cools, these vessels grow both smaller and denser, which makes the wood tougher and helps prevent deadly air bubbles from forming. The result of this process is that some layers of veiny flesh are thicker than others. By examining these "tree rings," scientists can determine the climatic history of past centuries, a practice called dendrochronology. Human history is written there too. Calvino writes that he was fond of visiting an exhibit in the Jardin des Plantes in Paris that featured a crosswise slice of an old sequoia tree. On various rings of the tree "the great historical events of the last two thousand years" were "marked on little copper tags": the destruction of Pompeii, the First Crusade, the American abolition of slavery, and so on. In 2012, while studying the carbon-14 isotopes embedded in the rings of an ancient cedar, a Japanese scientist named Fusa Miyake discovered evidence of a massive solar storm in 774 CE, which other scientists around the world soon confirmed in other ancient trees. Using Miyake's method, scientists were later able to pin down the exact year Norse sailors settled in North America, a question that had long eluded historians.

+

If only humans were so easy to read. Instead we must infer their pasts from tiny details about their appearance and their comportment. Or we must ask questions of them. Either approach is flawed.

Before interviewing Kimura, my translator, a bonsai artist and writer named Makiko Kobayashi, insisted that I send her all of my questions in advance so that she could approve them. I sent her twenty questions. She replied: "Numbers 3, 4, 6, 7, 13, 14, 16, 20 might be hard to ask him. I will try to ask him very carefully...."

+

When you look at a tree, allowing your eyes to move from top to bottom, you also travel back in time. A tree grows from the bottom up, each layer of growth building upon the last. This is what causes the trunk to taper as it rises. "Think of a candle getting thicker by being dipped again and again in hot wax," write Suzuki and Grady.

"In a tree, the new layer of hot wax is the cambium, and the layers of cooled wax are the tree's heartwood, the rings of its earlier growth." It is this peculiar, layer-by-layer growth process that leads to the mechanism of gnarling: Every strange bend a tree suffers in its long life is preserved, fossil-like, somewhere within its layers of tissues.

+

The magician of bonsai, I learned, did not set out to be a bonsai artist. He originally expected to become an engineer and inventor, like his father. But when he was eleven years old, his father was murdered. It was 1951, and the nation was still recovering from the war. The family fell into poverty, and Kimura was forced to get a job as an errand boy. This was a period of his life that Kimura largely refused to discuss, except to say that it was, in his words, "hell." When he was fifteen, Kimura's mother announced that she would be sending him to apprentice at Toju-en, a famous bonsai garden in Omiya, then the epicenter of the art form. She had noticed that he was good with his hands, and she wanted to give him a profession that would make him happy. As an apprentice at Toju-en, Kimura worked seven days a week, 8 a.m. to 11 p.m., without a single day off for the first three years. His master, Motosuke Hamano, harshly corrected his every error; Kimura says his master even told him how to walk. Kimura was given five minutes to finish meals. He was allowed no girlfriends, no alcohol, and no cigarettes.

+

When a tree is bent over by harsh winds, or when another tree falls on it, the tree will react accordingly: It will grow asymmetrically in order to straighten up. This process differs in needled trees and leafy trees: In needled trees, the trunk reacts by growing tougher fibers, called "compression wood," on its underside, whereas in leafy trees, it grows more flexible wood, called "tension wood," on its upper side.

Both are forms of what is called "corrective growth": The crown of the tree is gradually pushed (or pulled) upward. But due to the gnarling process, the curvature in a tree's trunk will forever bear the mark of its trials. Loggers tend to hate bent lumber, because crooked trees can be more dangerous to fell and because they make for less valuable timber. For this reason, the Taoist philosopher Zhuangzi professed a special reverence for twisted, "useless" trees, which, being spared the axe, can endure for centuries. This ancient, gnarled quality later became a hallmark of the aesthetic of bonsai.

+

Kimura completed his apprenticeship when he was twenty-six. Lacking the money to launch a bonsai business, he instead opened a plant shop. It was successful, and after a decade or so, he had saved enough money to become a professional bonsai artist. Now married with two daughters, he was determined to catch up to his more privileged contemporaries. One day, after spending seven hours shaping a Shimpaku juniper, the thought occurred to him: *Why doesn't anyone use power tools to accomplish this more quickly?* Kimura soon developed an arsenal of custom devices—sandblasters, small chainsaws, and grinders—that had never before been applied to bonsai. A bonsai artist named Michael Hagedorn likened this innovation to the invention of the electric guitar. "The possibilities just go 3D," he told me.

+

Traditionally, bonsai was a sedate art form, with a vague air of old money about it, prizing patience, adherence to tradition, and an invisibly light touch. There are a number of informal rules that define good bonsai. The rules include that a trunk should taper from the bottom to the top, and *never* in the opposite direction; that branches should extend from alternating sides of the trunk, creating a feeling of balance; that a short branch should never reach directly toward the viewer (what's known as an eye poker); and that the crown of the tree should lean slightly forward, as if bowing in deference to the viewer. Some also say that enough room should be left between the branches to imagine "a bird flying through." And lastly, the roots should flare out to grasp the earth firmly, giving the tree both the semblance of old age and a feeling of stability. (The Japanese have a beautiful word, *nebari*, for this quality. It also means "stickiness" or "persistence.")

+

Kimura is sometimes said to have done for bonsai what Picasso did for painting—he shattered the art form, and then reengineered it. By using power tools, he was able to perform transformations so radical they seemed to border on the impossible, creating shapes that verged on the ethereal. Young trees could be made to look ancient in a manner of hours. Kimura could hollow out thick roots to coil them up in smaller pots, bend stout trees to make them appear smaller, split apart single trees to create many-trunked forests, and quickly sculpt deadwood into creamy whorls. One of his most famous tricks was to flip a tree upside down (a technique he called "reversing the earth and sky"): He applied special hormones to the branches to force them to grow new roots, and then he used his power tools to carve the roots into wispy, dead branches. Even as his status rose, Kimura recalls that he received "lots of criticism from bonsai VIPs at the time." Detractors derided his use of power tools as "noisy" (both literally and stylistically); others accused him of making "sculptures, not bonsai."

+

Trees can be sculpted because trees are mostly made up of wood. Other kinds of plants, like herbs, are able to stand upright only because the water pumped through their vessels keeps them taut; when the water runs out, they wilt. But true trees have evolved wood—a substance made up chiefly of two polymers, flexy cellulose and flinty lignin—which allows them to grow taller. It's the lignin that makes wood woody. Lignin is also what must be stripped *out* of wood, when it is pulped and processed, to make paper pliable. My friends have often pointed out the irony that this book about the beauty of trees is printed on the mashed-up corpses of slaughtered trees. It is an additional irony that to make this book of trees, someone first had to remove the very thing—woodiness—that makes a tree a tree.

+

Kimura developed a reputation for working faster, cheaper, and better than his competitors, and his business flourished. As he acquired wealth, he adopted a Hemingwayesque lifestyle, driving American muscle cars, piloting speedboats, and hunting wild boar (in Spain, with the Spanish prime minister, no less). He also began traveling the world to see great trees in the wild—the skeletal bristlecones of California, the monstrous olives in Puglia, the gargantuan camphor trees of Taiwan—to draw inspiration from them.

+

In the wild, the shape of a tree is the visual record of every moment of that tree's life—every wound, every ice storm, every new bounty of sunlight. Tristan Gooley writes that trees can also be interpreted to glean information about the land around them: the prevailing winds, the height of the water table, even the location of the magnetic poles. (One of the many handy survival tricks he imparts is that, in the northern hemisphere, one can orient oneself by counting the number of aborted branches on a tree. Since the sun tends to be in the south, trees will grow, and subsequently drop, more branches on their south side.) The shape of trees also reflects their latitude. Tudge notes that trees in the far north and the far south grow "tall and steeple-like to catch the light that comes at them from the side," whereas trees in the Middle East and Mediterranean acquire flat tops, "aimed at the sunlight beamed from overhead." Trees in tropical rainforests shoot upward, juiced with ample rainwater, while in drier equatorial habitats, like the African savanna, they "spread themselves like cats."

+

Kimura finally began to receive the recognition of the Japanese bonsai establishment in 1988, when he submitted a seven-hundred-year-old wild-collected Shimpaku juniper called *Toryu-no-mai* ("The Dance of a Rising Dragon") to a prestigious national competition. It won the top prize and is now widely regarded as one of the finest bonsai ever created. It was a great Z-shaped roil of living and dead wood, the trunk rising almost horizontally, first left, then right, involuting, curling, coiling, bulging, and tendrilling out, like dense smoke in hard wind. Atop this luscious chaos sat a neat but asymmetrical dome of foliage, a green cloud into which the dragon's head vanished. The tree stands in Kimura's garden to this day. I had the chance to inspect it closely, and it is as beautiful as everyone told me it would be. Its trunk moved in ways the eye cannot follow, leaving me awed and, inexplicably, somewhat melancholy—a soft kind of sadness, born of an encounter with something just beyond one's comprehension. The Japanese have a word for this feeling, which English entirely lacks. They call it *yugen*.

+

At the convention, I had met an American bonsai artist named Ryan Neil, who was the first foreigner to complete a six-year apprenticeship with Kimura, and who now owns a garden full of wild-collected masterpieces in Oregon. Ryan explained to me that traditional bonsai was designed to provide a "reprieve" from the clamor of daily life, since our brains instinctively understand that a healthy, symmetrical tree indicates it is growing in a stable, peaceful environment. But Kimura's style—and Ryan's—is to push the degree of asymmetry until the viewer becomes uncomfortable, evoking a tree's struggle for survival in wind-scoured mountains and on seaside cliffs. A young tree nearly always grows straight and symmetrical, and that's what makes them boring to look at. "The older it gets, the more asymmetrical it gets, because of the random acts and events that the natural environment is imposing on the tree," he said. "Humans are virtually no different."

Years later, Ryan and I would climb to the top of a giant coast redwood together so that we could admire a tiny tan oak that had somehow taken root atop one of the redwood's branches, more than a hundred feet off the ground. He estimated the tan oak, which was only a few inches tall, was at least thirty years old. It was a perfect distillation of the wondrous perdurability of trees. "I think the magic of trees doesn't necessarily relate to size," he said. "It relates to the unfathomable."

+

When I met Kimura he was nearing eighty years old, and although his artistic dominance remained intact, people close to him told me that his creative powers were clearly winding down. Already, his designs were becoming less daring, and his treatment of his apprentices was becoming less severe. A few years prior, he had been diagnosed with lung cancer. Sixty percent of his lungs had to be surgically removed. He spent ten days in the hospital and stopped smoking for one month, then resumed. I hoped to ask Kimura about his legacy. What would he do with his trees when he died, for example? Did he want them sent to a museum? How would he ensure their survival? When I put these questions to him, he shook his head curtly and muttered something. "He does not like to think about his own death," the translator told me. That was the end of that line of questioning.

+

Trees are serene in the face of death. Rather than shying away from it, they use it to strengthen themselves. The vascular tissues of a tree are fated to die long before the tree does. The phloem lives only a few months (or, in some cases, years), then dies, dries out, and lines the inner bark, whereas the xylem, which survives for an even shorter amount of time, eventually gets crushed down into heartwood. These layers of dead tissue accumulate, year after year, enclosing one within the next, as the tree grows both taller and thicker. In this way, the tree's circulatory system gradually becomes both its skin and its spine. By the time a tree reaches maturity, it is roughly 90 percent dead. "And so the tree continues, part dying and part being born," wrote Aristotle. "Hence their long life."

+

When I returned home to Canada from Japan, I continued visiting Gerald at his garden, once every year or so. As my bonsai grew and I tended to its needs, I noticed that I felt myself becoming more attuned to that day's weather, the rain and the heat and the frost; I had begun to experience the world, however abstractly, through the tree. But along with this awareness came the terrifying knowledge of the fragility of life, especially plant life, and the unbroken chain of care required to foster it. Gerald once told me a story about a former client of his, an "old, old man," who managed to keep a bonsai alive for seventy years. "So what does that say about his life? Through everything you go through in life, he never forgot to water that tree."

+

Certain trees have evolved to store large amounts of water in the tissues of their trunks, saving it for the dry season. Baobabs, the camels of the arboreal world, can hold the contents of an average backyard swimming pool. Because the water is mostly stored in the tree's vascular tissues, humans can't access it—the notion of tapping a baobab in the desert for fresh water is a myth—but thirsty elephants have figured out how to tear hunks off the tree and chew on the wood, sucking out its moisture. Other trees, like magnolias, are said to hold so much water in pockets in their trunks that when arborists use chainsaws to cut into them, they occasionally get sprayed with a thick, red, tannin-rich liquid that eerily resembles blood.

+

A bonsai, being pot-bound, naturally has access to far less water than a wild tree. This means that, as the climate warms and heat waves intensify, the art of keeping tiny trees alive will become ever more difficult. One recent summer a record heat wave swept through Oregon. Ryan Neil later told me that, despite diligent watering, a number of his most cherished trees were either killed or badly maimed. "It was catastrophic," he said. For him, bonsai had always served as a microcosm for the beauty of wild nature. But now it had begun serving as a reminder of its fragility as well.

+

Inevitably, the time came when I forgot to water my bonsai. It wasn't entirely my fault. I was away on work for a few weeks one summer when yet another record heat wave swept through the province, parching every plant. My neighbors tried their best to keep the tree alive, but much of its foliage nevertheless turned brown and fell away. When I got back, it had taken on a raw-spined, mangey look, like a former show poodle gone feral. I sent a photo to Gerald. He sent back his condolences. Trees that badly damaged, he said, tend to enter a death spiral: There is not enough foliage left to support the roots, which then cannot send up enough stored sugars to push out new foliage next spring. He advised me to "plant it in the garden and see if it shoots back."

Here, I learned an oddly hopeful piece of arboreal arcana: When taken out of their pots and planted in healthy soil, bonsai can quickly grow into full-sized trees. Following Gerald's advice, I carried my supernatural little bonsai to a corner of my garden and planted it back into the earth, where it lives to this day, although, being a-tree-that-isn't-quite-a-tree, it is still no taller than my shin, and it never will be.

+

Looking at my little tree, I, too, see a microcosm of the wild, and it troubles me. We humans have seemingly bent the whole of the Earth into a kind of planetary bonsai, a thing we contort more or less at will, a thing above which we loom. And, like my little tree, that twisted, half-tame system is now beginning to falter.

Certain brave anarchistic souls say that the answer to our planet's woes is to do to it what I did with my juniper: to return it to nature and let it grow wild. I don't think it is so simple. In truth, there is not a single human society that does not "warp nature" to its needs, whether through fire, hunting, gardening, or aquaculture. To a certain extent, we *must* warp it to survive. The question then becomes: How do we contort other living things—and, just as importantly, contort ourselves *around* other living things—in a way that respects their unruly essence? What philosophy should we follow? How do we create, of the earth, a piece of careful, collaborative, and ever-living art?

+

Like the Taoist sages of old, I have grown to see bonsai as a kind of spiritual practice: a form of nature worship perfectly tailored to our post-natural age. This might sound strange. Some environmental thinkers regard bonsai as typifying an especially arrogant, manipulative, even cruel approach to the natural world. (The artist Julianne Skai Arbor half jokingly refers to the discipline as "hortitorture.") But bonsai artists, like arborists, tend to view their work as a form of collaboration, not domination. The landscape historian J. B. Jackson argued that arboriculture is spiritually enriching for precisely this reason. "The value of trees," he writes, "is not only that they can be beautiful and that they give us shade and privacy and coolness in the summer; they also demand our attention and care." It's an odd notion: The care that trees *demand* is a gift they *give* to us, not the other way around. But on deeper reflection, it makes sense. Caring for trees drags us out of the narrow confines of our humanity and into the broader community of life.

+

Gerald once told me that to create a healthy bonsai, you just need to "think like a tree."

I wasn't sure if he meant this literally or figuratively. Did he really believe trees have thoughts?

"How could they not?" Gerald replied. "The hugest, oldest living things on earth, and we think we're smarter than them? It's almost comical. We know they communicate with each other. We just don't speak tree."

+

In one sense, Gerald was clearly correct. Tree roots have been shown to form partnerships with fungi, through which chemical messages can spread; some trees like Doug firs, when attacked by insects, transmit "stress signals" to nearby trees, prompting them to emit toxins to ward off pests. Trees have also been shown to spread warning signals through the air. But can it really be said that trees send these messages on purpose? Or are they merely automatic responses, no more meaningful than ripples in a pond?

+

In *The Hidden Life of Trees*, the German forester and author Peter Wohlleben famously (and controversially) argued that trees make decisions, feel pain, have affinities, and, perhaps, consciously experience the world. In 2018, while on vacation in Berlin, I arranged to meet up with Wohlleben. A gracious, lean man who smelled faintly of woodsmoke, he took me on a hike through the ancient beechwood forest he had long managed, outside the tiny village of Hümmel. Being an ardent proponent of the (economic as well as ecological) value of slow growth, he took pains to cut down each tree individually and haul it out using horses, rather than heavy machinery, to avoid churning up the networks of roots and fungi beneath the soil.

On our walk, Wohlleben confessed that he was by no means certain that trees are sentient creatures; he merely wanted to open his readers up to that possibility, in order to widen their imagination. To illustrate his point, he led me to the stump of a beech tree whose roots had fused together with those of another, nearby beech. He bent down and scratched at the base of the stump with his fingernail, revealing a layer of living, green wood hidden beneath. The stump, miraculously, was still alive. I asked him why, evolutionarily speaking, one tree would bother to keep another tree on life support, as it were. Wasn't that a colossal waste of resources? Wasn't it, in fact, the opposite of intelligent behavior? He hazarded a guess that the stump had retained a sort of genetic memory of past hardships, which it was able to share with the other tree via the roots. Or, he said, "perhaps it's just to be social."* Noticing the skeptical expression on my face, he cautioned me against dismissing such possibilities out of hand. When investigating scientific questions, before one begins the rigorous business of pruning away false hypotheses, he said, "it's better to be open-minded."

---

*Jürgen Bauhus, a professor of silviculture at the University of Freiburg, put forward a leaner theory: The other trees are not sustaining that stump to glean its memories; they are keeping it alive to draw water through its vast root system—an act of pure, unthinking opportunism.

+

A tree is open-minded by its very nature. Unlike so many of us, it does not solve problems by imagining a single solution and then pursuing it with laser-like focus, nor does it solve it through blind guesswork. Instead, it employs a systematic process of trial and error, or more accurately, *trials and errors*: by growing many branches *simultaneously*, dropping some and retaining the rest, which gather their own share of sunlight while also supporting one another and the tree as a whole. Computers and economic marketplaces routinely run these kinds of tree-shaped operations, testing out many options, then allowing the better options to winnow out the less optimal ones in a Darwinian fashion. Great authors tend to write profusely, scribbling hundreds or even thousands of pages only to throw most of them away. (Tolstoy was said to compose his novels in precisely this profligate manner; his genius was powered by what the literary critic Viktor Shklovsky called "the energy of searching freely.") Professional bonsai artists, too, almost always work in an arborescent fashion, fostering many trees, trusting that the brightest of their creations will one day garner acclaim, while the rest will continue growing in obscurity.

+

If brevity is the soul of wit, then branchiness is the soul of genius.

+

Alex Shigo, a biologist who was often called the father of modern arboriculture, also believed that to truly understand tree biology, a person must begin "thinking like a tree." However, unlike Wohlleben, he never suggested that trees might possess sentience; he merely urged his readers to imagine what a tree *might* want, given its unique biology. In other words, it is possible to think like a tree even if trees don't think.

This form of cogitation, I've found, bends the brain into a new shape, a "cast of mind" (to borrow Kant's useful phrase) that can feel a bit unnatural at first, but in time proves to be highly fruitful. Tree thinking, put very simply, means seeing growth not as a one-way street, but as something that is multidirectional, open-ended, and endlessly self-revising. In the words of the ancient Chinese tract known as the *Vegetable Roots Discourse*, this shape of thought is both "grounded . . . lofty and broad."

+

Back at Gerald's garden one spring afternoon, I decided to entertain the notion of tree sentience, if only as a means of expanding my imagination.

"Do you think the tree is going, *Ow!* each time you prune it?" I asked him.

"No, I think they're going, *Aaahh* . . ." Gerald said, sighing contentedly, as if being massaged. "Can you imagine sitting in one of these pots for thirty years, getting fed and watered and groomed and cared for?"

"But then, every once in a while, someone cuts one of your limbs off!" I pointed out.

"See, you're thinking like a human. You're not thinking like a tree," he replied. "They're going, *Thank God, now I can get some sun in there!*"

3. ASCENDING

BY THE time I reached my late thirties, I had become one of those odd creatures: a Tree Person. I spent most of my day either thinking about or interacting with trees. The majority of these arboreal encounters were decidedly unspectacular—I read tree books, struggled to memorize local species, and tended to my little bonsai—but every now and again, whenever I ran across a tree with nicely spaced branches, I would take leave of the earth and scamper into its crown. I liked the way climbing trees made me feel (wilder, humbler), which was almost an exact inversion of the feeling I got from caring for my bonsai. Soon, however, I had exhausted the relatively small supply of trees in my local forest with limbs low enough to grab hold of from the ground. I found myself yearning to climb yet-taller trees, the ancient ones with long straight trunks, trees that grew so tall they seemed to scratch the underbelly of the clouds.

The problem was that to climb very tall trees required not just bravery and balance but also the type of expensive gear and technical skills usually reserved for scaling sheer rock faces. I learned this fact while reading *The Wild Trees*, Richard Preston's thrilling book about a group of elite tree climbers and scientists attempting to locate the tallest tree on earth. Preston intrepidly follows these climbers on their expeditions to a place called Hyperion Grove, at times climbing hundreds of feet in the air to reach the upper spires of giant redwoods. He memorably describes the sensation of floating around in "redwood space," navigating these otherworldly ecosystems high above the earth.

In the back pages of the book, Preston mentions that he learned this arcane skill from a world-renowned technical tree climber named Tim Kovar. I wrote to Kovar, asking if he might teach me as well. He said that he had a single slot left on an introductory tree-climbing course he was teaching that August. I signed up, caught a bus down to Oregon City, and spent a week living on his property, learning to climb up and down trees on ropes, using low-tech metal devices. That week an oppressive heat wave, followed by a grayish-yellow tide of wildfire smoke, washed over Oregon. It felt strange, but also strangely thrilling, to climb up and down and around the branches of trees amid that *Blade Runner*–tinted haze, like some kind of cyborgic arachnid.

After the course, I bought a full tree-climbing kit, including three hundred feet of static climbing rope, a giant slingshot to shoot lines into the tops of trees, an arborist's "saddle" (only tree-climbing neophytes call it a "harness," I learned), two handheld mechanical ascenders for clawing up the rope, a rappel device for gliding down, and a backup rappel device in case I accidentally dropped the first one. I practiced by climbing some of the biggest trees in my area. Slowly, I became comfortable floating in the open air, a hundred or more feet off the ground, my life held by a slender rope, which dangled from a branch, which could break off at any moment. I couldn't help but feel there was something quietly transformative about these slow hours I spent aloft, lost in what Kovar calls "tree time." Much like sitting in silence on a meditation cushion, tree climbing doesn't really do much, in terms of making the world a better place, but it does a hell of a lot *to you*. Recovering addicts often talk about the benefits of handing your life over to a higher power, how it frees you from egotism and helps you feel less alone. As an atheist, I've often struggled with this. But each time I climbed a big tree, I knew—in a deep, visceral, animal way—that I was placing my life in the hands of a being far more powerful and patient than I could ever hope to be. I also knew that the tree's life (and, by extension, my own) depended upon yet greater powers: the soil to which that tree was rooted, the rain clouds that fed it, and everything beyond.

Following my trips to England and Japan, I had been trying to conceive of my life as a process of arborescent growth, the aim of which was to strike a wise balance between wild branching and careful pruning. But at a certain point I realized I was missing something crucial. A tree grows ever toward the sun, even when it is only a tiny seedling floating around in a spaceship. Everything it does is ultimately directed toward this goal: to gather a bit more light. But I had no such goal, no higher value, toward which I was reaching. What, I wondered, was the summum bonum of a life well lived? Was it to cultivate virtue or to maximize power? To create beauty or experience pleasure? To get into heaven or to escape from samsara? Eventually, thinking about Ben Atkinson risking his life to protest climate change, and that "old, old man" who kept his bonsai alive for seventy years, I felt I had found the rough outline of an answer. The overarching aim of a good life, I thought, would be to foster the flourishing of oneself, of other people, and of other species.[*] Any time I found myself lying in bed, in the oceanic blackness of the night, paralyzed by that

---

[*] "Flourishing," a favorite term among contemporary philosophers, stems, fittingly, from the world of plants. It shares its root, the Latin *florēre*, with the word "flowering."

all-encompassing question—What's the point of it all?—I tried to reorient myself back to this goal of coflourishing, like a sailor aiming for a pinprick of distant light in the darkness. To grow, and to help grow: Could there be any higher calling?

+

On my tree-climbing course that week in Oregon I met a curious individual named Steen Christensen. He was a great sunburned grizzly of a man, covered all over in light brown hair. He was one of only two other students in my course, so we ended up spending a lot of time getting to know one another. When he told stories, which he loved to do, he spoke in the low, slow, happy drawl of a lifelong outdoorsman, lightly but perpetually stoned on fresh air.

Steen was a quintessential child of the American West during the twilight years of the American century. Growing up, his family drifted through a slew of working-class neighborhoods in Colorado and California. He described his younger self as a "dumbass good old boy," a once-talented athlete and uncommitted student who, like a young Ken Kesey, carefully deranged himself into a mystic. After high school, Steen joined the navy, where he served as a mechanic on a salvage dive ship. While on shore leave in Hawaii, he tried LSD for the first time, and his mind never returned to its original shape. He quit drinking, he began visiting a Zen temple in Japan and a Lutheran church in Arcata, and he took thousands of trips to the seashores and forests of California, where, while surfing and hiking, he communed with the waves and trees. He liked to say he was "seeking a deeper ecology."

Steen was also, surprisingly enough, a successful businessman. Back in college, he and a friend founded a company that sold little trees to gift shops. Their first product was a sequoia sapling that came packaged in a transparent plastic tube. Customers loved it. Part of its appeal lay in the way that it neatly encapsulated the paradoxical, almost miraculous nature of sequoias, which start out as some of the smallest seeds of any tree species, exist for a time as slender and rather unremarkable saplings, and then rapidly expand into the most massive trees on earth. By the time I met Steen, his little company had likewise grown into a sprawling affair. He managed two tree nurseries, growing a million and a half seedlings of more than a dozen species on his two properties in Humboldt County, California.

After the course, Steen and I kept in touch, talking on the phone for hours on end. During these conversations, he mentioned that he and his employees regularly embarked on "cone-collecting trips," traveling across the West to climb big trees and harvest new seeds straight from their branches. So when I received a cryptic voicemail from Steen one morning later that fall inviting me on an "epic trip," I assumed that's what he was calling about.

I was wrong. What he was proposing was even more exciting.

Steen had just learned that a crew from the BBC was preparing to film a segment in the giant sequoias for a television series called *The Green Planet*, hosted by Sir David Attenborough. Steen had been invited to join the crew to help rig up the trees and haul gear around. There was one more spot left on the team. Steen asked if I would be interested in joining them. I wouldn't be paid, he explained, but I would be able to climb some of the oldest, largest trees on earth, in Sequoia National Park, a privilege normally reserved for the handful of people who have been granted special research permits.

I didn't even check my calendar.

"Sign me up," I said.

"Groovy," said Steen.

+

Why is it that so many people, from cold-eyed rationalists like me to big-hearted mystics like Steen, sense that there is something divine—a higher calling, a higher power, a higher plane of existence—in trees? When I set out to write this book, this was one of the big questions I'd hoped to explore. I had some vague outline of an answer already in mind—something to do with the startling juxtaposition between their hugeness and longevity, on the one hand, and our tininess and ephemerality, on the other. In a forest, notes John Fowles, we sense that "we stand among older, larger and infinitely other beings," which he deems "very like the only form a universal god could conceivably take." Psychological studies have shown that looking at big trees naturally produces feelings of wonder, gratitude, and compassion. It seemed logical to me that trees would have acted upon the brains of our earliest human ancestors in much the same way—perhaps even more intensely, since those ancestors, who likely climbed big trees in search of fruit or honey, would have known their full grandeur in a way few people today do. We seem to be hardwired for a love, even a worship, of trees.

However, as I came to learn, every culture's way of loving trees branches off in slightly different directions. It is those differences, and what effect those differences have on our actions, that fascinate me most. Jesus infamously cursed a fig tree to wither away for failing to give him any fruit. This, concludes St. Augustine, is proof that "there is no community of rights between us . . . and trees." Followers of the Persian prophet Mani, by contrast, believed trees possessed souls, and that they would bleed when cut. (In a fitting twist, anyone who injured a tree was said to be reborn as a tree in their next life.) In Thailand, it is believed that killing an old tree can cause you to fall ill and die, whereas in Taiwan, the parents of a sick child will sometimes tie a red ribbon around the branch of an old tree, believing that the tree will soon die, granting a long life for the child.

The particular form of tree worship that I was raised with turns out to be less than three hundred years old—which is to say, it's younger than many trees currently alive today. I was struck by this fact while reading a work called *The Philosopher of the Forest* by Philip Freneau, which was serialized in *The Freeman's Journal* beginning in 1781. The text—a strangely unclassifiable work, halfway between a novella and an essay—has since fallen into obscurity, which is a shame, because it contains a fascinating glimpse into the minds of eighteenth-century Americans and how they viewed trees and wild land.

Freneau, a leading intellectual light of the Revolution, was once known as the "father of American poetry." He was raised in the countryside of New Jersey, on a small estate called Locust Grove. After graduating from Princeton, he moved to Saint Croix, the lushly forested Caribbean island then known as Santa Cruz, to hide from the oncoming war and work on his poems. While there, he saw the horrors of plantation slavery firsthand. It was also there, on that "sweet verdant isle," that Freneau apparently experienced a spiritual awakening to the glory of the natural world. He returned to find that his hometown had been ransacked by the British; enraged, he enlisted in the New Jersey militia. He later joined the crew of a privateer (a kind of glorified pirate ship), hoping to simultaneously impoverish the British fleet and enrich himself. This venture was a spectacular failure; he was almost immediately captured and then spent six weeks in a hellish prison. In virtually all of his subsequent writings, he devoted himself to exploring the three themes that had so far shaped his young life: liberty, nature, and violence. Fortunately for him, these would soon prove to also be the abiding obsessions of America itself.

The Philosopher of the Forest explores all of these themes (and more) at length, often quite brilliantly. What interested me most, though, was how the book begins. As a young man, the philosopher flees his idyllic childhood home in Switzerland and subsequently wanders the earth for decades. In a typical novel of that time, he may have been forced out by an evil stepparent, or an improper tryst, or poverty, or war. But this young man is different. He is compelled to leave home because a neighbor destroys a "beautiful grove of ancient oaks" that grew along the property line. Hearing the trees fall, the young man is overwhelmed by "grief." That grove had provided his soul with a kind of sacred stillness—an ineffable quality that he couldn't live without. "There is something in woods and solitudes congenial with my nature," he writes. "It is in these that I conceive the mind still finds itself in the best humour to contemplate, in silent admiration, the great and inexhaustible source of all things."

He tries to explain all of this to his neighbor, who responds by calling him a "fool" and a "madman." And indeed, the philosopher acknowledges, most readers of the time would have been inclined to agree with the neighbor; his pain at seeing the trees felled, he notes, will "appear to most men to be little better than imaginary."

Today, the tree-loving philosopher no longer looks so foolish. In the intervening two and a half centuries, a sea change in consciousness has swept across the Western world—a kind of Green Revelation—which has led us to view trees, forests, and many other wild landscapes in a new and holy light. Modern nature reverence is distinct from other religions in that it roots itself in scientific findings rather than scripture, but it emphasizes the findings that support its essential ethical beliefs—that all life is interconnected; that arrogance is humanity's greatest sin; and that we are both custodians and children of the living earth. Within this worldview, we tend to view old trees as sacred (or quasi-sacred) beings in themselves, and the forests as organic "temples of nature." I grew up within this faith, without ever knowing its name. But the odd thing about this religion, I've noticed, is that it doesn't *feel* like a religion. To many of its adherents, myself included, it simply feels, well, natural.

In *Second Nature*, his study of the ways that plants shape human behavior and human behavior shapes plants, Michael Pollan charts the series of metaphorical transformations trees have undergone in the Western imagination. First, he writes, they were seen as homes for spirits, demanding reciprocal action; then they were seen as fuel for empire and impediments to growth, something to be slashed back so that ships could be built and farms expanded; then they were politicized, like the "liberty trees" beneath which revolutionaries like Freneau once rallied; and then, only once trees appeared to be vanishing due to overlogging, did Americans learn to sacralize trees in a new way, shaped in large part by Romantic poetry and transcendental philosophy. "In the contemplation and company of the Romantic Tree—self-reliant, abiding, reaching ever heavenward—we could find an antidote to our mean commercial culture, and open ourselves to the infinite," Pollan writes.

Thinking through the long arc of this intellectual evolution, a different, toothier set of questions began to take shape in my mind—not why trees inspire reverence, but rather where that reverence leads us. In an age of catastrophic climate change, when every old tree on earth is endangered by fire and drought, what had that sacralization ultimately gotten us? Had it *really* changed how we treat the earth, or had it merely created some lovely parklands to delight and distract us? Why had our love of the shady green forest landed us in such a hot and perilous world?

+

The following October, Steen and I drove east out of Oakland in his old green pickup truck. It was packed with our tree-climbing gear, four backpacks in total. Over the truck bed was a pop-up camper, which contained the barest of necessities: a mattress, some cookware, some water jugs, enough food for a week, and precisely one fork, one spoon, and one knife. Steen periodically drove this truck down to Baja and lived out of it for monthslong surfing expeditions. The interior of the cab was coated more or less evenly with a mix of ocher Californian dirt and coarse glittering Mexican sand.

As we turned southward, we were absorbed into a field of aureate light. The sky above was the same sallow shade as the ground below; wildfires were burning in Sonoma County, and the haze had stalked us from the city to the Central Valley. The hills resembled nothing so much as the hunched backs of crouching lions. All was yellow, yellow, yellow.

Farther south, the dry grasslands gave way to rows of starveling trees: almonds, oranges, olives. We passed the time by playing an informal game. I pointed out a certain tree, and Steen would first identify it, and then expound upon how to best gather and grow its seeds. I never managed to stump him, and he frequently noticed odd species that I had missed. "I just look at the world in trees," Steen said. "I really do."

Many of the trees down here in the Central Valley were dying from a recent drought, Steen noted. Some farmers, unable to access enough water, had simply stopped irrigating them, leaving the fields to go fallow. Steen was concerned we were seeing the beginning of a second Dust Bowl.

As the road began tilting up toward the Sierra Nevada, the land darkened from yellow to gray green. On one hillside stood vast stands of dead pines, their bare branch tips as fine as fish bones against the sky. The trees were the victims of a pine bark beetle outbreak a few years earlier, Steen said. For thousands of years, the beetles and the pines had been battling: The beetles fed on the sugary phloem of the pines, and the pines defended themselves by flooding the beetles with toxic resin. But in the past fifty years, especially the past ten years, the conditions had tipped in favor of the pine bark beetles. The warmer weather helped the beetles breed and mature more quickly, droughts had left the pines without enough fluids to defend themselves, and a century of artificial fire suppression had allowed those pines to grow more densely. Making matters worse, timber companies, following "scientific forestry" methods meant to maximize profit, had for decades been clear-cutting diverse forests and replacing them with evenly spaced stands of the same fast-growing conifer species—a strategy known as "pines in lines." All of this allowed the beetles to rapidly spread across entire forests, moving among a biologically indistinguishable mass of trees like fire sweeping through a field of dry wheat. The result of these coinciding forces was that an estimated one hundred million pine trees had been killed in a single decade in California.

By this point in my life, I was accustomed to hearing these kinds of arboreal horror stories, but normally they were brought on by an invasive species, like the emerald ash borer or the chestnut blight fungus. What was most disturbing to me was that the pine bark beetle was not an invasive species. The pines had known how to handle them for millennia. Such is the uncanny nature of the climate crisis. Each passing year we make the earth alien to itself.

+

Trees are our most visible emblem of environmental destruction. Other types of ecosystem degradation—topsoil erosion, water pollution, species loss—often take place all but invisibly. But the sight of a one-thousand-year-old stump, or, worse still, an entire field of such stumps, is impossible to ignore.

That being said, if the cutting is done slowly enough, the gradual disappearance of a nation's forests can escape people's notice for a surprisingly long amount of time. Ecologists refer to this phenomenon as "shifting baseline syndrome": Each generation mistakenly assumes that the environment it was born into is normal, no matter how degraded it may be. Some places, like Iceland and the Faroe Islands, became entirely deforested before anyone apparently thought to curb the decline. Others have come perilously close. In *Landscape and Memory*, the historian Simon Schama notes that, even before William the Conqueror took over England in 1066, "no more than 15 percent of English territory would have been wooded." The remaining forests, many of which became protected by royal decree, were islands of green surrounded by civilization, rather than the inverse, and they only continued to shrink with time. Shakespeare, who grew up beside the Forest of Arden, must have witnessed this slow-motion vanishing firsthand, but in his corpus of richly forested plays, he seldom comments upon it. By 1664, a polymath named John Evelyn finally began raising the alarm; in a tract called *Sylva*, he described the felling of the nation's forests as evidence of shortsightedness and "avarice." In 1713, the poet Alexander Pope published an ode to one of the "green retreats" he had grown up playing in as a boy, the Windsor Forest. What is notably missing from his description of the forest are two features that would become commonplace in poems of this sort written in America: an abundance of ancient trees (Pope mentions only "thin trees . . . that shun each other's shades") and a sense of wildness. By the time Wordsworth began openly calling for forest preservation in the nineteenth century, his pleas were mostly in vain: The vast unbroken forest known as the "greenwood" had become a place of myth and distant memory.

In America, by contrast, the felling of the forests took place so rapidly and on such a vast scale that it was all but impossible to ignore. The trouble (from the trees' perspective, at least) was that most settlers saw that clearing as something to celebrate, rather than something to mourn. Trees stood as an impediment to farms and towns, and they harbored fearsome Native warriors. John Muir—the famed nature writer, who was born in Scotland and grew up in what was then still heavily forested Wisconsin—describes the settler mindset this way: "In the blindness of hunger, the early settlers, claiming Heaven as their guide, regarded God's trees as only a larger kind of pernicious weeds, extremely hard to get rid of."

In time, those "weeds" would turn out to be all too easy to get rid of. As wave after wave of settlers sailed across the sea and marched across the land, the ancient forests retreated westward. Behind them, the settlers trailed hyphae-like trade networks that then connected to global markets, whose hunger for certain resources, like timber, fur, and ore, was bottomless. Their advance was bolstered by laws that defined landownership by one's ability to clear it of its forest. Up until the signing of the Timber and Stone Act in 1878—and indeed, due to widespread skirting of this lax regulation, long after—politicians on both sides of the aisle cheered at the sound of a falling tree. In the words of Aldo Leopold, "A stump was our symbol of progress."

The giant sequoias were no exception. The early European settlers posed for gleeful photos beside the felled giants. They carved bowling alleys from their trunks. They danced atop their stumps. The sequoia groves were soon littered with millions of board feet of hacked-off limbs and broken trunks. It was sheer carnage. "Waste, waste, waste," wrote Walter Fry and John R. White in their 1930 natural history of the sequoias, *Big Trees*. "Probably not one-half of the trees destroyed . . . ever reached the mill to get converted into lumber; quite possibly not one-third." The historian Hank Johnston has described this period as "the greatest orgy of destructive lumbering in the history of the world." It seemed that the fever would not break until every last old tree was felled.

+

The next morning at dawn, with cool, dark, sweet air streaming through the open windows of Steen's truck, we drove out to an area of national forest called Freeman Creek. The BBC had selected that spot for the first few days of filming, I was told, because it contained a large grove of ancient giant sequoias and, unlike the nearby national park, there were fewer regulations on climbing trees or flying drones.

In the parking lot, we were joined by two of our team members: a pair of sequoia specialists named Anthony Ambrose and Wendy Baxter. They were one of those rare couples who manage to work together every day and somehow remain married to one another. Anthony, who had the hard little face of a skate punk and the unevenly graying beard of a young dad, had studied under Steve Sillett, the father of redwood canopy research, before receiving his PhD from Berkeley and striking out on his own. Wendy was a lean, calm, dark-haired woman, dressed in dark clothes, who had received her master's degree in the Netherlands. Over the coming days, I was delighted to learn that beneath her scrupulous demeanor lay a surprisingly perverse sense of humor, including a taste for the raunchy early films of John Waters. With Steen's help, Wendy and Anthony had founded a nonprofit organization called the Ancient Forest Society, which was dedicated to studying and preserving the world's big trees. As part of this work, they routinely climbed sequoias to monitor their health. It is quite possible that over the course of their careers, they had climbed more giant sequoias than any other scientists on earth.

We each grabbed two bags of climbing gear and set off along a winding little trail. The forest was unremarkable at first, just stands of pines and firs growing out of the dusty soil. I was, foolishly, expecting a giant sequoia grove to be composed exclusively of giant sequoias. In fact, even within these refugia—the small pockets where the climatic conditions (balmy, arid summers and mild, snowy winters) suit sequoias—the giants dwell in even smaller refugia. Hermetic beasts, these.

We soon dropped down into a small glade, so cold and dark in its depths that a stream curving through it was clouded with ice. There, among the darker, scragglier trees, I finally saw them: two enormous sequoias, glowing muscularly in the early-morning light. They were, quite simply, an astonishment.

All at once, my thoughts fell away.

Their size was the first thing I noticed. It was impossible not to. They existed on a scale more congruous with objects of industry—cooling towers, silos, cranes—than with other living things. But I was prepared for their gigantism. What surprised me was their creatureliness. Looking up at their crowns, I felt very much like a mouse standing between the forelegs of some impossibly tall woolly mammoth.

Down where they entered the soil, their legs, or rather their trunks, terminated in great knuckled feet. I walked up to the trunk of one tree and petted it, pressed my fingers into its spongy depth. The bark almost exactly resembled fur. It was a color—not quite orange, not quite red—that dog breeders refer to, rather prettily, as "golden rust." It had the smooshed, whorled texture of a grizzly bear's coat, matted from sleep. When I peered closer, I saw the bark was made up of tiny hairs, which, I would soon learn, had a maddening tendency to float down, land inside my shirt collar, and make my skin itch.

In 1871, Emerson visited a grove of giant sequoias with a young, eccentric, as-yet-unpublished local writer named John Muir serving as his guide. Muir later recalled that Emerson wandered the grove solemnly, saying little, "as if under a spell." Finally, Emerson turned to Muir and recited a line from Genesis: "There were giants in those days."

Steen joined me. We stood for a long while, just staring up at the trees.

"There's not a lot you can say," he said. "It just kind of falls out of the box. And then when you get up in the branches it gets even worse. You're like, 'Oh shit, I'm awful small. . . .'"

+

History has shown that a sense of divine reverence (whether poetic or supernatural) is one of the few forces on earth powerful enough to displace the hard, hungry logic of the market. Jared Farmer, our greatest chronicler of the history of trees, argues that the earliest known form of wilderness preservation was the setting aside of sacred groves, a practice dating back to ancient Mesopotamia, classical Greece, and Warring States–era China. As a general rule, the feeling of reverence that premodern people had for ancient trees was born out of a mixture of fear and respect, a balance of forces both light and dark. Animist traditions often held that certain trees were believed to house spirits or deities, which had the power to exact retribution for harming them.

The American settlers reached their form of nature worship by an entirely different route. The early colonists arrived with little or no belief in nature spirits, which had been largely extirpated by the church. However, by the seventeenth century, both in response to and in revolt against the coldly mechanistic findings of the Scientific Revolution, a reverence for nature had begun to creep back into the Western psyche. Philosophers like Baruch Spinoza argued that God was nature, and nothing more—a beautiful idea, for which he was accused of "abominable heresies" and excommunicated. But this idea nevertheless spread, especially among the educated classes. Indeed, the Declaration of Independence grounds its "self-evident" truths in what the founders call "Nature and Nature's God."[*]

Around the same time, the European Romantic movement flared to life. A love of mountains, mists, mysteries, paradoxes, provocations, botany, geology, and melodrama began to whirl around the continent. Much of this can be understood as a knee-jerk response to rapid urbanization and industrialization. Amid the coal fug of the metropolis, the artificial looked corrupted, and the natural, divine. "This change of attitude towards 'nature,'" writes the historian Chris-

---

[*] Contrary to popular belief, America was not founded exclusively on Christian principles. As Matthew Stewart argues in his brilliant book *Nature's God: The Heretical Origins of the American Republic*, many of the founding fathers, including George Washington, Thomas Jefferson, and Benjamin Franklin, were not really "deists" (believers in a distant, hands-off, clockmaker-style God), but rather scientifically literate, earth-loving pantheists—believers in "nothing that we commonly mean by the term 'God,' but rather to something closer to 'Nature'"—which, in the eyes of their pious contemporaries, would have made them little better than "wicked" atheists.

topher Thacker, "is as vast a change as any in the whole history of human attitudes."

In the late eighteenth and nineteenth centuries, Romantic influences wafted across the Atlantic, where they were eagerly inhaled by a class of American intellectuals repulsed by both the brutality and banality of modernity. The "father of American poetry," Freneau, was disgusted by the new nation's reliance on plantation slavery and its taste for empty piety. A generation later, the father of American nature writing, Henry David Thoreau, wrote with despair about watching his neighbors go whole months without traveling anywhere other than "shops and offices." European Romanticism was reborn as a quintessentially American religion, transcendentalism, which preached peeling one's soul away from church doctrine and ushering it toward a direct experience of the universe's baffling infinitude.

The ground was tilled, as it were, for a new form of nature worship. Industrial capitalism and hidebound tradition had walled off the soul from the wild, green world. But even still, for many people, a feeling of alienation was not—is not—enough to germinate a change in political consciousness. Something else was needed. Something godlike.

+

Once we had hauled all of our gear into the grove, we set to work. Anthony and Wendy began rigging ropes high in a pair of sequoias on one side of the glade, while Steen and I rigged another nearby tree. The last time Anthony had climbed this tree, he had left behind a thin, inconspicuous piece of black cord running up over a high branch, so all Steen and I had to do was tie a climbing rope to the end of the cord and hoist it up and over that branch. It was a straightforward task, not unlike raising a flag on a flagpole. Nevertheless, the sheer height of the tree made it a sweaty, time-consuming chore.

When the tree was securely roped up, Steen and I had no other duties that day, so Anthony suggested we climb it. I went first. I attached a pair of caving ascenders—chunky steel devices resembling staple guns with teeth—to the rope. One had a loop for my feet; the other was connected to my harness. The ascenders were designed to slide up the rope easily, but to grip it tightly when I rested my body weight on them. Climbing the rope was, in theory, quite simple: Slide one ascender up the rope, then the other, and repeat.

In practice, however, it proved to be hard going, in large part because this tree was roughly three times higher than any I had ever climbed. The half-inch-thick, six-hundred-foot-long climbing rope stretched with each movement I made, sending me bouncing and spinning. Talented tree climbers use this bounce to get into a rhythm and climb more quickly. Untalented climbers, like me, flail about like hooked fish.

It took me fifteen minutes to reach the first branches, which formed a lacy screen, blocking my view of the tree above. When I thrust my head up through them, I discovered I still had a long way to go. As I navigated around a series of waist-thick branches, it occurred to me that when we look up at sequoias from the ground, they appear to have oddly small, ovoid clouds of foliage. But I now realized that was an optical illusion, created by our usual vantage point. The crown is in fact both big and complex. Up close, a few of the branches were as wide around as whole trees, and some extended out far from the trunk, while others grew upward, or even downward. There was a small forest up here, agglomerated into a single beautiful chimera.

By the time I got to the topmost branches, my arms were aching, and my mouth had grown so dry that my lips had begun to chap. I was now 210 feet in the air. I looked down, saw the ground far below, and felt an adrenaline rush so strong that I tasted metal.

I sat down on a small U-shaped bench between two of the higher branches and tried to calm myself. In the distance were the Sierras, pale rock pushing up through the soil like tooth against gum. A cold wind blew across the top of the tree. I took a few deep breaths. The sky smelled green.

While Steen lumbered up the rope, I had time to inspect the tree more closely. The bark up here was thinner and less hairy than at the base; it now had the consistency of peeling house paint. Each inch was a slightly different hue of pink, brown, and gray. At the base of the branch I was seated upon, the bark flaked out in psychedelic patterns. Attached to it were neon-yellow wolf lichens, which came loose with the lightest brush of my hand.

From talking with Wendy and Anthony, I had been learning all about the new science of tree-canopy research. It was once mistakenly believed by scientists that the tops of redwoods were an "ecological desert," virtually devoid of life. But when Anthony's mentor, the botanist Steve Sillett, began climbing ancient coast redwoods in the late 1980s to study their canopy, he discovered that they contained a world of ecological richness beyond anyone's imagination. On top of branches hundreds of feet in the air, he found layers of soil three feet deep, created by centuries of decomposing redwood needles and other plant matter. Growing out of that soil were ferns, berry bushes, and various trees. He also noticed odd aquatic animals—salamanders, crustaceans, mollusks—the ancestors of which may have originally hitched a ride on the furry underbelly of a squirrel. In total, he and his team counted forty-nine species of plants growing in the canopy, along with dozens of mosses and hundreds of lichens. They also learned that the needles and even the bark of redwoods are capable of trapping and absorbing fog like a sponge, which rehydrates the top of the tree without having to hoist that water all the way up from the roots.

Since the early 1980s, all over the world, scientists—led by a pair of pioneering researchers named Meg Lowman and Nalini Nadkarni—had been climbing trees and finding unknown species, weird ecological dynamics, and a shocking profusion of life. Nadkarni amazed the scientific community when she discovered that certain species like big-leaf maples, which accumulate deep layers of soil and moss on their limbs, have evolved to extend roots out of their branches to access this aerial storehouse of nutrients. In terms of biodiversity, the canopy is less like a desert than a rainforest—a rainforest atop a rainforest. According to Lowman, "upward of *half* of all terrestrial creatures live about one hundred feet or more above our heads, not at ground level as scientists previously assumed." (This statistic sounds impossible, until one considers that most terrestrial creatures are insects.) Of these arboreal species, Lowman writes, approximately 90 percent remain unclassified by science.

Steen eventually made it to the top of the tree, panting and smiling.

I pointed out that he had a long gash on the back of his arm. Blood was running down his elbow.

"Ah, I'm always bleeding, man," he said.

He seated himself on a branch a few feet above me and began filming a video on his phone. I was worried he would drop it—I envisioned it hitting the ground, far below, and bursting into shards—but he managed to return it safely to the pocket of his pants. We sat for fifteen minutes or so, enjoying the last light touches of the sun, the faint wind sway.

Steen looked down at the forest floor with his pink-and-blue seaborne eyes.

"We're a long way from earth," he said.

+

An archetypal moment in the history of American nature worship occurred one day in 1874, when a windstorm blasted through these very mountains. John Muir, ever on the lookout for what he called "scootchers" (little adventures), climbed to the top of the highest ridge he could find. Then he climbed to the uppermost branches of a Douglas fir. He stayed up there for a long while, swaying back and forth, enjoying the sight of a whole valley convulsing in the wind, like a "wild sea of pines." What struck him most forcefully, though, was the tranquility he felt. "All seemed strong and comfortable, as if really enjoying the storm," he later recalled. "We hear much nowadays concerning the universal struggle for existence, but no struggle in the common meaning of the word was manifest here; no recognition of danger by any tree; no deprecation; but rather an invincible gladness as remote from exultation as from fear."

It was upon the power of moments like these that the genre of nature writing was born. It began as a hodgepodge of free-flowing first-person observations, which grew directly out of Romantic poetry and transcendentalist preaching. Like these antecedents, most nature essays did not aim simply to describe nature, but to present it in such vivid language that it would rush over the senses like a hallucinogen, jarring loose epiphanies.

Those epiphanies would tend toward a certain familiar, quasi-mystical shape: Again and again, nature writers reminded their audience that the Earth, and perhaps even the cosmos, is alive—*truly alive*—and that each of us is one mere part of that awesome living whole. This notion can seem irretrievably abstract when presented flatly, as I just have. But when folded into a flow of quicksilver-bright prose, set in spectacular locations (which most people back then would never get the chance to visit), it had the power to evoke a feeling of synthetic, secondhand awe almost as powerful as the real thing.

For nature writers past and present, trees have provided one of the most reliable delivery mechanisms for that particular type of awe. Take, for example, Emerson's description of walking through a field and being stopped short by the sight of the branches of a tree waving at him. A feeling of surreality is quickly replaced by one of communion: "I am not alone and unacknowledged," Emerson writes. Likewise, Thoreau, beset by a wave of loneliness one day beside Walden

Pond, suddenly perceives "an infinite and unaccountable friendliness" in every pine in the forest. No place, he realizes, no matter how "wild" or "dreary" it may appear, is truly alien to us. The eighteenth-century poet/painter William Blake and the twentieth-century poet/essayist Annie Dillard both had similar arboreal epiphanies. For Dillard, one numinous experience with a tree—"the backyard cedar . . . charged and transfigured, each cell buzzing with flame"—gave rise to a sense of *unio mystica* that would persist, flickeringly, throughout her life.

In his book *Awe*, Dacher Keltner describes his decades of research into the science of wonderment. His findings show that awe "allows us to get outside of ourselves, and integrates us into larger patterns—of community, of nature, of ideas and cultural forms." He has found that experiences in the natural environment—what he calls "wild awe"—are especially transformative. Wild awe, by loosening the grip of the ego and promoting a sense of connectedness, seems to promote "the reverential treatment of nature." In other words, awe leads to love, and love to protection. This is what the scholar Warren Tormey, writing about the birth of environmentalism, calls "wonder as an ethical force."

+

The following day, we returned to the icy glade at the base of the big trees. The BBC crew—a group of pale, polite, worried, cheerful people dressed in puffy down jackets—had been there since before dawn, searching for the time of day when the sunlight would strike the sequoias at precisely the right angle and brightness. Nature documentarians, I quickly learned, are sun worshippers. Their Lord giveth and He taketh away.

The team was led by a producer named Rosie Thomas, whose pockets were stuffed with walkie-talkies and other electronic devices that squawked and beeped at her throughout the day, and whose mind was similarly crammed with logistics.

The BBC's Natural History Unit, Rosie's employer, was famous for the outlandish lengths they would go to capture footage. In the filming of their flagship series, *Planet Earth*, camerapersons reportedly braved hundred-mile-an-hour winds in Antarctica to film penguins, hid in a sweltering blind for three hundred hours in Papua New Guinea to film a bird-of-paradise perform its mating dance, and spent three months living in the freezing mountains of northern India to record a single shot of a snow leopard sleeping. Rosie herself had once spent a total of four years filming footage of chimpanzees to create one (riveting) episode of a series called *Dynasties*.

The plan that day was to film Anthony and Wendy as they collected branches from the top of a pair of adjacent giant sequoias. Rosie explained to me that she had chosen this sequence to highlight the hugeness of the trees. The difficulty is that sequoias tend to look much smaller on a television screen than they actually are. Rosie's solution to this conundrum was to use human bodies—in this case, Wendy's and Anthony's—for scale.

That morning, Anthony and Wendy climbed to the very top of the tree, until their heads were protruding above the upper canopy. Then, two BBC staffers piloted a drone, roughly the size of a bald eagle, high above the tree. One man steered the drone itself while the other controlled its camera; the images were instantaneously relayed to an iPad the second man wore strapped to his chest. By watching the iPad, we were able to look down on Wendy and Anthony through the drone's camera, hovering high above the forest, as they pretended to collect samples from the branches. From that vantage, they looked like two little monkeys grooming for lice atop the head of a Kong-sized, green-furred gorilla. The drone pulled closer. Rosie radioed to Anthony, asking him to please turn a bit more to his left so they could catch his face in the light. He did. The shot was stunning.

"I think I like filming people," Rosie said. "You get a lot done really quickly."

"I guess you can't tell a chimp, 'Turn your head toward me,'" I said.

"No . . ." she said, with evident regret.

While all this was going on, the team had also set up a time-lapse camera to film some nearby sequoias. These kinds of shots were first introduced in 1910 in the short film *The Birth of a Flower* and were made famous by a 1995 BBC series called *The Private Life of Plants*. They involved taking thousands of photographs over an extended period of time and then stitching them together so that one can watch blossoms blossoming or ferns unfurling in mere seconds rather than days. They are some of the more fantastical moments in any nature documentary.

In recent years, I'd noticed that the shots had become even more magical. Now, the viewer gently moved *toward* the plant as it blossomed in fast-forward. Earlier that morning, I had finally learned how this effect is achieved: A camera, rigged up to a taut wire suspended between two trees, robotically inches closer to one tree with excruciating patience as the camera steadily clicks away over the course of a few days. This particular shot was designed to capture the passage of shadows as they swept across the sequoia trunks throughout the day, as if we, the viewer, were ambling calmly through this time-warped land.

As I watched the crew go about their work, it occurred to me that the art of the nature documentary is the exact offspring of nature poetry and nature writing. The purpose of all three art forms is to fuse together science and lyricism into an awe-inspiring portrait of the earth. But for the public, nature writing has since been almost entirely supplanted by nature documentaries—a hypervivid, multisensory medium, against which mere words on a page appear cold and pale. I can no longer read Muir without a cynical voice whispering in my head that his prose is purple and his philosophy Pollyannaish. But watching a BBC nature documentary, I am quite often overwhelmed with a feeling of cosmic wonder and tragic dread. I am not alone. Keltner writes that when he and his colleagues want to quickly induce a state of awe in their subjects, one of the most reliable methods is to show them a five-minute clip from *Planet Earth*.

Watching the drone float above the top of the sequoia and the time-lapse camera inch along on its wire, I suddenly began to understand why nature documentaries are such effective conduits of awe. While the content is scientific, the framing is emphatically spiritual. The world is shown from the vantage of an omniscient observer who looks down from the clouds and up from the soil, for whom a sequoia can look as small as a stalk of broccoli, for whom a flower can bloom in mere seconds, and for whom the flick of a chameleon's tongue can be slowed down to a pink ooze. And while these sublime, ecstatic, occasionally gruesome visions of life and death unspool, swelling music is played by some celestial orchestra off-screen and words are spoken by a disembodied narrator whose intonation—deep, ancient, gently commanding—is more or less exactly how one might imagine the voice of a loving God.

+

Two days later, the voice of God arrived. His name was Sir David Attenborough, and he had just flown in from London.

In some sense, Attenborough was both the progenitor and the living embodiment of the nature documentary. As he describes in his memoir, *Life on Air*, he began his career at the BBC during the 1950s, as a young Cambridge graduate and navy veteran. The first show he hosted was one of his own invention called *Zoo Quest*, in which he, a cameraman, and a zookeeper would travel to a foreign country, capture footage of an animal in the wild, trap the animal, and then ship it back to the studio, where they could show it in detail using larger, more powerful cameras. As the technology progressed and the budgets were increased, the scope of the documentaries was widened to encompass the entire globe, first with his groundbreaking "mega-series" *Life on Earth*, then *The Living Planet*, *Blue Planet*, *Planet Earth*, *Frozen Planet*, and now *The Green Planet*. These documentaries, unlike the first-person *Zoo Quest*s, tended toward the God's-eye point of view, jumping from aerial shots to nearly microscopic close-ups. On this new planetary scale of filmmaking, Attenborough gradually receded from view, serving mostly as a disembodied voice. At the end of nearly every episode, and even more forcefully at the end of every series, Attenborough would appear on camera and make a heartfelt plea for the protection of all these natural wonders. As these entreaties grew more forceful in the past two decades, he had become arguably the world's most prominent figure calling for wilderness preservation, much as Muir had been in a previous century. In a public poll in 2014, Attenborough was voted Great Britain's "most trustworthy person." (Queen Elizabeth, who had knighted him on two separate occasions, was ranked fifth.)

David arrived that chilly morning wearing a green safari jacket. His white, corn silk–fine hair was blown wildly about his head. (Before filming, he would make a brief, half-hearted attempt to smooth it down; such was, apparently, the entirety of the crew's hair-and-makeup team.) Traveling with him was a coterie of other BBC employees—a cameraperson whose job it was to film him, a producer whose job it was to coach him through his lines, and a personal medic whose job it was to keep him alive. David was then ninety-three years old, but he seemed remarkably hale, both in body and mind. A few years earlier, I had read an article in which he told the interviewer, "I see no reason whatsoever why I can't live past 100." Death evidently did not bear down upon him with the same weight as it did the rest of us. He seemed able to simply rise above such things.

Our filming location was an area of Sequoia National Park named the Giant Forest, a mountainous tableland occupied by one magnificent sequoia after another. Within walking distance of where we sat lived five of the ten largest trees on the planet. Muir had taken credit for naming this grove, remarking that "no forest could equal this." For once, he was not exaggerating.

We had established ourselves at the base of an impressive tree named Andromeda. Far above, it sported a mazily complex crown, while, at the ground, it had an A-shaped, fire-charred cavity running through the base of its trunk, which was large enough to walk through. (As long as there are still vascular tissues running from the roots up to the leaves, most trees can survive having a hole bored—or burned—through the center of them.) Near the base of the tree, David's assistant set up a blue camping chair emblazoned with his name in white letters. David gratefully took a seat and gazed up at the tower of living wood before him.

At one point that day, during a lull in the filming, Wendy asked David if he had ever been here to see the sequoias before.

"Yes, some twenty-five years ago," he said.

"Are the sequoias the most magnificent trees you've seen?" Steen asked.

"Oh, they're the most magnificent things on earth," David said. Then he paused, as if scanning through his vast mental catalog of wonders, and, with a Cantabrigian aversion to overstatement, added: "Well, you know, it's an awfully big world."

+

A feeling of awe is what finally turned the growing American fondness for wild nature into a political force. And no tree evoked more awe than the giant sequoia. As the largest trees on earth, as well as some of the oldest, the giant sequoias, put simply, broke people's brains. "The majesty of their gigantic trunks is incommunicable," wrote the great Western nature writer Mary Hunter Austin. Standing before one, she writes, she was overwhelmed with a "stifling sense of awe."

In 1852, a bear hunter named Augustus T. Dowd stumbled upon a stand of sequoias in the Calaveras Grove. The story of his "discovery" was recounted ten years later in a popular book entitled *Scenes of Wonder and Curiosity in California* by James M. Hutchings. According to the author, when Dowd saw the big trees for the first time, he could hardly believe his eyes. "Surely, this must be some curiously delusive dream," he thought. When he returned to his camp and told his friends about these giants, they didn't believe him either. But word soon leaked out to the public, and by the following year, the largest of the sequoias in the Calaveras Grove was already being referred to as the Eighth Wonder of the World.

"No other native tree of the American West has cut so wide a swath through the human consciousness," argues William C. Tweed in *King Sequoia*, his history of the species. Tweed makes the case that sequoias helped inculcate America with the nature philosophy of Emerson and Muir: We came to view wilderness as something worth guarding—something worth protecting from fire and pests and industrialists—in part by learning to protect these monstrous, furry, ancient, almost unreal trees.

The news of the felling of giant trees in the 1850s shocked and horrified the public, resulting in what the scholar James Tackach dubbed "perhaps the first national environmental protest in the United States." Newspapers across California, and then across the nation, began running alarmed stories, detailing the destruction. "To our mind it seems a cruel idea, a perfect desecration, to cut down such a splendid tree," announced one popular magazine of the time. "In its natural condition, rearing its majestic head towards heaven, and waving in all its native vigour, strength and verdure, it was a sight worth a pilgrimage to see." Note the carefully selected verbiage: "desecration," "majestic," "heaven," "pilgrimage." This is the language of scripture. Muir was yet more messianic: "Behold the King of Glory!" he wrote. "For is he not the greatest light in the woods; in the world?" Even the members of the Kaweah Colony, a Marxist commune that attempted to carve out a utopian settlement among the giant sequoias in 1886, stopped short of cutting the largest, oldest sequoias, which they deemed "sacred."

Sequoias had one other crucial asset: In addition to being considered priceless, they were also basically worthless. This was not true, for example, of the coast redwood—the taller, thinner cousin of the giant sequoia—which produces good, hard, rot-resistant timber. Coast redwoods were cherished by lumbermen because they provided high-quality urban building materials, railroad ties, storage tanks, and pipelines to transport water and oil across the state. The lumber of giant sequoias, by contrast, was oddly brittle; when the trees fell, being so large, they tended to shatter on impact, ruining the wood's commercial value.

In short: A sequoia had enormous worth while left alive, and very little when dead. Faced with this overwhelming logic, the nation's berserk war against the forests suffered its first major defeat. During the height of the Civil War, nearly a decade before Yellowstone became America's first national park, a California senator named John Conness proposed that the federal government acquire the Yosemite Valley and a nearby forest of giant sequoias known as the Mariposa Big Tree Grove and set them aside "inalienable for all time." When one of Conness's fellow senators pointed out to him that there was no precedent in the nation's history for taking such action, he replied: "There is no parallel, and can be no parallel. . . . The Mariposa Big Tree Grove is really the wonder of the world." The bill passed, paving a foundation for the national park system to come: an array of natural wonderlands, set apart from the ever-growing wastelands of civilization, which would soon sweep across the entire planet. John Muir pushed tirelessly (and successfully) to have the boundaries of the park expanded, writing articles with titles like "In God's First Temples: How Shall We Preserve Our Forests?" In 1892, he helped found the Sierra Club, one of America's first and still one of its most influential wilderness preservation organizations. When it came time for the Sierra Club to choose a logo, they did not pick Half Dome or Yosemite Falls or some other iconic geological feature. They chose a giant sequoia. Over the past 125 years, that logo has been revised numerous times, but the big tree has always remained right at its center.

+

The scene we filmed at the base of Andromeda took the better part of two days to set up. First, Anthony and Wendy used a crossbow to shoot a fiberglass arrow (tied to fishing line) over a high branch in the tree. Then they pulled up a rope, climbed it, and affixed a pulley, so that a camera could be lowered down the full length of the trunk in one smooth movement. As the camera swooped earthward, it would capture David down on the ground (a tiny white speck, growing larger every moment) until it reached his eye level.

It took many tries to get the timing of the shot just right. The producers, meanwhile, were visibly anxious about David's safety. Sequoia branches have a terrifying tendency to drop at random intervals, with a sound like calving glaciers, and he was walking directly beneath the tree without a helmet on. Steen assured the crew that if any branches came down, he would hurl himself onto David and shield him from any harm.

The final sequence was the moral pivot: the moment, familiar to any viewer of the genre, when the wonder-inducing scenes of science turn to an ecological call to action. The subject of the episode was how plants—from snow-encrusted conifers in the boreal forests of Finland to warty hammer orchids in Australia—had evolved in concert with the regularity of the changing seasons. That rhythm was becoming erratic, and it promised to become ever more so. The environmental thinker David Farrier calls this phenomenon a "chronoclasm," a cataclysm born of misaligned timing, when "the long-held relationships that weave species together around shared needs fray."

Sir David Attenborough stood in front of a grove of sequoias, the honeyed light of the magic hour radiating divinely behind him. With a look of careworn sagacity in his crinkly eyes, he stared through the camera's lens and, it seemed, right into the viewer's soul.

"The question is," he said, "can we curb climate change sufficiently to ensure that the seasons will continue? Only if we can do that will the future of seasonal plants, including these magnificent trees, be assured."

Afterward, a young park ranger, who had been standing off to the side during the taping, said, "That was awesome. It actually healed a bit of my broken heart."

To my surprise, I found myself curiously unmoved by David's words. I imagined the viewers at home hearing this speech, wiping their befogged eyes, rising from the couch, turning off the TV, and then sliding right back into their old grooves, as the planet grew hotter and deadlier each year. The voice of God could command people to change, but He alone could not make it so.

+

The sequoias are some of the world's toughest trees. They are clad in asbestos-like bark—a three-dimensional matrix of fibers, as much as three feet thick, which insulates them from fire and cushions them against rolling boulders (a not-inconsiderable concern in the avalanche- and mudslide-prone Sierras). That bark is also rich in insect-repelling tannins. And they have enormous root systems, which can extend laterally for hundreds of feet. These defenses have allowed them to reach ages exceeding that of almost any other tree. So it is all the more alarming to realize that they are now in peril. Anthony and Wendy's research was finding that, during the region's increasingly long, dry, fiery summers, the sequoias are less able to ward off attacks by a flourishing population of native bark beetles. In other words, though the sequoias are unusually impervious to pests, fire, and drought, they are not immune to the combination of all three. And that deadly combination, unfortunately, is precisely what climate change—which is to say, the carbon economy—is fostering.

I am tempted to lay the blame for the current plight of the sequoias entirely at the feet of avaricious industrialists. However, according to environmental historians, some of that blame belongs to none other than John Muir. In a bitterly ironic twist, it was in trying to preserve the trees that Muir helped doom them. "Fire," he once declared, "is the arch-destroyer of our forests, and sequoia forests suffer most of all." If he had bothered to speak with a Sierra Miwok or Western Mono person about the ecology of the region, they may have informed him that they had been setting low-intensity wildfires in the sequoia groves on a regular basis for centuries, and far from harming the sequoias, they actually *helped* them. Sequoia cones are sealed with resin, which melts with heat, opening up like a wax-sealed envelope held above a candle. This ensures that seeds take root in recently burned soil, which has been swept clean of detritus and cleared of competition. Oddly enough, Muir seems to have been (at least dimly) aware of this science. He writes that fire "furnishes bare, virgin ground, one of the conditions essential for its growth from the [sequoia] seed." Nevertheless, to the end of his life, Muir was still calling fire "the great destroyer of sequoia." The forest service, heeding his (and others') dire warnings, instituted a nationwide campaign of fire suppression in the early twentieth century, which allowed piles of woody debris to build up, providing the fuel for today's giant-killing megafires.

Calamity, in hindsight, was inevitable: We stockpiled tinder in our forests for a century while, at the very same time, making the atmosphere warmer. Now, the marriage of those conditions is giving birth to something infernal. During the summer of 2020, the worst fire season then on record, as many as ten thousand sequoias were immolated—an alarming number when one considers that the entire global population of giant sequoias is just around eighty thousand. That summer, news reports featured surreal, futuristic images of sequoias in the Giant Forest, their trunks wrapped in silvery foil to protect them from being scorched.

In a tragic turn, about a year after our trip to the sequoias, Steen informed me that a forest fire had killed Andromeda, the enormous tree at whose base we had filmed Sir David Attenborough delivering his lines. The monarch of *The Green Planet*, which had stood for two millennia or more, enduring countless fires, was brought down in a single day.

+

To celebrate the successful conclusion of the shoot, the whole crew ate dinner together in the restaurant of the Wuksachi Lodge, a faux-rustic hotel located within the park boundaries. We ate plates of stuffed acorn squash and drank bottles of good, cheap Sonoma red wine. As we ate, David regaled us with tales from his various travels. His work had taken him to arguably all of the world's great wildernesses (with the sole exception, he has said, of the Gobi Desert), often at a time when both the regions' ecosystems and Indigenous cultures were comparatively unaltered by colonial capitalism. He recalled one particular trip, to "quite a remote part of Vanuatu," in the late 1950s. In those humid equatorial forests one can find a species of bioluminescent mushrooms. "It's wonderful when there's a sudden flush of them and the forest is lit with these little toadstools," he said. He recalled one night in particular, in a village called Sulphur Bay. "That evening, they started beating the drums, and—it sounds like a Hollywood movie—out of the forest came the women, with these luminous mushrooms stuck on their faces with perspiration, and they were dancing and dancing, with their faces illuminated with this ghostly glow. I tell you, it was really creepy, and unforgettable."

At one point, I turned the conversation to the problem of climate change. What, I asked him, should other storytellers—writers, filmmakers, artists—be doing to address the climate crisis? How do you inspire people to make social change without sounding preachy and turning them away?

David's voice became soft, almost a whisper. "I have no idea, really," he said. "One is going to do what one can do. If you can write, then you write. If you can make films, then make films. If it's public speaking, then public speaking, I guess."

"But it's changed so much, hasn't it, the way that we tell stories about the natural world . . ." I said.

"Well, I suppose in technological terms, yes. But how you tell it?" He shrugged. "The message has always been the same really. And there have been people who delivered it much more powerfully. People like John Muir."

I felt like quibbling with him. It seemed to me that a great deal had changed since Muir's time: the rise of globalization, the postmodern erosion of the concept of nature, the ever-growing doom cloud of climate change. But upon further reflection, I realized he was right. The message of the Green Revelation was that an ancient forest was a source of both health and awe, a natural cathedral filled with strange wonders, and, perhaps, a portal to God. For those lofty reasons, as well as the more mundane exigencies of personal health and ecological stability, the wild was worth protecting. This sermon, delivered for the better part of two centuries, through sparkling prose and hyperreal cinematography, had saved a number of spectacular forests from clear-cutting. But it hadn't radically altered the larger economic and political systems that were now incinerating those same forests.

Perhaps it was time for a new message.

+

When I returned from my adventure with Steen, I went back and started rereading the classic works of nature writing, many of which

I hadn't read since I was a teenager. Right away, certain blind spots began to jump out at me. It is hard, for example, reading Muir, not to see the disgust with which he views the migrant shepherds who befoul his beloved Yosemite, or the condescending way he writes about the "well trained" Black people he meets on his walk to the Gulf. In Thoreau and Emerson, one now cannot ignore the high-nosed manner with which they describe their less-educated neighbors. "To speak truly, few adult persons can see nature," Emerson writes. The rise of a poetic sensibility as a new realm of cultural capital punished those who, toiling to survive, could not afford to cultivate such refined sensibilities. This elitist strain in the Romantic spirit would later haunt the environmental movement's attempts to save the old-growth forests of California and the Pacific Northwest, pitting what many perceived as earthy, hardworking loggers against rich, airy-fairy urbanites. The old nature films had their blind spots as well. In some cases, these blind spots were quite literal: The filmmakers tended to crop local people and human infrastructure out of the frame, creating the illusion of an unpeopled wilderness.

On the whole, the nature conservation movement was a movement *away* from people. As Thoreau once wrote, "I love Nature partly *because* she is not man, but a retreat from him." The problem with this way of seeing, as has been noted by thinkers like William Cronon, was that it cleaved the human realm in two (pristine wilderness on one side and despoiled human landscapes on the other), with no viable vision for how people might live sustainably *within* the wild world.

Countless beings—humans and nonhumans alike—suffered from this exclusionist philosophy. However, perhaps none suffered more grievously than Native communities—the very people who tended the lands that nature worshippers claimed to venerate. It is notable that, in the face of the ongoing genocide of Native people, the great nature poets of America remained largely silent. Freneau, who decried the "rav'nous nations" that "conspir'd to rob [Indians] of their native soil," nevertheless failed to make any public demand that Native people be allowed to retain their land and left in peace. The nature poet William Cullen Bryant, going a step further, publicly supported the brutal removal of Cherokee people known as the Trail of Tears. Thoreau idolized Native wisdom—he even compiled a three-thousand-page work of unpublished research he called his "Indian Notebooks"—but he was often left embittered when actual, living Native people failed to live up to his expectations. While paddling through the wilds of Maine, he noted that the local Penobscot people preferred hunting moose to sketching pictures of them. "What a coarse and imperfect use Indians . . . make of nature!" he griped. "No wonder that their race is so soon exterminated."

Muir, too, spoke highly of some Indigenous groups he met, such as the "natural dignity" of the Huna Tlingit people of Alaska, but he despised the "dirty" Miwok and "ugly" Mono who refused to evacuate his "clean" Sierras. In *The Mountains of California*, Muir recalls passing a group of Mono people dressed in rabbit skins, who were hiking over the mountain passes into the Yosemite Valley to fish for trout and collect acorns. He portrays them as almost subhuman beasts—"hairy beings . . . lumbering toward me with a kind of boneless, wallowing motion like bears"—whom he viewed with open contempt. "Somehow they seemed to have no right place in the landscape," he writes, "and I was glad to see them fading out of sight down the pass."

+

The following morning, Steen and I decided to extend our trip to the sequoias by a day. Instead of driving straight back to San Francisco, we stopped off at the home of a Native American man named Charlie Castro, who lived in the town of Three Rivers, just on the edge of the national park. I had first run across his name years earlier while researching giant sequoias in an online newspaper archive. In the

1960s, he was known for climbing dead and dying sequoias to safely cut them down and, on one occasion, to snuff out a crown fire. It was horrifically dangerous work. Numerous stories had described him as the finest, toughest, and most daring tree climber ever employed by the National Park Service.

When he hobbled out of the house to greet us, Charlie revealed himself to be nothing like the sinewy, iron-eyed firefighter I had been imagining. He was a genial, boyishly handsome man in his late eighties, with a round, suntanned face, huge ears, and white hair. The only clues to his former life as the king of giant sequoia tree climbers were his hands, which were meaty, wrinkled things, like the deflated pecs of a former bodybuilder.

"Howdy!" he called out, shaking each of our hands. His head barely reached my chin.

He welcomed us inside and we sat on his couch, which was covered in a turquoise doily. Over the course of a few hours of pleasant conversation, he unspooled his life story. He had been born and raised in Yosemite National Park. His father was half Miwok, and his mother was a Paiute. They lived in the Yosemite Indian Village, a collection of twelve small cabins housing the Native families who worked in the national park.

One recurring theme of Charlie's life story was fire. He recalled his elders telling folktales around campfires. His mother cooked the family's meals over a woodstove: acorn porridge, pine nuts, venison, raccoon, porcupine, groundhog, marmots, squirrels, pigeons—anything edible their family could catch or gather outside the park boundaries. And he fondly recalled watching the "firefall," a nightly event when park rangers pushed hot embers off the edge of a cliff on Glacier Peak, creating the impression of a river made of incandescent sparks. "God, that was amazing," he said.

Charlie's ancestors had likely inhabited the Yosemite Valley for some four thousand years, with intermittent interruptions. In 1851, in order to claim the region for gold mining, a group of white soldiers known as the Mariposa Battalion had marched into Yosemite, burned the villages and food stores of the local people, killed two dozen individuals, and captured dozens more, who were sent off to reservations. Charlie's family were victims of this atrocity. He grew up hearing stories about how his grandmother fled to a nearby cave, where she hid for three or four days without food or water until her parents retrieved her.

"The genocide of Native Americans was nowhere more methodically savage than in California," writes the journalist Ed Vulliamy. Spanish and (later) American settlers subjected them to waves of slaughter, enslavement, disease, and ecological disruption due to the introduction of foreign livestock. The Miwoks (Charlie's ancestors on his father's side) are estimated to have once numbered more than eleven thousand; by the early 1900s, their population was reduced to less than five hundred. Those tribes who remained living in the Yosemite region were looked upon as the lowest of the low. They were often derided as "Digger Indians," supposedly because they dug for tubers for sustenance, although the rhyme with the hateful term for Black people would have been hard to miss. As the anthropologist Allan Lönnberg notes, some settlers harbored a pseudoscientific belief that they were traveling backward in evolutionary history as they pushed farther west, until, at the Pacific coast, the tribes were "sunk almost to the darkness of the brute."

As Native populations declined, the Euro-American fear of "Indians" softened into a patronizing romanticism. Within a span of only a few decades, the fearsome enemies of pioneers and cavalrymen became the heroes of the Boy Scouts. Following this trend, the park service stopped trying to oust the Native inhabitants of the Yosemite Valley and began using them as tourist attractions. In 1916, an annual event was instituted called the "Indian Field Days," in which local Miwok and Yurok people were encouraged to wear feathered headdresses and pose in front of canvas tepees, both of which were alien to their culture.

Native Americans worked a number of hard jobs within the park on a seasonal basis. Their labor was integral to the functioning of the park for decades. Even still, park officials seemed to regard the very existence of "Yosemite Indians"—within the park, or elsewhere—as a problem to be solved. As park superintendent Charles Thompson once wrote, the government hoped "to break them up as a racial unit and, in time, to diffuse their blood with the great American mass." Charlie remembered being rapped on the knuckles in school for "talking Indian" to his friends. He recalled his teacher saying to him, "We don't do that here. This is a white man's school." He admitted, somewhat mournfully, that he now remembers no more than a handful of words in either of his parents' native languages.

This war of cultural attrition went on for decades. Finally, in the 1960s—when Charlie had already grown up, moved out, and started a family of his own—rangers began quietly evicting the remaining families from the Indian Village. In 1969, when the houses were all empty, they burned the village to the ground, supposedly as part of a firefighting training exercise—a haunting, if unintended, echo of the attack by the Mariposa Battalion a century earlier.

+

Charlie's first real job was working for the park service, fighting wildfires. One of his bosses, noting Charlie's potential—he was strong, tireless, and unafraid of heights—taught him to climb trees using ropes, and Charlie soon proved his talent as a "hazard tree faller," climbing and carefully disassembling big trees that were in danger of toppling over and injuring people or damaging property. By the late 1960s, he was the leader of a small crew of elite tree climbers, mostly other local Native Americans, and the park service had begun sending them all over the West—from Alaska down to Arizona, and from Wyoming over to Hawaii—to handle unusually difficult and dangerous situations. He also assisted a team of scientists led by Richard Hartesveldt in their landmark study of fire ecology among giant sequoias. Their report found that fire suppression was killing off sequoia groves, because it prevented their cones from opening and new saplings from sprouting up. This finding would help change the fire policy of the entire nation—the beginning of what the journalist M. R. O'Connor calls the "fire revolution," a widespread (though perhaps not yet widespread enough) project of burning off the underbrush on wild land, just as Native people had, centuries earlier.

The most memorable fire Charlie ever encountered, he says, was in 1967. While fighting a wildfire in Montana, he was called back to Sequoia National Park for an emergency. A giant sequoia called the California Tree, one of the largest in the park, had been struck by lightning, and incandescent debris was now raining down, threatening to start a massive conflagration.

Charlie was asked to climb the burning tree and put out the fire from above, something no one had ever done before. He did so by climbing a nearby fir, throwing a rope into the branches of the sequoia, and swinging across, before climbing to the top of the burning tree, some 250 feet in the air. As he weaved among the charred branches, he could feel the trunk vibrating from the sheer energy of the fire churning within. (One quirk of sequoia biology is that when they are struck from above by lightning and fire bores down into the tree trunk, the same bark that insulates them from wildfire can help keep a fire smoldering within the tree for months or even years.) Charlie clambered into position and hauled up a fire hose, which he aimed down into the glowing cavity of the tree. As soon as he opened the hose's nozzle, a plume of vapor and ash came roiling out of the hollow trunk, momentarily blinding him, but he remained up there for hours, his face singed by embers and his hands numbed by the cold water. Finally safe back on the ground, some twelve hours later, he was rewarded with a six-pack of beer from his boss. The California Tree still stands, more than fifty years later, and park rangers still tell stories about Charlie Castro, the legendary savior of giants.

+

At the end of our visit with Charlie, Steen pulled out his phone to play a video he'd taken from the top of one of the sequoias we'd climbed that week. Charlie leaned in and peered closely at the screen. He grew quiet, admiring the sequoias from an angle he hadn't seen in decades.

"Golly sakes, isn't that wonderful?"

"It's just fantastic," Steen said. "It's like a gift from God."

"I know it. There's not a lot of people who can do what you and I can do," Charlie said. "And you figure, by God, we're special to have the right to be up there."

"I always thank the tree," Steen said.

"That's the Indian way, too," Charlie said. "Thank him, thank the Great Maker for keeping you safe, and wish for that big beautiful tree to live on forever."

I would later look back upon this moment often, rolling it around like the pit of a plum on my tongue. Both Steen and Charlie sincerely loved the sequoias; both even expressed gratitude to them. And yet, one way of loving trees—what Charlie called "the Indian way"—had resulted in millennia of careful stewardship of those forests, while the other way—Muir's way, and Steen's, and, indeed, my own—had precipitated a strange Baudrillardian crisis, wherein we worship trees in nature documentaries and national parks while, just out of sight, the emissions of our daily lives incinerate forests to ash.

It is no secret that what Charlie calls "the Indian way" of relating to land differs starkly from that of Euro-Americans, but non-Indigenous scholars have often found it hard to pin down exactly what that difference is. In 2017, the University of Victoria hosted a conversation between the philosopher Umeek, also known as

E. Richard Atleo, a hereditary chief of the Nuu-chah-nulth people, and the Euro-Canadian political philosopher John Ralston Saul. Saul began by attempting to lay out the fatal flaw in the colonial view of nature as he saw it:

> Cities can be wonderful places, but one of the outcomes of the cities has been to accentuate the worst of the colonial relationship to place. People live in condos and in apartments.... They're in favour of 'environmentalism,' but they actually know little about the environment.... Some of them love going to national parks and saying, 'Look at those trees! Aren't they wonderful?' But they can't name any of them. They don't know anything about the properties of the trees.

Umeek agreed, but he added that merely learning the names of the trees, or even their scientific properties, wouldn't fully fix this problem. What was needed, he argued, was a shift toward an Indigenous paradigm of thought. Pressed to define this paradigm, he replied simply: "It's relationships."

When I later reached Umeek by phone, we spoke at length on this topic. Within the Nuu-chah-nulth worldview, he said, all living beings—which share a common ancestry through the Creator, Qua-ootz—are united by complex relationships that have been deepening for tens of thousands of years. "We ask one another for help because we are related," he said. "It's very much like if you're my brother and you're an electrician, and I'm doing something electrical, and I say to you, 'Brother, can you give me some advice?'"

In the woods, I have often felt a sense of wild awe. But I don't think I've ever felt what Umeek calls *isaak*—a respect born of "a consciousness that all creation has a common origin." When I think back on the countless hikes I have taken through forests in my life, all the books of nature writing I have read, all the shimmering documentaries I've watched, it occurs to me that none of these things have made me feel truly *related* to the living beings around me. Relationships, argues the Anishinaabe writer Patty Krawec, are built on reciprocity, on a sense of give-and-take. "For Indigenous peoples," she writes, "kinship means responsibilities." But what had I given back to the earth in all of those moments of reverie? Aside from a few pieces of litter I'd picked up now and again, the answer was: depressingly little.

I'd come to suspect that one reason I've never fully felt at home here on Earth is because being at home ultimately means being nestled safely among kith and kin. The modern worldview reduces the earth, our raucous and crowded abode, into, as R. Buckminster Fuller famously argued, a "planetary spaceship": a sphere of humanity floating all alone in a chilly void. Besides a handful of species we keep as pets, other living beings are largely seen as resources to be mined (for food, for wealth, for pretty photographs), not true relations. This worldview leaves many of us feeling both deeply unnatural and deeply, existentially lonely. The purpose of the Green Revelation, I was realizing, was to surround us with a feeling of presence at once natural and divine—"an invincible gladness as remote from exultation as from fear"—so that one would never have to feel alone. The irony was that, in trying to preserve that wild nature, we ended up setting it aside in parks and preserves, far from our daily lives. And so, except in brief flashes of communion, we found ourselves even more lonely than before.

How, I wondered, had we ended up like this? Who or what severed all those earthly relationships? How had we grown so dangerously unrooted—both from one another and from the planet beneath our feet?

4. GNARLING

ONE DAY in 2018, while back home in the suburbs of Chicago, I sat down with my dad to trace our family tree. In hindsight, I can see that this day marks a cardinal bend in the course of my life, but at the time it felt like no big deal. It was one of those languorous summer afternoons when life flows along weightlessly, as if atop a slow, brown river. We sat on the back porch of his home, sipping glasses of iced tea. The air shimmered with the mating calls of cicadas, which, after waiting patiently for seventeen years, had recently clawed free from the soil and clambered up into the nearby oaks.*

Growing up, I had never given much thought to my ancestors.

---

*Most cicadas appear aboveground on a yearly cycle, but certain species go dormant on longer cycles, waiting as many as seventeen years below the surface before reemerging. During their long dormancy, the nymphs survive by sucking the sap from the roots of trees. Scientists believe the nymphs may be able to keep track of time by tasting differences in the tree sap, as it grows sweeter and more plentiful in the spring and summer, and thins out in the fall and winter.

They are dead and gone, I thought. *Who cares who they were, or how they lived?* It was only once I began traveling abroad that I started to see how strange this genealogical amnesia was. While backpacking through Southeast Asia in my early twenties, for example, I noticed that local people routinely made offerings to ancestral spirits, known as *phi* or *neak ta*. A similar custom is practiced in many animist and syncretic cultures around the world: One's progenitors are felt to be vitally, even dangerously, present in one's own life. The dead, these traditions hold, are never *really* dead, because even after death, they continue to affect our lives. This belief makes intuitive sense to me. Our ancestors shape us, both through their genes, which become our genes, and through their actions, which molded their children, who in turn molded their children, ad infinitum.

The belief that these ancestral influences don't matter, that each person can be born fresh into the world and make of themselves whatever they choose, is a quintessentially American delusion. We are taught to worship Great Men, not great-grandmothers. In school, I had been forced to memorize the name of every American president in chronological order—I always stumbled around Rutherford B. Hayes—but I didn't know the names of any of my ancestors beyond my own grandparents, and worse, I didn't care. I began to suspect there was something perverse, something almost inhuman, about the way that I was taught to relate to the world. What does it say about my sense of relationality (to borrow Umeek's incisive term) that I didn't even know the names of my own relations?

All of this was somewhere in the back of my head that summer's day when I asked my dad if we could try to chart our family tree. I knew from the outset that tracing our ancestry would prove more difficult for our family than for most. We had drifted here and there across the continent for generations, blowing about like dandelion fluff. Virtually all I knew about our European roots was that our surname—Moor—gestured to the damp peatlands of Scotland and

England. (John Muir, whose name has the same derivation, quipped that he had "tinctures of bog juices . . . oozing through all my veins.") Of course, there is another meaning of "moor"—an antiquated word for dark-skinned North Africans, which persists in the names of Mauritania and Morocco. But that word, though spelled the same way, bears no etymological relation to the other, and a DNA test my father had taken years earlier showed we Moors bore no Moorish blood.

Our roles that day were clear: My dad excavated scraps of genealogical information from his memory, while I plugged it into the computer. I began by signing us up for an account on Ancestry.com, a website devoted to cataloging family history. Next I asked him to list all of the relatives he could remember, which didn't take long. He had no siblings and only one cousin. Of the relatives whose names he knew, he knew surprisingly little, though what he did know was by turns colorful and somewhat tragic. He knew that his mother had performed on the vaudeville circuit. He knew that his father had once been so poor he slept on park benches and ate popcorn three times a day (and later, after a failed attempt to strike it rich in the oil business, almost went to prison for tax evasion). And he knew that his grandmother had spent her final decades living in the Northwest Texas Insane Asylum. The gaps in his knowledge proved as interesting as the knowledge itself. He didn't know his own father's birthday, for example, nor did he know his father's father's first name.

We tried to use Ancestry's database to locate more relatives, but rather quickly, we found ourselves floundering in murky possibilities— the names Moore and Moor were often used interchangeably until the rise of mass literacy in the 1850s, and there were too many of us to count—so we soon called it a day.

In the end, we decided to just pay a genealogist to do the research for us. He returned with his findings after a few weeks. What he found surprised us both—though, in hindsight, perhaps it shouldn't have.

The genealogist, a man in Utah named Nick Sheedy, reported that he had managed to trace my father's line as far back as a farmer and country doctor named Hezekiah Balch Moor. Hezekiah was born in Tennessee in 1793, served as a physician in the army, and then later moved to Alabama, where he became one of the founders of a town called Leeds. He had seventeen children with his first wife, and then, after she died, two more with his second. For decades, Hezekiah sold crops and bought more land. To work that land, he bought enslaved people. By 1860, the genealogist reported, he had amassed considerable wealth, but "the bulk" of that wealth was "the ten slaves he owned, seven females and three males under 6 years old."

This news was not a complete shock to me; from our online research, I had gathered that our family had been roaming around the American South for centuries, and over that expanse of time, it was almost inevitable that some of them would be slave owners. But at the end of the section on Hezekiah, the genealogist noted something else: In the 1860 census, Hezekiah was listed as owning a twenty-four-year-old Black woman. Ten years later, the same woman was living next door to him, without a husband, and three of her four children were listed as being "mulatto." The Black woman's name was Lucinda Moor.

I wrote to Sheedy to clarify if this meant what I suspected it meant. "The context certainly suggests that he could be the father of her children," he wrote back. As most Americans now know, this situation—where a white slaveholder impregnated an enslaved woman he owned—was exceedingly common. Virtually all African Americans whose ancestors were in America before the Civil War have at least one white ancestor and, Y-DNA testing has shown, most of the time that ancestor was a man. The implication, as the journalist Michael White notes, is obvious: "Widespread sexual exploitation of slaves before the Civil War strongly influenced the genetic make-up of essentially all African Americans alive today." Though chattel slavery was long ago abolished, its legacy is engraved, indelibly, in both human bodies and in the body politic. As James Baldwin memorably wrote, "People are trapped in history and history is trapped in them."

+

Curious to learn more about Lucinda, I searched for her name on Ancestry. After a few minutes I came across a page that made my pulse quicken: Someone, using a private account, had created a family tree connecting Hezekiah and Lucinda, as if they were husband and wife, and listed all of their descendants, up to the present day. I sent a message to the owner of that private account, and a few hours later, I had a response waiting for me. It was from a Black woman named Gia Gray.

"Hi Rob. Yes, I am the ggg granddaughter of Hezekiah Balch Moor and Lucinda," she wrote. (She had made her account private, she later told me, because some distant white relatives had blocked her from joining their family group on Ancestry when they saw that she was Black.) "So yes, you have plenty of African-American cousins," her message concluded. "I am one. Nice to meet you."

Two days later, I called the number Gia had given me. We ended up talking for three hours that afternoon, and many hours after that. It all came pouring out, the diverse tributaries of past lives—family history, personal history—combining into a torrent. I listened, rapt, as she recounted stories about her ancestors, passed down through three or four generations, precisely the kinds of stories that my family had allowed to decompose.

A few months later, while on a work trip down to San Francisco, I took a detour to the town of Danville to meet her in person. She greeted me at the door of her large suburban home. A youthful-looking woman in her late forties, she was dressed in a chic navy tunic, white pants, Tory Burch sandals, and big gold earrings shaped like twisted clouds. Her bright dark eyes held a glint of something warmly confidential, as if we had known one another our whole lives.

Outside the air was acrid with wildfire smoke, the sky the color of a singed fingernail, so we passed the afternoon indoors, drinking white wine and discussing the joys and frustrations of genealogical research. I was impressed by her ability to keep multiple branches of her family tree in her head at once, stretching back many generations, and I noticed that she spoke about her great-grandparents with a sense of intimacy, as if she'd known them personally. She also spoke of her yet-more-ancient relations—"the Ancestors"—as an almost divine force, who she believed were "watching over us."

It gave me a vertiginous feeling to think about how Gia's family had made their way from Alabama to Illinois, taking a totally different path than the one my family had taken, only to arrive at a neighborhood less than an hour's drive from where I had grown up. All around us, I realized, are distant relatives, following their own winding courses through history.

+

Humankind is far more closely related than it may appear at first glance. At some point in our evolutionary past lies a single common ancestor to every person living on Earth. However, according to geneticists, in order to meet that common ancestor, you would not need to time travel all the way back to the dawn of our species. You would only need to travel back about three thousand years. "In the time of Egypt's Queen Nefertiti, someone from whom we are all descended was likely alive somewhere in the world," the science writer Scott Hershberger notes. When I first encountered this fact, it was hard for me to wrap my head around. Traveling back a mere three thousand years would seem too recent to account for, say, a tribe who has been living in a remote corner of the Amazon for the past five millennia. However, as a geneticist named Adam Rutherford explains, "genetic information spreads rapidly through generational time." Because no society can be perfectly insular without becoming dangerously inbred, even the most remote communities are forced to sometimes marry outsiders, and thus genes tend to "drift" from one community to the next. Beginning in the early 1500s, some European people had children with Indigenous people in South America, and those children had children with other people, and on and on, the genes spreading gradually across the continent and around the world.

Given this deep kinship between various peoples, it is worth pausing to ask: If humans are all part of one big family, how did people like Gia and me ever come to see ourselves as being distinct from one another in the first place? Who or what chopped up the human family tree?

+

Gia was born and raised on the South Side of Chicago. It was less than forty miles from where I had grown up, but culturally, it was another country. Whereas every one of my neighbors had been white, every one of hers was Black. "Growing up, I always felt a little bit different," Gia told me. Just by looking in the mirror, she could tell that she was born of mixed racial ancestry, but her parents, both of whom identified as Black, and both of whom looked more or less like her, never discussed it with her.

She described her childhood as a happy one. Her mother was a school principal and entrepreneur, and her father was a police officer who coached youth sports teams in his free time. They raised four children, three girls and a boy. Her father was also proud to have played a small but important role in the civil rights movement. Gia later sent me photos of her father, in a trilby hat and a suit coat, standing directly behind Dr. Martin Luther King Jr. during a rally held before thirty thousand people in Soldier Field, looking equal parts dapper and tough.

King had come to Chicago vowing to "smash" the city's long-standing practice of "slumlordism," and Gia's dad had volunteered to act as his personal bodyguard. In one of the marches later that summer, through the all-white neighborhood of Marquette Park, Gia's father did his best to shield King while a white mob pelted him with rocks, bricks, and cherry bombs. Afterward, King told reporters, "I have seen many demonstrations in the South, but I have never seen anything so hostile and so hateful as I've seen here today." Despite the fact that he and many of his fellow campaigners had suffered injuries, the march had been a success, he explained, because it helped "bring the evil out into the open."

+

When Gia was three years old, the TV miniseries *Roots* aired. The show, based on the bestselling book by Alex Haley, told the story of seven generations of Haley's family, beginning with Kunta Kinte, who was abducted from the Gambia in 1767 and sold into slavery.

At the time of its airing, *Roots* was the most watched show in history; reportedly, the streets of New York were eerily empty when it aired, because everyone, white and Black, was glued to the television. Gia watched it with her parents. She recalls two things in particular: the scene in which "slave hunters" tie Kunta Kinte to a tree and chop off his foot with an axe, and the scene in which Kizzy, Kunta's daughter, wails in pain after being raped by a white slaveholder.

One of the many unforeseen effects *Roots* had on the public was that it created an explosion of interest in genealogy, especially among Black families looking for ways to trace their lineages back to Africa, just as Haley claimed to have done. Near the end of the book, Haley spends many pages describing his research process, which spanned twelve years and half a million miles, ranging from his ancestral village in the Gambia to archives in London. But subsequent investigations by historians and reporters concluded that much of what Haley wrote was either erroneous or invented.

What is worse, in fabricating these facts, Haley had instilled an unrealistic hope in millions of Black families. Sheedy, the genealogist my father and I hired—who has worked as a researcher for the PBS series *Finding Your Roots*—told me he regularly has to deflate the hopes of clients wanting to trace their genealogies back to Africa. In fact, he has succeeded in closing that gap only once, for the musician Ahmir Thompson, also known as Questlove. Thompson, Sheedy discovered, was descended from one of the enslaved people brought over in the *Clotilda*, the very last slave ship to land on American shores. When Thompson was presented with these documents, on an episode of *Finding Your Roots*, his eyes welled up with tears. "Until an hour ago, I didn't know who I was," he said.

Gia eventually became a doctor of family medicine and moved to the town of Danville, California, where she married and had two children of her own. Her interest in her ancestry, which had been growing slowly throughout her childhood, flowered one day at her clinic at Kaiser when a medical assistant came into her office and closed the door so they could have a private conversation.

"Dr. Gray, what *are* you?" the medical assistant asked. "We were all talking, and there's just something different about your look."

"I'm Black," Gia replied. "My parents are Black."

The medical assistant (who, to Gia, looked either Latina or Filipina) seemed unconvinced, and the question lingered in Gia's mind.

+

It is common these days to hear people say that the idea of race is a fiction, which was formulated in large part to justify the act of enslavement. This is partially true. The fuller truth is that race is a complex and fantastically gnarled concept, a notion made up of layer upon layer of beliefs that have been accreting over the course of centuries.

Long before one's race was seen as being skin-deep, it was believed to reside in the blood. In the centuries predating the transatlantic slave trade, Europeans generally used the word "race" as we might now use the word "bloodline." The notion of blood race, which was largely metaphorical, became terrifyingly real in the fifteenth century, when Spaniards began carrying out the Inquisition, an act of ethnic cleansing against the area's Jews and Muslims, following a policy known as *limpieza de sangre,* or "cleanness of blood." When the "clean blood" of a person was being investigated, the Inquisitors would summon the oldest Christian men living in a given town and ask them a series of questions about the suspect's family history, hoping to locate a secret Jew or Muslim. The Spanish word for race, *raza,* therefore had concealed within it a double meaning: It meant both breeding (as in the raza of an expensive horse) and *raça,* which refers to a flaw in a gem. We can still hear the double meaning in one Spanish nobleman's stipulation in his will in 1473 that his sons and grandsons could not marry anyone "infected with the bad raça of Moors or Jews or any other bad blood."

Up until this time, there was no concrete notion of racial "blackness" as we know it today. This is not to say that people did not notice skin color. The presence of dark-skinned Africans in Europe was frequently remarked upon throughout antiquity. In ancient Greece and Rome, dark-skinned Africans were lumped together as "Aithíops," meaning "people with burned faces." The term referred to people from a particular (if vaguely understood) place, not an abstract scientific category. Likewise, in medieval Europe, Black people were most often referred to as either "black Saracens," or "Moors." In other words, there were no "Black" people, only various dark-skinned *peoples.*

This began to change when, with the rise of larger trade networks and then overseas colonies, Arabs and Europeans began capturing and purchasing large numbers of enslaved people from sub-Saharan Africa during the Middle Ages. In *Inhuman Bondage,* the historian

David Brion Davis writes that by the fourteenth century, the Arabic word for slave, *abd*, had come to be synonymous with dark-skinned Africans. (Previously, enslaved people throughout Europe and the Middle East had been captured from a wide variety of populations, including a great many Slavs, hence the English derivation of the word "slave.") Arabs tended to view themselves as being "white," while Africans were seen as "black." The increased visibility of enslaved Africans also led medieval Europeans to independently invent the idea of a Black and a white race. The art historian Madeline H. Caviness has noted that around the twelfth century, Europeans began painting themselves not in various shades of pink, but in a stark shade of white.

A binary was emerging between whiteness, which Arabs and Europeans conceived as innocent, pure, and noble, and blackness, which was associated with wickedness, mystery, and savagery. It almost goes without saying that this classification system was in no way inevitable; black and white are merely two abstract colors we project onto a wide range of skin tones. In many parts of India, a common term for white people is *tāmramukha*, meaning "people with copper-colored faces." When the Vikings first encountered African people, they described them as being blue.

During the colonial era, when Europeans began importing millions of enslaved Africans into the Americas, this polarized racial binary would prove to be a terribly useful tool for segregating and subjugating the labor force, especially in the Caribbean colonies, where white indentured servants worked alongside enslaved Black people. Following a series of revolts by both white and Black laborers, colonial overlords discovered that enslaved white laborers could be granted greater privileges than Black ones, winning their loyalty and ensuring they could be relied upon to help quell any Black uprisings.*

---

* The artificiality of these racial categories becomes clear when one looks back at

The concept of epidermal race was gradually layered over that of blood race, though not entirely neatly. Owing to the widespread rape of enslaved Africans by white plantation owners, there was soon an enormous population of so-called "Negros" whose skin colors varied drastically from one end of the spectrum to the other. Indeed, the phrase "colored people" (and, I was surprised to learn, the phrase "people of color") came into widespread use in the nineteenth century precisely because white people had begun to acknowledge that Black people often contained a large amount of "white blood." In the state of Alabama, for example, the law defined a "person of color" as someone who had "any Negro blood" in their ancestry for five generations. Other states adopted the "one-drop rule," in which even a single African ancestor at any point in history was considered a stain, which legally prohibited that person from marrying someone white. (The Nazis, who studied American race law closely, reportedly considered adopting this rule, but ultimately found it, in the words of one Nazi author, too "unforgiving.")

In the nineteenth century, scientists would concoct yet another definition of race, which sleeved neatly over its antecedents. Blackness, they now declared, ultimately resided not in one's blood or one's skin, but in one's bones. Taking calipers to skeletons, scientists purported to find racialized features in the width of nostrils, the height of foreheads, and, especially, the size of crania. The American physician Samuel George Morton attempted to rank the various races

---

how whiteness was defined during the colonial era. Benjamin Franklin expressed a prevalent (if not universally held) belief of his time when, in 1751, he wrote that "the Number of purely white People in the World is proportionably very small. All Africa is black or tawny. Asia chiefly tawny. America (exclusive of the new Comers) wholly so. And in Europe, the Spaniards, Italians, French, Russians and Swedes, are generally of what we call a swarthy Complexion; as are the Germans also, the Saxons only excepted, who with the English, make the principal Body of White People on the Face of the Earth."

based on cranial capacity; he placed "Caucasian"* brains at the top of the hierarchy and "Ethiopian" (i.e., African) brains at the bottom. The French naturalist Georges Cuvier likewise claimed to have discovered a "cruel law" that "condemned to eternal inferiority the races with cramped and compressed skulls." Darwin, too, subscribed to this myth, writing, "The belief that there exists in man some close relationship between the size of the brain and the development of the intellectual faculties is supported by the comparison of skulls of savage and civilized races." Scientists now know that cranial capacity is only weakly correlated to intelligence. What it is strongly correlated to is body size, which correlates to childhood nutrition, which correlates to wealth—a perfectly circular logic, if one wants to prove that the dominant race is biologically fated to be so.

Today, most scientists agree that the human family tree simply cannot be carved up into neat categories known as races, because there are no clean breaks between one group of people and the next. This new, far messier understanding of race is primarily based on genetic science, which has been layered—again, not entirely neatly—on top of the older racial definitions based on blood, skin, and bones. It has led to some surprising and even comical revelations. There have been numerous news stories in the past two decades of people who had labored under the belief that they were one race, based on their skin color, only to find out, following a DNA test, that they were another. The most gleefully schadenfreude-laden of these stories concerned the fervent white nationalists who discovered, to their

---

*The word "Caucasian" is a term coined in the late eighteenth century by a German philosopher named Christoph Meiners, who divided humanity into two overarching "tribes": the "higher tribe" of "white-skinned and beautiful" Caucasians—for reasons that are almost too muddled and nonsensical to bother recounting, Meiners had concluded that all white people were descended from inhabitants of the Caucasus region—and the "dark-skinned and ugly" people he called "Mongolians," a catchall category for every non-white ethnicity on Earth.

horror, that they had Black ancestry; they argued that the results were "rigged" to "spread multiculturalism," and began speaking of "noise DNA" that didn't really count as a racial signifier.

Other stories are less easy to laugh at. A woman named Ingrid Johnson, for example, grew up believing she was half Black, half Italian (which, in her mind and in the minds of those around her, made her a Black woman), but when she took a DNA test, the results came back informing her that only 2 percent of her genes were of African origin. (Of course, in the long run, *all* human genes are of African origin, but DNA tests work on a genetic time frame reaching back about five hundred to one thousand years.) When Johnson took a second, more comprehensive DNA test through Ancestry.com, it revealed that she was roughly one-third African, one-third European, and one-third unknown. Then Ancestry quietly updated its secret algorithm, and overnight, Johnson learned that she was now nearly half Black, just as she had grown up thinking. According to a story in *The New York Times Magazine*, when learning the news of her African ancestry, which had so recently been put in doubt, Johnson teared up. "I'm so relieved to see the African part, that I really am a black woman," she said. And yet, from those same results, she could have easily felt precisely the opposite. As the author notes, "Many African-Americans . . . upon seeing how much of their lineage is European, are not necessarily surprised or doubtful about the results, but they feel gut-punched by the bald reminder that even their genes carry slavery's legacy."

+

Shortly after she was confronted by her coworker about her racial background, Gia decided to take a DNA test. When the results came back, weeks later, they announced that she was 34 percent white. Rather than shock or sadness, she was overcome by a burning sense of curiosity. She began staying up late on her laptop, hunting for clues about her ancestors. ("It went from more of a hobby to an addiction," she said.) On her mother's side, she discovered that she was related to an enslaved man who worked as a Confederate quartermaster under General Nathan Bedford Forrest, who would later become the first grand wizard of the Ku Klux Klan. Gia also discovered she was related to a white family that stretched back to Virginia in the 1770s, which allowed her to join the Daughters of the American Revolution.

Next she investigated her father's side, where she slowly uncovered the story of Hezekiah and Lucinda. First she tracked down photos of Lucinda's daughter (and Gia's great-great-grandmother), Isadora, who, she noticed, had strikingly light skin. She scrutinized the census records. Finally, by matching her DNA with multiple white descendants of Hezekiah she found online, she was able to confirm her suspicion: Lucinda had been raped and impregnated by Hezekiah.

Gia began asking family members if they knew anything about Hezekiah. Her older relatives told her fragments of information their ancestors had passed down about him, the kinds of things a census wouldn't capture, and none of them were positive. Gia told me that her family often spoke in terms of "good" slave owners and "bad" ones, which were, the irony in Gia's voice made clear, relative terms, not absolute ones. Hezekiah was said to be one of the bad ones: Family lore describes him as "mean" and "a drunkard." Gia also noted that her family members who traced their lines back to him, when compared with other lines of her family tree, tended to have markedly harder lives; at least three of them had died violently, two by gunshot and one by strangulation. While she and her three siblings had managed to achieve a relatively happy, stable, bourgeois existence, the generational progress they'd made had been hard-won. Many of her cousins had not been so fortunate. "Each generation should be building," she said. "But they didn't start off life with anything. You need to have a little something to get more."

As Gia described it, there are two chief challenges to researching Black genealogy. The first is that, for obvious reasons, it is far more emotionally "heavy" than it is for white people. The second is that the historical record is riddled with lacunae and erasures. Before the Civil War—what is known as the genealogical "brick wall"—enslaved people were not named on census records, nor were they named on the manifests of slave ships. And many of the unofficial records that might hold information about a Black person's ancestors—the farm schedules, the photographs, the family Bibles, account books, diaries, almanacs, birth records—were, and in many cases still are, owned by white families. "We need your help," Gia said. "We have oral history, which is wonderful. But the part we don't have is anything written."

Back home, I emailed Gia with a proposal: What if we took a trip to Alabama to conduct some family research? The itinerary I proposed was a simple loop: We would fly into Atlanta, drive together to Leeds, then make our way through Birmingham, Selma, and Montgomery, visiting important civil rights monuments along the way.

I half expected Gia to decline. During our conversations, she had told me that she was wary of ever going to Alabama, parts of which she had heard were still dangerously racist. And anyway, if she *did* want to go, why would she need me, a virtual stranger, tagging along?

Within a few hours, I had a message back from Gia in my inbox. "Yo!!!!! I would totally be down for it!" she exclaimed.

Next, I wrote to the Leeds Historical Society and informed them that I would be coming to town on a genealogical research trip with a "distant cousin." Margaret Little, the treasurer of the historical society, received the news enthusiastically. She said she would be happy to show us around town and take us on a tour of the local history museum, which had a portrait of Hezekiah hanging on the wall. "I have also contacted some Moor descendants who would like to meet you and share some family history," she wrote.

I booked my tickets south, and Gia booked hers.

+

One morning the following spring, Gia and I drove west along the highway from Atlanta to Leeds. As we left the city, our rental car—a gray whale of an SUV—passed into and then out of a blinding squall. We glided into Leeds over empty, rain-polished streets. The town was sleepy, even somewhat comatose; aside from a few new cars, there was almost no visible evidence that we were in the twenty-first century rather than the twentieth. We drove past a cement plant, past a library with an extensive collection of VHS tapes in its window, and past a store that sold pants, whose sign read, simply, "Pants Store." The downtown was about three blocks long.

With us in the car were Gia's two sisters, who were also family-history buffs. Her big sister, Jennifer, who was dressed in a crisp white blouse and a bright yellow blazer, had the faintly airbrushed aura of the host of a morning TV program. Her little sister, Susan, dressed all in black, was quiet, bespectacled, and cerebral. They made a good team: Jennifer did most of the driving, Gia did most of the talking, and Susan did most of the genealogical research, keeping our various findings neatly cataloged on her laptop.

At a café in Leeds, we met up with Margaret Little, a charmingly forceful older woman dressed in a jacket monogrammed with her initials. She led us to a white clapboard house that served as the local history museum. It was old, quaint, and tidy, with the smell of all old, quaint, tidy places: of ancient dust that caulks the narrow gaps between floorboards, of layered wallpaper, of windowsills that have been painted so many times they take on the texture of frog skin. We wandered around, admiring the exhibits. On one wall hung a series of photos of local military veterans; on another was a signed poster of the basketball player Charles Barkley, the town's most famous son. In the next room over, as promised, hung a charcoal portrait of Hezekiah.

Gia and I stared at Hezekiah.

He stared back at us.

A sign beside the portrait read "Dr. Hezekiah Balch Moor."

"He was a doctor. *I'm* a doctor," Gia said. "So that's kind of interesting."

In his portrait, Hezekiah has big, bright, boyish eyes, a button nose, and an odd, old-timey beard. A young man, dressed in an army uniform, not quite sure what to do with his hands.

For the first time, I found myself thinking about Hezekiah not as an ancestor or an abstraction, but as a living person, a being trapped in the flow of time. The portrait was drawn around 1813, when he was twenty years old. One year earlier, he had married his first wife, Gincy. One year later, he would be camped out in the dark forests of what is today eastern Alabama, battling Native people.

It occurred to me that this young man had no idea what his life would one day hold—the bloody settlement of Alabama, the death of his first wife, the Civil War, emancipation, Jim Crow . . .

He didn't know that he would one day rape an enslaved woman he owned. He didn't know that she would bear his child. He didn't know that he would then enslave that child as well.

He didn't know that, from that child, an entirely new branch of his family tree would sprout.

Nor did he know that the descendants of that branch would one day return here, to this very corner of the earth, to reckon with his legacy.

+

A few feet away from Hezekiah's portrait hung a large framed illustration of the genealogical tree of another old family of Leeds, the Lees, which stretched all the way back to the early 1600s. I'd never seen a family tree quite like it. It was about three feet tall and densely illustrated, apparently by hand, with dozens or even hundreds of ancestors arrayed along the branches and roots. Instead of the typical series of square brackets, it was drawn to look like an actual tree, with a stout trunk and curving branches, including some that stretched across the trunk to merge with other branches, to mark the marriage of two cousins. By my count this happened at least eight times. Of course, this was not an unusual occurrence back then. A seventh-generation Alabaman I had met years before told me that his family had so many such intrafamilial marriages that his family tree looked more like a "family wreath."

Family trees tend to come in one of two shapes: Either they branch downward from a single, distinguished ancestor (Charlemagne, say), showing each of his many descendants, or they branch *upward* from the person who paid to have the family tree made, charting the many ancestors who led to the present generation. (The family tree of the Lees of Leeds, unusually, branched in both directions, which for some reason met at the trunk in the figure of a man named Needham Lee Sr., who was born in 1770.) A truly accurate family tree, though, would not resemble a tree at all. Reaching back to the very beginning of humankind, it would also show the trees of every other relation, a webwork of endlessly diverging and incestuously recombining branches—less a tree than a tangled forest. In 2018, researchers attempted to do just that, using genetic data from thirteen million people harvested from the genealogy website Geni: Even a fraction of the resulting graph, which sprawls in all directions, like a hunk of moss, is so dense and complex that it hurts my head to even contemplate it.

It makes sense, then, that the earliest genealogical records were not trees but unitary bloodlines. They consisted of lists of names—usually the male ancestors of kings or chieftains—which were recited or sung. As any reader of the Bible knows, the Old Testament often becomes mired in exactly this type of ancestral list making: Adam begat Seth, who begat Enos, who begat Cainan, who begat Mahalalel, and so on. This form of genealogy was remarkably common, in large part because it conforms to the linear nature of speech, which cannot branch out the way a written work can. In precolonial Hawaii, a designated genealogist would recite the *Kumulipo* (Beginning in deep darkness), a two-thousand-line song tracing a chief's origins all the way back to the first spark of life in the universe. The ancient Scots employed a similar figure, known as the *sennachy*, or royal bard, who recited the ancestors of the king. Sometimes these "family chains" took the form of carved trees: The masterful Salish totem poles of the Pacific Northwest, for example, portrayed genealogical (as well as mythological) history, interweaving the stories of humans, other animals, and spirits.

It wasn't until the Italian Renaissance that genealogical records began mimicking the shape of trees; such a chart was sometimes known in Latin as an *arbor consanguinitatis*, "a tree of shared blood." Such diagrams were especially useful for wealthy families trying to work out complex inheritance schemes. Around 1568, the writer-scholar Scipione Ammirato began creating luxury genealogical charts for noble families, inserting their ancestors' names in the branches of vividly rendered oak trees. These new trees invested one's genealogy with a kind of mythic power: The family was no longer a series of fathers and sons and grandsons, like a chain of dominoes falling, but a single, vast, ancient, ever-living thing, reaching its roots into the past and budding in the present.

+

Margaret ushered us to the front of the museum, where our relatives were gathered, waiting for us. There was the briefest of pauses, a kind of fluttery caesura. None of us knew how this meeting would go. I had read that when the descendants of President Thomas Jefferson and Sally Hemings, the enslaved woman with whom he famously fathered six children, were invited to a meeting of the Jefferson family in 1999, it broke into open hostility. Despite DNA evidence proving that Hemings had given birth to Jefferson's offspring, some white descendants demanded yet more proof. ("We're not racists," said one Jefferson descendant, in his own defense. "We're *snobs*.") Gia and I had talked this all through in advance, but now that the plan was unfolding, I could tell she was nervous as well.

We shook hands with three smiling men. Each had grayish hair and a reddish face, and each was dressed in a button-down and slacks. (In these men's rosy cheeks I thought I spotted a family resemblance to me and my father, though perhaps it was just a shared aversion to sunscreen.)

We all stood in a circle and introduced ourselves. They were: Eddie, a local retiree; J.J., a school principal; and Cliff, a lawyer.

After an awkward lull, J.J. asked, "So do y'all know which of Hezekiah's children you're descended from?"

"Yes, sir, yes we do," Gia said delicately. "We are from Lucinda. She was an enslaved woman, and we see in the census she was living next door, with her mulatto children."

"Really," J.J. said amiably. He was carrying a spiral-bound book of Moore family history, written by his great-aunt Willie Alma Moore White, which he had brought to show us. "I bet *that's* not in here," he said, holding up the book.

Everyone laughed.

"No, that part's not in there," Gia said.

She explained how she had worked her way through the DNA results, matching the various lines back to Hezekiah, and about how Hezekiah had been mentioned in her family's oral history.

"Is that right?" muttered Eddie, in wonderment.

"See, I learned something today," J.J. said. "He had an enslaved woman living next door who he had children with . . ."

After a beat, he added: "Which would have been common."

"It was so common," Gia agreed.

"Thomas Jefferson," J.J. said.

"Thomas Jefferson," Gia agreed.

(Later, when I interviewed him over the phone, Cliff told me that he had heard rumors about Hezekiah's Black offspring swirling around Leeds for as long as he could remember. "The Moores always were prominent, and that's the kind of shit that people would like to talk about," he said. "I just always dismissed it as gossip.")

Margaret led all of us into an adjoining room, where Hezekiah's portrait hung on the wall. We all sat down at a long table, the four of us on one side, and the four of them on the other.

Gia recounted what little she had managed to learn about Lucinda Moor. Her older family members told stories that described how her family had left the town of Leeds around the year 1900. Old newspaper stories she'd found show that, the previous year, a dispute had broken out between Black and white coal miners, and two Black miners had been shot. Family lore holds that Gia's great-great-grandmother, who was close to the slain miners, feared her family would be next, so they fled town in the dead of night, having wrapped their horses' hooves in burlap to muffle the noise. They made their way to Oklahoma, known then simply as Indian Territory. The next generation moved to Chicago during the Dust Bowl, following the tidal wave of immigration northward known as the Great Migration. It was unclear, however, whether Lucinda had escaped the town of Leeds with the rest of her family, or whether her children had left her behind. Gia was never able to locate a death certificate for her. After the 1880 census, she simply vanishes from the historical record.

Next, Randy Ray, a local amateur historian Margaret had invited to join us, gave a talk on Hezekiah and the history of the town. Hezekiah, he explained, had fought in the War of 1812 and then, the following year, in what's called the Creek War—a civil war between two factions of the Creek Nation, which Andrew Jackson deviously exploited to seize tens of millions of acres of Indigenous land, about half of modern-day Alabama. For his service, Hezekiah was granted forty acres, as well as a pension, which he used to acquire his homestead in what would later become Leeds. He built a two-story home—the second floor was reportedly designed to double as a fort, in the event of an attack by "Indians"—and set about building a profitable farm using enslaved labor.

"It's said Alabama was built on stolen land, on the backs of stolen people," Randy said. "And there's a lot of truth to that."

However, Randy also wanted to point out that the form of slavery practiced in Alabama had not been as harsh as in some other states. He explained that certain basic rights were set out for enslaved people in the Alabama Constitution of 1819.

"You had to properly clothe, properly medicate, properly feed, and you couldn't beat," he said. "That was the law."

I glanced over at Gia and saw her eyes narrow.

"What happened if the slave master didn't follow the law?" Gia asked mildly.

"They could be punished with fines," Randy said.

"Hmm," Gia said.

By the onset of the Civil War, there was roughly one enslaved Black person for every white person living in the state. Slavery was not just the backbone of the economy; it formed its skeleton, its musculature, and arguably, its beating heart. So, like many enslavers, when Hezekiah's sixteen captives were emancipated, he was afraid he would be left destitute. Willie Alma's book of family history includes a letter that Hezekiah sent to his daughter just after the end of the Civil War. In it, he complains his farm was in ruins. "Outlyers"—free Black people, who often hid out in forests and swamps—had killed his hogs and burned his thresher, and Yankee soldiers had seized his horses and his saddle, as well as corn, bacon, flour, dried fruit, salt, and money. "I worked about sixteen negros, and they have freed them and left me in poverty, and not able to work," he goes on. "I am in so much trouble that I can hardly write."

Nevertheless, fifteen years later, when he died, Hezekiah had amassed enough money to leave each of his youngest children a college fund, as well as a horse, a cow, and a pig. Such are the gnarls of history. Even when the powerful lose their wealth, the world is shaped to helped them win it back.

+

By the end of his life, Hezekiah had acquired enough land to donate a large parcel to the nearby Cedar Grove Baptist Church so they could build a new cemetery, where he and both his wives were later buried.

After lunch, we traveled to that cemetery, a grand hilltop full of large marble headstones overlooking the strip of highway where most of the town's corporate chain restaurants were clustered. Hezekiah's headstone stood in a place of prominence, as did those of a number of other Moors (and Moores).

At one point, Cliff pointed out the curious fact that on Hezekiah's gravestone, the word "Baptist" was practically "bigger than his own name."

He began to explain why, then paused. "Y'all aren't going to get sensitive on me now?"

"No!" Gia laughed. "We're the least sensitive people, to be honest."

Cliff explained that Hezekiah had previously been a Presbyterian, but he "got mad" and renounced his membership because the church had taken a position against slavery, so he helped found a Baptist church instead.

All across the South in the antebellum period, Christian churches were riven by the question of slavery. Some factions, like the Quakers and Methodists, became staunchly abolitionist. Their preachers frequently quoted a passage from the book of Genesis stating plainly that "every nation of men," all being descended from Adam and Eve, is made from "one blood." Proslavery Christians, like the Southern Baptists, tied themselves in knots trying to counter this clear and forceful argument. Some, taking a paternalistic stance, argued that slavery was divinely ordained—often citing a line from Ephesians calling slaves to "obey your earthly masters with respect"—because it was in the best interest of Africans, who were believed to be naturally childlike. Others argued that Black people, being descended from Noah's disrespectful son Ham, bore an eternal curse to be "the servant of servants." A few believed that Black people were not children of Adam at all; rather, it was argued that the snake in the Garden of Eden was a coded reference to a Black person who tempted the innocent Eve to commit the original sin. The fallacies undergirding these arguments—Black people are childlike; Black people are genetically stained; Black people are sinister—can still be heard today, albeit in slightly more coded forms.

We wandered down among the gravestones to the church itself. Inside we met a friendly old woman named Carolyn Ryan, who talked about how it had once served as a hospital during the Civil War. In a nearby vase, in lieu of flowers, there stood an arrangement of cotton bolls.

As we walked down the aisle of the church, Carolyn informed us that the pews were carved from the wood of local cedar trees—the same trees, we realized, that Hezekiah would have once walked beneath. "This cedar is beautiful," Gia exclaimed, stroking it. She said that just thinking about it—the tightly coiled solidity of time, the tangible presence of the past—gave her the chills.

+

The following morning, in Birmingham, we stopped off at the city courthouse and spent hours digging through crates of old documents and paging through an enormous tome marked "MARRIAGE INDEX, FEMALE, BLACK, 1882–1940," hoping to dig up some new information on Lucinda. But, as elsewhere, she was nowhere to be found. It felt as if she were hovering just beyond the veil of the historical record, calling silently to us, like a specter.

Later that morning, we visited the city's famous civil rights museum. Across the street stood the Sixteenth Street Baptist Church, where, in 1963, four young Black girls were killed by a bomb placed by members of the Ku Klux Klan. Later that day, in Selma, we crossed the Edmund Pettus Bridge—named after a Confederate general and grand dragon of the KKK—where Dr. King and other peaceful protesters were beaten with truncheons, trampled with horses, and sprayed with tear gas. On the bridge we met a pair of butch Black women who asked us to snap their picture as they posed on the median between two lanes of traffic, with fists raised to the sky.

We arrived in Montgomery by midafternoon, our windows sealed tight against the city's viscous heat. Rather than going to our hotel and dropping off our bags, we drove straight to a place called the National Memorial for Peace and Justice, hoping to slip in before it closed for the evening. The memorial, which was first envisioned by the famed civil rights attorney Bryan Stevenson, aims to preserve the memory of the thousands of Black people who died by lynching throughout the Jim Crow era. I'd often heard it spoken of as something like a secular American temple—a "reverential space," writes the artist and writer Masud Olufani, dedicated to an "unspeakable horror."

We entered the memorial through a metal detector. On our left was a sculpture depicting enslaved men and women held together in chains. Susan noted that the manacles had been fashioned from corten steel, which oxidizes, so that, over time, they would drip sanguineous rust down the bare chests and backs of the statues. Blood as rust, rust as residue. A stain that cannot be wiped away.

We climbed a ramp toward a modernist, open-air pavilion and stepped inside.

The memorial was austere. It consisted of row after row of rectangular rusted steel pillars. That was all: just pillars. Each pillar was about six feet tall; above it was a thin metal stalk that extended up to the ceiling. On closer inspection, we discovered that on each pillar was inscribed the name of a different county in the South, and below the name of each county were listed the lynching victims of that county. We moved slowly between the pillars, reading the names on each. Gia noticed that the slab for Jefferson County, where Lucinda had lived, had more lynching victims than anywhere else in Alabama.

As we moved deeper into the pavilion, the genius of the memorial's design revealed itself to us: The wooden walkway gradually began slanting downward, but the pillars remained at the same height, so that as we descended the ramp, the pillars seemed to lift up off the floor, suspended by the thin metal stalks connecting them to the ceiling. The lower the floor went, the higher the rectangular slabs rose overhead, until they were hanging just above our heads. When the wind gusted, the slabs swayed gently from side to side.

A chill passed over me; a taste of bitter salt.

The "pillars," I realized, were no longer pillars. They were dead bodies, dangling from the limbs of trees.

+

A tree is not just a tree. It is also, always, a symbol. For white Americans, forests have almost entirely happy resonances, calling to mind fresh air and cool shade, tranquility and adventure. It is not so simple for many Black people. During the Jim Crow era, white Southerners deliberately refashioned trees into murder weapons— murder weapons that lived on for hundreds of years, often in places of prominence like the town square—to remind the town's Black residents to remain subservient. A postcard from the time shows Black lynching victims hanging from a dogwood tree (which mobs preferred for its long lateral branches). Beneath the photo is a poem that reads:

> *This is only the branch of a Dogwood tree;*
> *An emblem of white supremacy . . .*
> *The negro, now, by eternal grace,*
> *Must learn to stay in the negro's place.*
> *In the Sunny south, the Land of the Free,*
> *Let the white supreme forever be.*
> *Let this a warning to all negroes be,*
> *Or they'll suffer the fate of the dogwood tree.*

In *The Lynching*, the journalist Laurence Leamer describes how, in 1981, a group of KKK members decided to kidnap and murder a nineteen-year-old Black man named Michael Donald, who had never been accused of any crime; he was chosen merely for being Black. They brought Donald to a secluded forest, bludgeoned him with a tree limb, and slit his throat. What is most telling is that the killers then drove Donald's corpse back downtown and hung his body from a camphor tree, a purely symbolic act. Something similar had happened, almost fifty years earlier, during the lynching of a man named Claude Neal in Florida. Neal was taken to a forest outside town and tortured, castrated, and killed. Then his dead body was brought back into town and hung from an oak tree on the courthouse lawn. When a sheriff cut down the corpse, a mob of two thousand white people demanded it be strung back up; when the sheriff refused, the mob began to riot. That tree stands in front of the courthouse to this day.

The poet Glenis Redmond confesses that when she looks at a tree, she sees the grand beings she climbed and loved as a child, but she also sees the lynching tree that terrorized her ancestors. "I am simultaneously enchanted and haunted by trees," she writes. This paradoxical, haunted view of trees recurs throughout modern Black literature. In Toni Morrison's masterpiece, *Beloved*, she describes how Sethe, an enslaved woman who escaped to freedom, prefers to remember the beauty of her former plantation, rather than the violence that took place there. And yet, the violence lingers behind the memory of the trees, like a menacing shadow seen in the corner of the eye: "Boys hanging from the most beautiful sycamores in the world . . ."

+

We moved through the coiled innards of the memorial. Lining both walls of the walkway were plaques bearing the names of various lynching victims, along with the justifications for their murder. Gia read each aloud, in a voice that grew increasingly incredulous:

"Arthur St. Clair, a minister, was lynched in Hernando County, Florida, in 1877, for performing the wedding of a black man and white woman.

"Jack Turner was lynched in Butler, Alabama, in 1882, for organizing black voters in Choctaw County.

"After Calvin Mike voted in Calhoun County, Georgia, in 1884, a white mob attacked and burned his home, lynching his elderly mother and his two young daughters, Emma and Lillie.

"After a white man attempted to assault Jack Brownlee's daughter in Oxford, Alabama, in 1894, Mr. Brownlee was lynched for having the man arrested."

We read on and on. Many of the victims had been killed for only the most minor of social infractions.

". . . for knocking on a white woman's front door."

". . . for speaking disrespectfully about some white people."

". . . for 'frightening' a white girl."

". . . for 'standing around' in a white neighborhood."

". . . for addressing a white police officer without using the title 'mister.'"

". . . for insisting that a white coworker return his shovel."

". . . for reprimanding white children who threw rocks at her."

". . . for refusing to hand his teenage son over to a mob."

". . . for protesting the lynching of another black man."

For the victims of lynching and their loved ones, the pettiness of the supposed crimes combined with the cruelty of the punishment to create a kind of awful absurdity, designed to instill a fear that even the slightest transgression could reap deadly results. The same trick is used by abusive parents and authoritarian governments. Rational violence, however unfair, can be predicted and ultimately avoided. But chaotic violence comes on like a terrible wind; one is forced to live stooped in fear or bent in supplication.

The outpourings of rage—and even glee—that these lynchings provoked among the crowds of white people who attended them, sometimes numbering in the thousands or even the tens of thousands, are nauseating to look back upon. Having convinced themselves that Black people were little more than beasts, white people behaved in the most beastly way imaginable: They cut body parts from the dead and pried teeth from their skulls, to serve as keepsakes. Entire families, children included, picnicked beneath the dangling bodies.

We rounded a corner and stood before a long wall down which a perpetual sheet of water ran. The wall was made of concrete crafted to resemble wooden beams. It called to mind water seeping through the walls of slave ships, of rain pouring through the leaky roofs of slave cabins, of sweat running down foreheads, of blood running down backs, of tears, of thirst, of rage, of sorrow, of grief, those most liquid emotions, which, long pent, can suddenly no longer be contained.

"I'm a little overwhelmed," Gia said, her voice breaking.

I stepped away to give her some privacy.

Outside, in the stark sunlight, exact replicas of each of the pillars were now laid out in horizontal rows. The pillars, which had become bodies, had now become coffins. Bodies, finally laid to rest.

+

In *The Properties of Violence*, Sandy Alexandre argues that lynching was not simply an outpouring of white rage; rather, it was part of a widespread and deliberate effort to sever Black landowners from their land. A single lynching could intimidate entire communities. Walter White, a courageous undercover investigator of these crimes, described how, after the lynching of Mary Turner in 1918, "more than 500 negroes" fled the town of Valdosta, Georgia. Hundreds of such instances have been documented. "The threat that blacks would somehow gain socioeconomic ascendancy over whites through landownership had to be quashed," writes Alexandre, "and lynching violence against blacks served whites well in this regard."

Gia's family had experienced this kind of intimidation. Her cousins' grandmother, a woman they all called Mama Georgia, was a widow who lived on a farm in Mississippi. Every day a white man would drive his car up her long driveway and simply sit, staring at her house, for hours. "He wanted the land," Gia said. "So Mama Georgia finally got sick of it and she got her shotgun and she ran out of the house and yelled, 'You get on out of here! You're not going to take my land!' She jumped in her car and chased him off. And he never came back." Gia's great-great-grandfather, a formerly enslaved man named Preston Roberts, was not so fortunate. He, too, had acquired a small farm, but one day, according to family lore, a white man appeared on his doorstep and told him it was time for him to leave. "If he didn't leave, he knew what would come next," Gia said. "The white robes and horses, and a tree with his name on it."

Just as the practice of lynching stole physical land from Black families, it also stole land, in the broader sense, from the Black imagination. The author bell hooks has written that, from the present vantage point, it is "easy for folks to forget that black people were first and foremost a people of the land." Prior to their enslavement, most of the Africans who were kidnapped and shipped to America in chains would have had an intimate and exquisitely detailed knowledge of their ancestral land. The enslaved descendants of those Africans, in their way, lived close to the land as well. Most enslaved people spent their days working the soil. They also expertly tended personal garden plots bursting with okra, milo, eggplant, collard greens, watermelon, yams, peas, tomatoes, beans, squash, peppers, onions, cabbage, sweet potatoes, corn, peanuts, tobacco, and indigo. They felled trees for firewood and to clear new farmland. They hunted possums, squirrels, raccoons, birds, deer, and even bears in the forest. They fished, caught crawdads, and collected oysters and mussels. They healed themselves with herbal medicine, and they ate clay pulled from the ground to replenish the minerals their diets lacked (a practice that horrified ignorant white observers).

In their scant free time, sometimes in the dead of night, enslaved people snuck off to places in the woods known as "hush arbors." In these invisible churches, preachers led rounds of ecstatic prayer. Out of the sight of their overseers, enslaved people also availed themselves of "rootworkers"—so named because of their use of medicinal roots and other plants—who drew upon ancient African animist traditions to heal physical and spiritual wounds. Some Black escapees, known as "Maroons," made homes in wilderness areas like the Great Dismal Swamp, intermarried with Native communities, and lived there for generations.

Following emancipation, millions of Black people migrated northward, and in the process, found themselves driven from the land itself. Up north, Black people largely transitioned from working outdoors to working indoors, often in industrial or service jobs. Through housing policies known as "redlining," they were forced into the most treeless neighborhoods of big cities; as white people fled these newly integrated urban neighborhoods, they gravitated to "leafy" suburbs like the one I grew up in, which were actively hostile to Black families. The outdoor-oriented groups that white people began joining as a response to urban malaise—summer camps, the Scouts, hiking clubs—were overwhelmingly segregated. Black people were also banned from visiting many national and state parks, trips that, even if one could afford to take them, would have involved passing through dangerous rural towns.

By the 1970s, most Black people had stopped working outdoors, stopped hunting, and stopped gathering wild foods. It became a point of pride to live an urban or suburban middle-class life, far from the farms where one's ancestors had been forced to work. As Eldridge Cleaver once said, "In terms of seeking status in America, blacks—principally the black bourgeoisie—have come to measure their own value according to the number of degrees they are away from the soil."

Gia has lived through the very tail end of this centuries-long transition. She recalls that her grandmother, who was born in Tennessee, kept chickens in her yard in Chicago, and she knew how to cook rabbit and "maybe squirrel." But by the time Gia was born, her parents had moved into a home on the South Side with only a small yard, and many of those old ways were gradually forgotten. Her relationship to wilderness was complicated. In the city, she said she grew up without "any connection to nature." Then her family would travel up to a cabin they owned in northern Wisconsin, and she would find herself transported to another world; it almost felt like "make-believe," she said.

The lake house was a small log cabin, with an outhouse instead of an indoor bathroom, surrounded by tall woods. Up there, Gia's father and brother, Barry, rose before dawn and spent most of the day outside, hunting and fishing. When I spoke with him on the phone, Barry told me he had always felt a sense of "freedom"—a word I noticed both he and his sisters used in a particular way, suggesting a quiet refusal to allow white society to hem them in. "Don't get me wrong, I understand the struggles that we have," Barry said. "But I never felt *caged*." Gia said she had always greatly admired this quality in her brother. But, as a girl, she felt that her own freedom was a bit more circumscribed. At the cabin, she and her sisters mostly stayed indoors, reading and playing board games. Sometimes she walked around the perimeter of the property, collecting pine cones and leaves, which, ever the genealogist, she'd iron and then preserve in scrapbooks.

Beside Gia's house in California, which sat at the end of a cul-de-sac in an affluent corner of Danville, I had noticed a beautiful hill, covered in yellow grass and oak trees with wide-spreading branches, which I would have been tempted to climb as a kid.

I asked if her children ever played up there.

She said that they kept asking to, but she wouldn't let them. "I just don't want them to get too much out of my sight," she said.

+

On our last day in Alabama, we made our way to what is surely one of the nation's finest history museums: the Equal Justice Initiative's Legacy Museum in Montgomery. Its elaborate exhibits trace a roughly four-centuries-long arc of Black history, showing how slavery evolved into the sharecropping system of the Jim Crow era as well as the modern prison system.

In some cases this evolution was shockingly naked. The Louisiana State Penitentiary, for example, was built on a former cotton plantation; the first inmates slept in slave cabins and picked cotton seven days a week. Today, nearly 80 percent of the men imprisoned there are Black, a significant portion of whom spend their days toiling in the fields of the old plantation, harvesting cotton and other crops that are sold on the open market, just like generation upon generation of Black men before them. In *How the Word Is Passed*, Clint Smith describes visiting the prison and seeing Black men working in those fields. "The parallel with chattel slavery made it feel as if time was bending in on itself," he writes. "There was no need for metaphor; the land made it literal."

Beginning in the 1840s, prisons in the South also began a program called "convict leasing," in which they loaned out their prisoners to nearby plantation owners for a fee. One beneficiary of this system was Gia's ancestor's boss, Nathan Bedford Forrest. In the final years of his life, Forrest leased farmland on President's Island, Tennessee, and then he began leasing (mostly Black) convicts from a nearby prison to work the land—operating a slave plantation in all but name.

We wandered on: past a row of mock prison phone booths where one could hear the haunting testimonials of death-row inmates; into a luminous, copper-ceilinged shrine room dedicated to Black civil rights heroes; and finally into a small contemporary art gallery. On the wall hung a piece of folk art, painted onto a canvas of brown leather, showing rows of prisoners picking cotton. The composition was brilliant, as was the choice of materials: By choosing to paint on leather rather than white canvas, the painting's default background became the earthy hue of sunbaked skin and fresh-tilled soil.

The painting was created by a man named Winfred Rembert. The son of sharecroppers, Rembert grew up picking cotton on a plantation in Georgia. As a fiery, rebellious teen, he joined the civil rights movement. During a march in 1967, to escape two white men chasing him with a shotgun, he stole a car and drove off. He was subsequently arrested, spent a year in jail without charges, then escaped, was arrested again, and then narrowly survived a horrific attack by a lynch mob. He spent seven years in prison, including a backbreaking stint working on a chain gang, and finally won his freedom.

Recollections of his life, like the one published in *The New York Times* shortly after his death, typically end there. But Rembert's story was somewhat more complicated. After returning to society, to support his wife and eight children, he turned to selling heroin, eventually amassing enough money to purchase a large home in a Connecticut suburb and a gold-trimmed Mercedes. He was arrested again and was facing another fifteen years in prison, when a judge, after hearing an impassioned plea from Rembert's wife, chose to release him.

Newly freed, Rembert gave up the drug trade and dedicated himself to leatherworking, a skill he'd picked up in prison. He began by creating reproductions of famous works of art, but he found his voice when he turned to depicting scenes drawn from his memory: vibrant, geometric arrangements of men picking cotton, dancing in juke joints, working on chain gangs, swimming in rivers, and dangling from trees. The pains and the joys of Black life, all mingled together. "I want people who've lived in the South to talk about their history," Rembert later wrote in his Pulitzer Prize–winning memoir, *Chasing Me to My Grave*. "I want black people to be proud of what their families have gone through, and what they survived."

We stepped outside the museum into the blinding spotlight of a late-morning sun. Everything was bright, harsh. The concrete sidewalks glittered with flecks of mica. I felt subtly reconfigured, as if my mental furniture had been rearranged. The odd thing was that much of the information I'd encountered in the museum was already familiar to me. What felt new was subtle, subtextual; it took me a moment to figure out exactly what it was. I realized that the museum—which stands, poignantly, on the foundations of an antebellum cotton warehouse—both embodies and imbues a philosophy of what historical change is, how it takes place. Call it the arborescent view of history.

The present grows, always, upon the deadwood of the past. The crooked grain of that past—all its injuries, all its errant turns—remains forever as it was, just beneath the surface, warping the contours of the present, and constraining whatever shape the future might take. Wounds create gnarls; gnarls bend branches. This is how slavery grew into sharecropping, plantations into prisons. But it is also how a warehouse where enslaved men once sweated under sacks of cotton could be reborn as a museum dedicated to the cause of emancipation. It is how Winfred Rembert could transform his own scars, and those of his people, into cherished works of art. It is how John Lewis, the son of an Alabama sharecropper and the great-grandson of an enslaved man, could become a civil rights leader, a US congressman, and a recipient of the Presidential Medal of Freedom. It is why history has not one but many arcs, and it is how those arcs are bent.

Walking through the museum with Gia by my side helped drive this lesson home. At one point, she had stopped in front of a wall of glass jars. The jars were filled with soil, which ranged in hue from brick red to light beige to coal black. A nearby sign explained that the various soils were gathered from the sites of racial terror lynchings; each jar represented a Black person whose blood had been spilled on that very patch of earth. She pointed to one of the jars on the far right end of the wall. The label on the jar read "Jim Gaston, Kosciusko, Mississippi." She recognized the name right away. "That's my uncle's uncle," she said. "So this history is not far removed, to be honest."

+

That night, we had a farewell dinner at the hotel. Gia drank black coffee with dinner, a habit, she said, she'd picked up from her mom. She thanked me for organizing this trip. Even though we hadn't managed to track down the truth of what happened to Lucinda, Gia felt she'd learned a great deal more about her roots. We spent hours unpacking all we'd seen and heard.

The trip had put Gia in an oddly bifurcated state of mind: On the one hand, thinking about the horrors of slavery and Jim Crow had underlined how much progress had been made since then. But it also summoned memories of the many indignities, large and small, that she and her family still face today. She recalled how, on her first day at a mostly white college in Iowa, a professor, upon learning she was from Chicago, had asked if she was in a gang. How, on her first day working as a doctor, an elderly white patient had told her she was "pretty smart for a colored." How her mother had been called the n-word; how her son had been called a "monkey." How her brother, a pilot for United Airlines, had been tackled in his own backyard by police, after a neighbor mistook him for a burglar. How her parents had been the first Black couple to buy a house on their block, and how, within a few years, every single white family had moved away.

"As a Black person, you're born with baggage," Gia sighed. With every slight, every suspicious glance, every stolen opportunity, she felt this baggage, this peculiar weight of history itself, steadily accumulating.

I asked her how the US might finally remedy this lasting injustice. Reparations? A process of truth and reconciliation?

"It's not any one thing," she said. "It's just: an evolving."

+

A few days later, after paying a visit to some friends and family members who lived in the area, I boarded a flight home. As I stared out the plastic porthole, I found myself thinking once again about how history hardens around us, binding our lives to the curves of the past.

It was a gorgeous, cloudless day. As the plane glided beyond the ragged edge of the city, it began to pass over vast stretches of coniferous forest. Before my trip to Alabama, I would have been inclined to look down at those forests and view them, in some unconscious way, as an almost divine good. But traveling with Gia had given me what the poet Ama Codjoe calls a "double vision." All lands possess a history, which can be both nourishing and cruel. Once you begin seeing that checkered history, you can't unsee it.

In pine forests just like the one beneath the wings of my plane, enslaved people once performed the grueling and dangerous work of harvesting turpentine—making wounds in the bark of pine trees, collecting the resin in buckets, then hauling it to a fire and boiling it down, so it could later be sold as a solvent and a sealant. (One popular use for turpentine was in waterproofing the wooden hulls of early battleships.) But even after emancipation, life in the turpentine camps remained virtually indistinguishable from life under slavery. Workers, 80 percent of whom were Black, went unpaid (earnings were deducted from debt for the cost of housing and food, debt that, with monthly interest added, never seemed to diminish no matter how hard one worked). Laborers were frequently whipped, and escapees were hunted down and brutally punished. Multiple generations of Black families were born into, grew up in, and spent their lives working in the gloomy realm of the turpentine forests. The practice only ended in the 1950s, when the industry finally collapsed due to the rise of petroleum-based solvents.

Many of those turpentine forests, along with thousands of acres of former cotton plantations, were later cleared and converted into pulpwood plantations to feed the growing paper industry. This was good news for the forests up north, which were now spared the axe, but bad for many Black communities down south, who were mostly locked out of the profits of this new (highly mechanized) industry. Paper mills also tended to be located in predominately Black neighborhoods, so it was Black residents who were sickened by the waste products that were dumped into local waterways and pumped into the air. This phenomenon, known generally as environmental racism, extends far beyond the paper industry. Studies have shown that landfills tend to be located in Black neighborhoods, as are the dumping grounds for toxic products like coal fly ash. All across America, Black people have far higher rates of asthma and certain types of cancer than white people. It is no accident that the strip of land known as the Black Belt—a region of nutrient-rich "black" soils stretching from Georgia to Mississippi, where many slave plantations once stood, and where the descendants of enslaved Black people still live—is home to some of the nation's dirtiest drinking water.

Westward, westward we flew, over swamps and cattle ranches, snaky suburbs and steel-ribbed oil refineries, my mind drifting yet further back in time. In his book *Scars on the Land*, the historian David Silkenat argues that much of the nation's westward expansion, mythically explained away as the fruits of a Manifest Destiny, was in fact the direct result of plantation capitalism. The monocrop farming of cotton, wheat, corn, and (the especially ruinous) tobacco were known to rapidly diminish the soil's fertility, sometimes within as few as two or three years. "Many planters saw land as a disposable commodity to consume and abandon," writes Silkenat. The frontier system was riddled with myopic incentives: It was often cheaper to ruin one piece of land and then purchase (or steal) another than it was to invest in the soil's fertility. One formerly enslaved person, named Louis Clark, having witnessed this phenomenon firsthand, put it succinctly: "Slavery curses the soil."

Plantation agriculture's poisonous tendencies were exacerbated by the mining and timber industries, which also employed enslaved labor, also fouled waterways, and also degraded soil. As these forces combined and the land's yields waned, plantation owners pushed westward, seizing new lands. Forging ahead into these malarial wildernesses, enslaved people were forced to build roads, fell trees, drain swamps, and break the iron surface of untilled soil. Moving westward also required displacing and slaughtering Native peoples, "a quest that Southern slave owners pursued with vigor," Silkenat writes. Having no roots in this new land, plantation owners felt little guilt about exploiting it as totally as a cloud of locusts consumes a field of wheat. But that land, too, was soon despoiled, and so the cycle began again. The result was a rolling frontier that moved ever westward across the American South, propelled onward by the lash of a whip and the barrel of a gun. It was one such wave of land plunder in 1817, known as "Alabama Fever," that brought Hezekiah Moor to what would become the town of Leeds.

Karl Marx, who published a number of astute critiques of slavery in American newspapers before the Civil War, noted that seizing new lands served another useful function: It created a pressure release valve for the poor white farmers of the South, who dwelled in shanties while their neighbors lived in gleaming white mansions. Westward expansion promised "to tame them with the prospect of one day becoming slaveholders themselves." The class system back in preindustrial Europe, for all of its cruelty and inequity, had held both peasants and lords rooted to a single plot of land for generations. But in America there was a constant pressure to get ahead or get left behind. If that mad scramble resulted in the "naked, shameless, direct, brutal exploitation" of both people and land, then, men like Hezekiah thought, so be it.

Emancipation should have helped heal these ecological wounds, but it didn't. Indeed, for reasons that Marx lays out, the relationship between people and land grew even more gangrenous. One of the most quietly disturbing parts of *Capital* is the way Marx uses the word "freedom." A maximally efficient economy wants wage laborers to be "free" in two distinct ways. First, they should be "free" from slavery or serfdom, which prevents workers from traveling around at will, seeking employment wherever it is most needed. But just as importantly, they should be "free" from other modes of subsistence (farming, hunting, sharing food with friends) that would lessen their need for cash. If people are living happily on fertile plots of land, in tight-knit communities and stable ecosystems, what great desire will those people ever feel to go work in a factory or a slaughterhouse? Why would they abandon their extended family, and the comforts of community, and the coo of the doves at dawn, and the taste of wild meat and wild plants, and that knotty old oak in the backyard beneath which their grandfather is buried—the feeling, in short, of true kinship with a place—only to amass a slightly larger pile of gold?

To reach peak efficiency, a capitalist society must therefore apply a quiet but mounting pressure to forsake relationships for riches. The first generation might resist this pressure, and perhaps even the second, but eventually someone caves to it and moves to the city, a place where they have no roots. This dynamic is what propelled my ancestors across an ocean and then across a continent, and in a different, far more brutal way, it is what propelled Gia's family as well: Excised from the soil, we all drift around, seeking the places the market can best put us to use. In this way, over the course of centuries, even as it has seen opportunities narrow and delusions blossom and despotism rise, America has become—in both senses of the word—the Land of the Free.

+

In the years following our trip down south, Gia and I stayed in touch, periodically sharing family photographs and new fragments of family history. I later asked J.J. for a copy of the hand-typed book of genealogical records that he had brought to our meeting that day. He generously took the time to scan each page (eighty of them in total) and email them to me, which I forwarded along to Gia. Separately, we combed through it looking for clues. The book was filled with colorful trivia about Hezekiah and his white offspring, but no explicit mention of Lucinda or her children.

As is often the case in researching Black genealogy, the book was more notable for what it didn't say than what it did. I noticed, for example, that it lacked any mention whatsoever of the two enslaved women Hezekiah owned in 1860, even though they would have been right there on the census form that its author, Willie Alma Moore White, had surely read. I also noted that, though the book includes the 1850, 1860, and 1880 censuses, it was conspicuously missing the one from 1870, where three "mulatto" children are listed as living next door to Hezekiah. I imagined Willie Alma's hands hovering over her typewriter, considering whether to mention these uncomfortable facts. Omissions, silences, blind spots—these are all another kind of gnarling. In the moment, it may seem harmless, even polite, to leave an uncomfortable truth unmentioned, but as time passes, that omission becomes woven into the fabric of reality.

We often say that time "goes by." This phrase is profoundly misleading. It implies that time rushes past like the wind, leaving no trace. It would be truer to say that time accretes. It gnarls, and then it gnarls around its gnarls, endlessly. In the past two decades, one of the most enlightening concepts to emerge from progressive politics is the notion of structural racism: the ways in which past inequities are not softened or smoothed out with time, but instead become sclerified into structures—laws, policies, institutions, the boundaries of neighborhoods and districts—that shape generation after generation of human lives. Those structures often prove extremely difficult to reform, in part because they shape our thinking, and our thinking then shapes those structures, in a fantastically complex loop. Over time, those gnarls come to seem natural; then, they become invisible.

The American Dream is the luminous vision of a land unencumbered by gnarls, one vast smooth continental tabula rasa, where anyone can achieve anything. As an ideal to strive for, this dream is galvanizing; as a realistic description of the nation's past or present, however, it's fantasy. The arborescent view of history is tougher but far truer: The past shapes the present. Ignoring that past will not magically obliterate it. But with continual effort, we can grow *from* that past, toward something better. Even the most crooked branch can curve back to the light.

There are a great many people who do not want to accept that hard truth, preferring instead to remain within the dream. And so, a few years after Gia and I returned home from Alabama, I was disturbed, but not surprised, when self-proclaimed patriots began fighting to erase America's gnarled history from the public consciousness, cutting painful facts from textbooks and removing photographs of whip-scarred backs from museum walls. The past cannot be destroyed, but it can be obscured, until the next generation comes along and reveals it once again. So it grows, this tangled thing we call a nation, ever toward the light, and toward the dark.

+

Looking back on our genealogical pilgrimage, Gia and I agreed that the trip's high point was also, oddly enough, its low point. Following our visit to Hezekiah's grave that afternoon in Leeds, Gia, her sisters, and I set out for Scott City Cemetery, where most of the town's Black residents had once been buried. We were hoping to find Lucinda's grave.

The cemetery was located at the end of an unmarked dirt road on the outskirts of town. As we approached, Gia peered out the window. Two muddy ruts wound up a hill, disappearing into the forest.

"Are you sure that's a road?" Gia asked nervously. "This doesn't look right."

We drove up a steep hill, with tall grass brushing the undercarriage of the car. Beside the patch of flattened grass that served as a parking lot, someone had dumped their household trash, which lay strewn among the weeds.

We wandered among the gravestones for a long time. There were reported to be as many as a thousand Black residents buried there, but we saw less than a hundred headstones. Some of them were made of rough concrete, with the name written by hand as the concrete dried. Others were completely blank. Many were tilting at odd angles. None bore Lucinda's name.

We paused at one grave, which had been left untended for so long that a scraggly plum tree had taken root in the center of the plot and grown up to above the height of my chest.

The sun dissolved into a gold mist behind the hills. Gnats floated up from the grass and found their way to the corners of our eyes, the whorls of our ears.

Gia peered off into the distance, frowning thoughtfully.

"I mean, it's a beautiful place, but..." she said, her voice trailing off.

I sensed she was thinking not just about Lucinda but about all her ancestors, and about land, and memory, and respect—how, ideally, those things commingle in perpetuity, and how, too often, they do not.

"In a way, it's got a better view than the other cemetery," I said, searching for a silver lining. "It's not overlooking a strip mall."

She glanced around. A forest of stately loblolly pines and winged elms surrounded us on all sides.

"It is more peaceful," Gia sighed. "They don't have to be over there, with all that stress and drama. They're just, like, alone out here. It's almost like freedom."

5. SHADOWING

WHAT DOES it mean to be free? Philosophers have dreamed up hundreds of answers to this question, thousands perhaps. The ancients spoke of freedom as the opposite of enslavement. But that definition, concise though it may be, is merely a negation, a shadow of something real. I find myself craving something a bit more solid—something I can grasp, like the handle of an axe, and put to good use.

In my mind, the clearest definition of freedom I can summon is not a string of words, but an image: a wild, ancient forest. Back when I lived in a city, I would often catch myself daydreaming of one day slipping free from its cage of towers and retiring to a cabin in the woods, or, better yet, a yurt in the taiga, or a thatch-roofed hut on a tropical island. Amid ancient trees, I imagined, I might return to a simpler way of life, unfettered by laws, market forces, or social conventions—what Rousseau called "natural liberty." His portrait of primordial man, residing in "immense forests," still shimmers with romance. "I see him sating his hunger beneath an oak, slaking his thirst at the first stream, finding his bed at the foot of the same tree that supplied his meal, and with that his needs are satisfied."

This sylvan vision remains as enchanting for twenty-first-century tech workers as it was for nineteenth-century transcendentalists. It spans clear across the political spectrum, from the rich Reaganites who haunt the Bohemian Grove to the anarchic queer collective known as the Radical Faeries. It was especially powerful for Black people in the antebellum South. In one of history's most subversive lyrical twists, enslaved people frequently took an old Methodist hymn entitled "Ain't I Glad I Got Out of the Wilderness"—a song equating wilderness with wickedness—and brilliantly inverted it, singing, "If you want to find Jesus, go *in* the wilderness." To those in the know, the meaning was plain: In the forest lies liberation.

As a cosseted teenager in the suburbs of Chicago, I was initially drawn to Buddhism by the image of Siddhartha Gautama and his followers wandering barefoot through the forests of northern India dressed in tattered robes. I especially loved the tale of the monk named Bhaddiya. In his former life as a nobleman, Bhaddiya was pampered by servants and surrounded by armed guards, but nevertheless he felt anxious and fearful, so he gave up his vast wealth and began wandering with the Buddha. In the forest, he gradually became "unconcerned, unruffled, dependent on others, with a mind like a wild creature's." Bhaddiya was often seen sitting on the hard ground at the base of an enormous tree, muttering: "Ah, what bliss!"

Many people I know, and many of the writers I most admire, confess to feeling a similar desire to leave their lives behind and start anew among the trees. Steen often told me he fantasized about staging a treesit, living on a wooden platform placed high in the branches of a redwood, to halt the logging of an old-growth forest. Tim Kovar, the professional tree climber, said he dreams of constructing an entire treetop village, where he and a few friends could learn to live— hunting, gathering plants, and collecting rainwater—without ever coming down, like the puckish hero of Calvino's *Baron in the Trees*. The great Zen monk Bassui, who spent most of his life wandering the forests of Japan—and who would, on certain occasions, meditate in the branches of trees to sharpen his focus—urged his followers to free themselves from Buddhist tradition, with all its dusty temples and fussy rituals, and instead listen to "the voices of frogs and worms, the sound of wind and raindrops." The Trappist monk Thomas Merton, having cloistered himself in a monastery in the heavily wooded hill country of Kentucky, wrote: "Freedom ... this is what the woods mean to me. I am free, free, a wild being. ... It is the way everybody has lost."

+

When I imagine a life of true liberation, I tend to picture a treehouse. This is an image pulled directly from my childhood. But the treehouse I envision is not the slapped-together pile of plywood and two-by-fours one usually thinks of when one thinks of a "treehouse." It is a spacious, elegant, gently decaying structure in a far-off jungle.

I first saw this treehouse in an issue of *National Geographic* when I was about twelve years old. The cover of that month's issue featured an image of a mountaineer rappelling down a thin rope into a blue-black tunnel of glacial ice, which normally would have enthralled me. But scanning the table of contents on the right-hand margin, my eye was drawn away from the glacier to another story. The title read, simply, "People of the Trees."

I turned to page 34. The article described a tribe called the Korowai, whose lives were spent roaming the swampy forests of Papua (then known as Irian Jaya). I read on with steadily intensifying fascination. The Korowai wore only leaves and vines, as well as the occasional bone through their noses (specifically, "the thin bone of a bat's wing"). They hunted with bows and arrows, eating insects, reptiles, and birds. And, on rare occasions, they practiced ritual cannibalism, to "absorb" the "powers" of the slain person. I did not find this story unsettling, or even particularly surprising; its outlines had long ago been etched into my young mind, albeit crudely, by countless cartoons and comic books.

What did surprise me were the lofty treehouses in which the Korowai lived. The story opened with an image of a huge, somewhat decrepit hut built in the uppermost branches of an ironwood tree, more than a hundred feet above the forest floor. It was reached by climbing a long, spindly wooden ladder. According to the home's owner, he built it to "see the birds and the mountains and to keep sorcerers from climbing my stairs." I remember lying on the carpet of my room and staring at that photo and feeling an ache of yearning so intense that it bordered on bruise. This, I thought, was how humans were meant to live: far from the suburbs, deep in the jungle, high in the air, hidden away in a place where magic still exists.

Decades later, while sifting through various childhood relics, I ran across that old issue of *National Geographic* and read the story about the Korowai again. My callow love of the exotic had faded with time, but to my surprise, I found myself admiring the Korowai way of life for entirely new reasons. Their communities had no rulers, no police force, no prisons, and no bureaucracy. Until very recently, they relied upon no modern industrial products for their survival. They lived in small family units on large plots of mostly wild land, but they traveled widely throughout the forest so they could visit family members and exchange goods, stories, and songs. One's "wealth" (excess food, spare tools) was expected to be shared with anyone who needed it. The Korowai seemed to sincerely believe in the equality of all people and, more incredibly still, to actually behave in accordance with this belief. They also identified on a personal level with the forest around them, knowing that they needed to tend to it to keep it alive, just as it kept them alive.

Rousseau, who despised the foul air and stifling social conventions of "over-crowded cities," portrayed the "pure state of nature" as a fundamentally solitary existence; humans, being relieved of the bonds that hold one to another, are thus free from domination. But the Korowai way of life offered a stark rebuke to this notion. They were able to maintain an extraordinary level of freedom, it seemed, precisely because they were tied inseparably both to one another and to the forest. True freedom, seen in this sylvan light, was nothing more, and nothing less, than a state of wild coflourishing.

Once I finished reading the story, I paged through it once more, admiring the images of lean, gleaming bodies bent in postures of labor and leisure: an artfully blurred shot of a man carrying a dead cassowary, a woman pounding sago flour with a stone axe. At this point in my life, I was coming to see Western civilization as a monstrously gnarled thing, contorted around its past mistakes, teetering on the brink of collapse. It occurs to me now that these images moved me so powerfully because they portrayed a way of life that had survived wholly outside of that history; to even imagine it was to momentarily escape into something that felt somehow both fresh and unfathomably ancient. I had no doubt that the life of a forest-dweller was more difficult and more dangerous than my own. But wasn't it also freer, fairer, and in its way, richer? I felt its quiet pull, like a child finding an open door at the back of a house crowded with unpleasant guests, and through that door, a stand of tall trees glowing darkly in the dusklight.

+

One January, while spending the antipodean winter in Australia with Remi's family, and realizing that I was as close to Papua as I was ever likely to be, I decided to fly there, trek through the swamps, and visit the Korowai treehouses in person. After spending many months reading and watching documentaries about them, I was curious to learn if the reality of Korowai life—its flies and rashes and petty frustrations—matched up to the fantasy I'd constructed in my mind.

To get there required a lengthy journey, including three flights, a long ride in the back of a pickup truck, and a two-day trip upriver in a narrow wooden boat called a pirogue, followed by a half-day hike through the jungle. To help us get there in one piece, I tracked down a local guide named Bob Palege, who had led many tourists and journalists like me on this trip. When I spoke with him over the phone, Bob mentioned that he had recently received a similar request from a Ukrainian named Vlad Kutsey, who was a *National Geographic* photographer. It seemed a fortuitous pairing: I, a professional magazine writer, and he, a professional magazine photographer. We agreed to combine our little expeditions, in no small part because it would nearly halve the cost.

Remi and I left for Papua from Perth. On our penultimate flight, the plane touched down just after dawn for a stopover in Timika, a trade city near the world's largest gold mine. Sensing the wait might be lengthy, I rose to go to the bathroom. As I moved down the aisle, a hand reached out and waved me down. "Robert!" a man exclaimed.

"Vlad?"

Vlad shook my hand enthusiastically. He was wearing a little green army cap on his blond head; his nose, which protruded past the small brim of the cap, would over the coming days grow terribly sunburned. He was cheerful, voluble, and a bit clumsy, both physically and socially. He had seemingly been to every corner of the earth. Within moments of our meeting one another on the plane, he pulled out his phone and began scrolling through photos he had taken on past trips: volcanoes in Java, canyons in Cappadocia, ruins in Bagan. The photos were artfully composed, with a vibrant, almost surreal color palette. It was obvious he was talented and intrepid. But, as we talked, it also quickly became evident that he was not, in fact, a *National Geographic* photographer. His source of income was never exactly clear to me—he appeared to be some mixture of social media star / adventure tour guide / "brand ambassador" / part-time tech-industry worker, who also submitted photographs to contests on *National Geographic*'s website.

But if he was not really a professional magazine photographer, I realized, then by that same logic, I wasn't really a "professional magazine writer" either. In truth, I only published one or two magazine stories a year, while devoting most of my time to the writing of this book, a nebulous project that was taking many years to develop, largely out of sight—the exact inversion, in other words, of an Instagram post. So perhaps, I thought, being both wholly alike in some ways and wholly unalike in others, Vlad and I would prove to be a good fit after all, just as Bob had promised we'd be.

While Vlad and I chatted, his wife, Alena Veretennikova, sat beside him, pale and sleepy after their long flight. Her hair was twisted into two thick braids. One half of each was blond; the other was dyed a vivid cerulean. Over the coming days, she would reveal herself to be an ideal travel companion—tough, cheerful, and coolly competent—but since her English was considerably less nimble than Vlad's, he did most of the talking.

Our plane eventually took off again, flying over a landscape that resembled a rumpled green quilt, and landed in the city of Jayapura. In the baggage area, we met Bob, our guide, a squat Indonesian man with watery, smiling eyes. Atop his head sat a wide-brimmed leather fedora decorated with crocodile teeth.

As we left the airport, I struck up a conversation with Bob's co-guide, Marius Refideso, a slim Papuan who perpetually wore an apologetic smile. Like Bob, he had been guiding people on treks to meet the Korowai since the early '90s. I asked him what the Korowai were like back then. "Very scared of white people," he chuckled.

I heard something similar when I later spoke with Johannes Veldhuizen, the first European to encounter the Korowai. He said that when he made his way up the Becking River in 1978, the tribesmen he encountered shook with fear. One reached out and touched his leg, to see if it was warm. Because of his pale skin, they had assumed he was a *laleo*—a kind of walking corpse, a zombie.

Veldhuizen informed me that the Korowai also believed in the existence of invisible, hostile beings, known as "underneath people." These mysterious figures live in a shadow world exactly inverse to that of humans; when the Korowai are experiencing floods, the underneath people are said to be experiencing drought. The Korowai understand that, to the underneath people, they are the ones who are upside down. Parents warn their children that, should these two communities ever meet—should the great cosmic others be united—the world would abruptly come to an end.

+

For a long time, Europeans, too, believed the outside world was populated by monsters. The ancient Greeks and Romans thought that in the hinterlands lurked one-eyed people, headless people, goat-footed people, and people whose ears were long enough to use as blankets. Many of these people were depicted as being rather pathetic (like the cave-dwelling Troglodytae, who, according to Herodotus, "feed upon serpents and lizards" and "squeak just like bats"), but others were described with a tone of envy, such as the Hyperboreans, who lived in the far north, in perpetual sunshine. "No sickness or ruinous old age is mixed into that sacred race; without toil or battles they live," writes Pindar. One group of people, known as the Hylophagi, were believed to climb to the tops of trees and eat the tender branches that grow there. And then, of course, there were the Anthropophagi: the people who eat other people.

More than a thousand years later, writers like John Mandeville and Marco Polo claimed to have visited foreign lands where the people were only slightly less fantastical: men with the feet of horses, men who drank human blood, men who grunted like pigs. The great Moroccan traveler Ibn Battuta recounted visiting an island where the men "have mouths like those of dogs." They go naked (except for the occasional penis gourd for men and leaf covering for women), and they "copulate like beasts, without the least concealment." He deemed them "a vile race." A few of these tales seem rooted in truth, such as when Mandeville describes an island where "men and women go naked because of the great heat . . . hold all property in common, and are cannibals." However, even the more accurate-sounding accounts nevertheless drew from deep wells of myth and xenophobia. The image of the man-eaters, for example, was already a stock figure in the Christian imagination; the practice was ascribed to Scythians, the Huns, the Arabs, and the Mongols, the latter of whom were said to "devour human flesh like lions, but prefer it roasted." The overall lesson of these monstrous tales is that the farther one strays from one's home, the stranger the people seem to become, until they blend into animals and creatures from dreams.

When the Western world learned of the existence of the Korowai in the 1980s, writers and documentarians fixated on a single detail about their culture: the fact that they practiced a form of ritual cannibalism. Televised documentaries about the Korowai had titles like *Last Cannibals* and *Treehouse People, Cannibal Justice*. Indeed, the Korowai *did* once eat people, although this topic is considerably more complicated than most travel writers make it sound. The Korowai traditionally believed in male witchlike creatures called *xaxua*, who secretly steal organs from a person's body and replace them with sticks, leaves, and ash. To reclaim the stolen organs—to balance what anthropologists call a "flesh debt"—it was believed that the family of the deceased had to hunt down the xaxua, capture him, and force him to confess his crime. Then, they sent him to another clan, who would kill, butcher, and eat him. Therefore, the Korowai did not really see themselves as cannibals. From their perspective, they did not eat people; they ate witches. Which is to say, they slayed monsters.

+

Two days later, on the banks of the Brazza River, we boarded a wooden longboat, which was powered by a loud, smoky outboard motor. We sat single file, cross-legged on the floor. Marius sat at the bow, looking out for floating logs and hidden snags, which, Bob warned, could punch through the hull and sink us, leaving us prey to the crocodiles that lurked below. The sun grew so hot that the black plastic tarp we sat on became scalding to the touch.

We paused here and there to fish along the banks, hauling in fat, silver-brown, toddler-sized fish called barramundi, which Bob would later fry up for dinner. (On days when we failed to catch any fish, we ate nothing but plain rice.) Early that afternoon, we passed between two groups of men dressed in T-shirts and flip-flops standing on opposite banks of the river. They were shouting and brandishing bows and arrows at one another. "Later, we cannot pass," Bob said. "Because thousands of arrows."

As we motored upriver, Vlad peppered Bob with questions about the Korowai.

"Do they know the world is like . . ." Vlad drew a circle in the air with his finger.

"No, but now they are learning from the kids who go to school," Bob said.

"Are they still eating people?"

"Sometimes yes. But not so much anymore."

"But sometimes they are eating people?"

". . . Yes."

"Is the Korowai the most uncontacted tribe?"

"They have all been contacted now. They have many missionaries."

"But are they the most uncontacted tribe?"

". . . Yes."

"How many tourists go to Korowai? Not many, yes?"

"Tourists never go without guides," Bob said obliquely.

"So this is still like the most uncontacted place. We are like the most crazy people. For you and for them."

"They will like her hair," Bob said, pointing to Alena's blue-and-blond braids. "They will find it very beautiful."

"Is it true if they like a tourist, they will give him their daughter as a wife?"

"No. If a man takes their daughter, they will kill."

"Ah, so it is not true," Vlad said with a faint note of disappointment in his voice. "People on the internet are writing a lot of shit."

+

When Christopher Columbus landed by accident in the Americas and encountered its native inhabitants for the first time, he wrote home, with a note of surprise, that he "saw no monsters." Instead, what he found were human beings like himself, only with different customs than his: different (and less) clothing, different hair styles, different languages, and different ways of subsisting off the land. They also had different bodies—smaller, darker, less hairy—but not so different as to be disturbing. In fact, he found them "very handsome."

It is fascinating, today, to read Columbus's journals alongside the letters he sent home to his financial backers, because there is a noticeable gulf between what he perceived and what he portrayed. What he perceived were peoples with diverse responses to the arrival of his ship: some friendly, some afraid, some aggressive. What he represented in his letters, though, were people who were "guileless" and "marvelously timorous," people who "refuse nothing that they possess, if it be asked of them," people who shared everything they owned—people who (and here he comes to the underlying point) "should be good servants." But he also recounted rumors of a neighboring tribe who were "most ferocious" and "eat human flesh." This second group, who were variously referred to as "Caribs" or "Canibs," eventually lent their name to both the word "Caribbean" and the word "cannibal."*

---

* It is important to keep in mind that what we commonly call Columbus's "journals" are in fact a reconstruction of now-lost logbooks, written by the Spanish friar Bartolomé de las Casas, who was famously sympathetic to the

Columbus was constructing, more or less in real time, an image that would remain fixed in the European imagination for centuries: the savage, a word derived from the Latin *silva*, for "forest." The savage was always both fearsome and helpless, at once a monster and a child. This bipolar portrait struck a deep and resonant chord in the European imagination. Amerigo Vespucci, Columbus's rival, who arrived in South America seven years later, echoed it and then amplified it. He described a land possessed of "an infinite number of trees," where the people "have neither king nor lord, nor do they obey anyone, but live in freedom." Alongside these peaceable people, Vespucci portrayed—or, very possibly, invented—the most gruesome images of cannibalism in any of the explorers' letters home, including accounts of one man who "was popularly credited to have eaten 300 human bodies" and another who ate his own wife and children. European intellectuals fashioned their understanding of their own humanity—their intelligence, their virtue, their God-given mastery of the earth—around these warped visions of far-off, subhuman children and devils. As Sartre writes, "The European has only been able to become a man through creating slaves and monsters."

It was a matter of no little irony, then, that back home in southern Europe, the twin powers of church and state were ruling with inhuman brutality—ethnically cleansing Jews, enslaving Muslims, and condemning blasphemers (a term applied with terrifying flexibility) to be burned alive. For the explorers, this created a dilemma: On the one hand, this "new" land was full of "barbarians," who wore no clothes, had few metal tools, and knew nothing of the word of God; on the other, with its lush forests and white-sand beaches and egalitarian social system, it looked an awful lot like paradise. It was

---

plight of Indigenous people. It is therefore quite possible that I have it all backward, and it is Columbus's letters that accurately reflect his first impressions of the islands' native peoples, while the slightly more nuanced, humanistic portrayal in his journals is the exaggerated fabrication.

even theorized that somewhere in South America, explorers might stumble upon the biblical Garden of Eden; one of Columbus's more eccentric beliefs was that the earth was shaped like a woman's breast, and that on top of the planetary nipple, one would find paradise. The bitter irony, for the land's Indigenous inhabitants, was that the arrival of explorers—who soon instituted the practice of plantation slavery and introduced deadly new viruses—would transform large swaths of this earthly paradise into a living hell.*

With startling rapidity, images of childhood, paradise, and savagery were fused in the European imagination into a single image, which would affect the lives of millions of Indigenous people for centuries. Beasts or children; children or beasts. In the decades to come, European writers, in trying to divine the nature of "savage" people, would flip back and forth between these two poles. In either case, the conclusion tended to be that "savages" were fit only for work as either servants or slaves. The former were infantilized; the latter, dehumanized. Only centuries later would Europeans come to believe that Indigenous forest-dwellers deserve to be "protected"—left free from outside domination or despoliation, but open to occasional visits from anthropologists, documentarians, and well-heeled tourists—just like the forests in which they live.

+

Two full days we motored upriver, in the blistering sun. I hid beneath a wide-brimmed sun hat, sunglasses, and a white bandana, like Marlon Brando in *The Island of Dr. Moreau*. From time to time Vlad would

---

* It is estimated that the Indigenous population of South America was decimated between 1492 and 1650—dropping from around sixty million to just six million. The effects of this wave of mass death were so far-reaching that scientists have credibly (if controversially) theorized that the sudden growth of new trees on abandoned farmland—the birth, in other words, of a brand-new forest roughly the size of France—may have sucked up enough carbon in the following centuries to exacerbate the global cooling period known as the Little Ice Age.

force the boat to pause so he could send a drone camera high above the river, then he would lift a Ukrainian flag up with both hands and shout, "Papua Jungl-ay!"

The banks of the muddy river were walled off with tall trees. Bob pointed out the species: acacia, agathis, ebony, ironwood. Neat rows of corn were planted, incongruously, amid the chaotic verdure.

We arrived at our destination, the village of Mabul, amid a sudden rainstorm. Stepping off the boat in a bright blue synthetic rain shell, I thought: *We are going to look like extraterrestrials to these people.* After all, what kind of soft-skinned freaks must cover themselves in space-age fabrics just to keep from feeling the rain on their skin?

When we disembarked from the boat and scaled the riverbank, we discovered that every single person in the village was wearing Western-style clothing, and one little boy was wandering around with an umbrella. None of them remarked upon our rain gear.

The village of Mabul was a single red-clay road, bordered on one side by tin-roof shacks, and on the other side by fields planted with sago palms. The wooden houses were arrayed cheek-by-jowl, and strung together with power lines. In its orderliness and bland uniformity, it vaguely resembled a shrunk-down, low-cost, concrete-free version of an American suburb.

Most of the villagers seemed to spend the afternoon sitting on their porches, waiting for the day to pass. Some of them owned smartphones, although there was no cell service. (I later learned from a missionary that the phones came preloaded with music, movies, games, and pornography.) A number of the men worked, panning for gold or constructing a new airstrip, but most did not. Bob told me that this village received one billion Indonesian rupiah (roughly $70,000) a year, to be doled out to its residents for certain work projects. This was all part of an aggressive campaign by the government to settle the Korowai, motivated by a mix of paternalistic concern for their welfare and nationalist shame at their "backward" lifestyle.

I spent the afternoon sitting on the balcony of a tin-roofed home, above a general store stocked full of cheap Chinese foodstuffs and cleaning products, conducting taped interviews with whoever would talk to me. Beside me sat a Korowai boy no older than two who listened to the song "Baby Shark" on repeat through the speakers of a cell phone; whenever the phone was taken away from him, he began to fuss.

The interviews I conducted that day were not especially productive; the Korowai people I spoke with tended to be shy, and the language barrier was considerable. Every question required at least one and sometimes two translators, layers of communication that often resulted in answers coming back that were entirely non sequitur.

Much of what I now know about the Korowai was collected by a Cambridge professor of anthropology named Rupert Stasch, who spent two years living with them. In his book *Society of Others*, he outlines the Korowai's markedly egalitarian social structure, which, though idyllic in theory, has certain comical and even perverse aspects. For example, when a Korowai person's loved one dies, the neighbors will come to express their condolences. Only, instead of arriving bearing casseroles and flowers, they demand the surviving family member hand over some of their former loved one's possessions, a totally rational arrangement, which nevertheless strikes Westerners as upside down and rather callous. The Korowai are also very fond of teasing, a form of "social leveling" that is common among egalitarian hunter-gatherers. The anthropologist Jerome Lewis writes that among the Mbendjele people of the Congo, "individuals who hunt a lot will become a target for teasing and mockery, even cursing, if people perceive that the group is eating their production too often." Again, this struck me as absurd (why punish someone for bringing home the bacon?), but again, upon closer inspection, it makes sense, since it harshly discourages both overhunting and overinflated egos.

As one might expect, the recent shift to village life was proving difficult for people who were long adapted to living far apart and sharing everything. It turns out that one reason they could previously share everything, without driving one another crazy, was that they lived so far apart. Squabbles and theft now occurred frequently. The Korowai even have a saying—"It's not your food, I'm going to eat it"—for when a person strolls into your home and takes your stuff.

Within a decade or two, it seemed clear, the oldest generation of forest-dwelling Korowai would begin to die off, and like nearly all colonialized peoples, each subsequent generation would settle deeper and deeper into a life of consumer capitalism. I found this trajectory depressing, and not just because some childish part of my soul was sorry to see them abandon their romantic treetop existence. I had often read about other hunter-gatherer tribes throughout the region who had been bribed to settle into villages, only to then witness their ancestral forests clear-cut and converted into palm oil plantations against their will. I asked one of the young Korowai men I spoke with how he would feel if, once all of the Korowai were settled, the government stopped sending them those massive checks, which could force the Korowai to take low-paying jobs, like those offered on palm oil plantations. He said softly that would be "very not fair."

+

As I conducted these interviews, I couldn't help but feel like I was playing anthropologist, the way a child plays archaeologist by digging in the backyard. Real anthropologists typically do fieldwork for at least a year, and even then they come away painfully aware of how little they actually know about the culture they've been studying. Understandably, they seem to despise writers like me, who parachute into a place, spend a few days with a single family, and then pretend to speak about it with perfect authority.

The word "anthropology" literally means the study of humans, and for a time, that's what it was. While reading Kant's *Anthropology*, one of the earliest major works to deploy that term, I was surprised to find that it is just a book about people—all people, rather than any particular group. Much of the book is given over to listing the character flaws of his friends and coworkers, rather than the customs of far-off tribes. At one point, he lays out a series of ironclad rules for a "tasteful" dinner party (e.g., "not to allow deadly silences to set in, but only momentary pauses in the conversation"), and he judges that of the three vices—sloth, cowardice, and dishonesty—sloth is "the most contemptible." When Kant directs his attention beyond the limits of his hometown of Königsberg, he does so briefly, referring offhandedly (and secondhandedly) to the habits of "American savages" and so on.

In the nineteenth century, the "study of man" gradually transformed into the study of what the Germans called *Naturvölker*, or "primitive" peoples. This shift was born from the realization that Indigenous people were rapidly dying off, largely due to imported diseases. With the rise of social Darwinism and scientific racism, this observation became a prophecy: It was widely believed that Indigenous races were fated to go extinct. Darwin himself made such a prediction, writing, "Wherever the European has trod, death seems to pursue the aboriginal.... The varieties of man seem to act on each other in the same way as different species of animals—the stronger always extirpating the weaker." If this was the case, scientists reasoned, then the customs of those people should be recorded before they disappeared; the mission was of a piece with that of zoologists who went in search of rare animals, which they captured and shipped back to zoos. A new type of savage thus appeared in the Western imagination: what the anthropologist Renato Rosaldo calls the "vanishing savage."

The empires of Europe and the Americas sent out academics across the globe, collecting stories, sacred artifacts, and skulls. It was a highly romanticized—even eroticized—venture. "Nothing is more exciting for an anthropologist than the prospect of being the first white man to penetrate a native community," writes Claude Lévi-Strauss. But it was also somewhat mournful, since even when an anthropologist contacted a people for the very first time—before the missionaries could sweep in and begin dismantling their delicate culture—the anthropologist knew that, by introducing the people he studied to modern technology and foreign ideas, he was helping to hasten the demise of the very thing he sought to preserve. As Susan Sontag quipped, "Anthropology is necrology."

+

The following morning, we set out for the treehouses. We left the village and were immediately swallowed by a vast forest. We trudged along flooded trails, the brown water rising sometimes to our knees. The air was damp, dim, breezeless, and hot. Remi was loving it. "Reminds me of Queensland!" he said, taking deep lungfuls of the humid air. I, meanwhile, was flushed, itchy, and covered in a slime of sweat. Whenever we stopped for a rest break, I took off my shoes and dusted my feet with talcum powder to prevent fungal infections, a trick I'd read in a jungle-survival book. I also fanned myself, using an in-flight safety card I had stolen for precisely this purpose. Our small team of barefoot Korowai porters, for whom this hike was a stroll and this weather was comparatively mild, looked at me with pity and confusion, just as I used to look at the polar bear that lived in the Central Park Zoo, forever panting, its fur tinged green with algae.

So this is the jungle, I thought. I'd often noticed that something about jungles brings out a kind of morbid verbosity in writers. One recalls Aschenbach's equatorial delirium from *Death in Venice*: "a tropical marshland, beneath a reeking sky, steaming, monstrous, rank"; of Lévi-Strauss, in *Tristes Tropiques*: "as if some pathological disorder had attacked the riverscape . . . a terrestrial distemper"; of Ryszard Kapuściński, in *The Shadow of the Sun*: "sinking, slipping, into the labyrinths, tunnels, and underworlds of some alien, green, dusky, impenetrable realm"; and then, of course, of Joseph Conrad in *Heart of Darkness*, describing "the great wall of vegetation, an exuberant and entangled mass of trunks, branches, leaves, boughs, festoons ... a rioting invasion of soundless life."

The jungle I was walking through was not as overwhelming as the ones they describe. Perhaps, I thought, one had to travel to central Africa, as Kapuściński and Conrad had, or deep into the Amazon, as Lévi-Strauss had, to be truly horrified by the sheer profusion of plant life. Or perhaps they were just exaggerating.

In *The Forest and the Sea*, the zoologist Marston Bates argues that

> "rainforest" and "jungle" are frequently taken to mean the same thing. But I have never liked the word jungle. It has all the wrong connotations. You hack your way painfully through the lush vegetation of the jungle, dripping sweat in the steambath atmosphere; snakes hang from trees and lurk under foot; leopards crouch on almost every branch and there is always a tiger just beyond the impenetrable screen of foliage. There are hordes of biting, stinging and burning things. The jungle is green hell. I doubt that there is any place, outside of books and movies, where all these conditions are combined.

Rainforests, in other words, are real places, with discernible ecological patterns; jungles, on the other hand, exist only in the mind.

As I trudged through the jungle (or "jungle"), I began to think about how, over the course of centuries, the notion of the savage and the sylvan had been fused into a single concept, like conjoined twins. Consider how, in *The Maine Woods*, Thoreau writes of the "primitive forests, beyond the bounds of ... civilization, where the moose and the bear and savage dwell." The phrase "primitive forest" has since fallen wholly out of favor, as has "primeval forest," "virgin forest," "untrammeled forest," and "aboriginal forest," all of which were popular during the dawning of the Green Revelation. Now, those same forests are called "primary" or "old-growth." A similar transformation has taken place with the words we use to describe forest-dwelling peoples: They have evolved from "barbarians" and "savages" to "primitives" and "natives"; to "aboriginals" and "Indians"; and, finally, to "Indigenous" or "First" peoples.

It occurred to me that we can change which words we use, but the structural underpinnings of those words are much slower to change. So a relatively new term, like "old-growth forest," comes to absorb other, older words—"primeval," "virgin," "savage"—like a new layer of cambial skin draped over old heartwood. Concepts like savagery, though outmoded, inaccurate, and untrue, nevertheless become the scaffolding of the new. Peel away the latter, and within it you inevitably find the former. I know this because when I excavate my own mind, I feel the chisel of my intellect becoming pinched in the dense, unseen core of these bygone beliefs.

+

After four and a half hours of walking, the trees pulled back and the air brightened. Once my pupils adjusted, I found myself in a clearing filled with tall grass, ferns, and sago palms. The trail curved past two small huts that were raised only a few feet off the ground. Then I looked up to find a treehouse, hovering atop six sawn-off tree trunks and fourteen poles. It looked as if a house had grown spidery legs and lifted itself about thirty feet off the ground.

It was—and I felt guilty even thinking this, after coming so far to see it—less visually impressive than I had imagined.

I stood a moment, sweating with lagged and nonsensical force. Then I turned to find a sun-darkened man sitting on his haunches in the center of the clearing, smoking a hand-rolled cigarette. He wore a stern, distant expression.

I nodded at him. He did not nod back.

He looked about fifty years old, but his age was distributed unevenly: He had the deeply lined face of an old man but the taut, fatless physique of a teenager. Around his throat was a necklace made of pig's teeth, and around his waist was a rattan belt, which, in the absence of pants, served no discernible purpose. His penis was wrapped with a leaf into a small green tube; it exactly resembled the last bite of a stuffed grape leaf. While men throughout Papua traditionally cover their penises with gourds or hornbill beaks, effectively making themselves look bigger—sometimes cartoonishly so—the Korowai practice is to invert their penises back into their bodies and then tie the nub off with a leaf. Again, this practice initially struck me as absurd. But, I later realized, is the practice of wearing pants really all that different? Males in Westernized countries—with the exception of ballerinos, professional wrestlers, Fire Island party boys, and elderly French beachgoers—tend to choose clothes that disguise our genitalia behind flat expanses of baggy fabric, effectively rendering all men alike.

A few more eternal minutes passed while I sweated and the man smoked.

Finally, the rest of the group arrived. The man broke into a wide smile when he saw Bob and the Korowai porters. They began talking animatedly. Hearing the clamor, the man's wife and son emerged from within a nearby hut, and introductions were made. The man's name was Markus Nguali. His wife was named Gebil. She looked to be about Markus's age. She wore a sago frond skirt, a necklace made up of dog teeth, and no shirt. She had the thin, veiny arms of a professional rock climber. The expression on her face suggested that she was not thrilled to be topless in front of us. (Indeed, I later learned that she was a convert to Christianity, and she frowned on the old ways but put up with it for the sake of money.) Their son, Muatan, who was five years old, was wholly naked, and wholly unperturbed.

At the same time, my own clothes were drenched in sweat, so I began searching for somewhere to change into something dry. There was nowhere to hide: Everything was either out in the open or private and off-limits, like Markus's house. While the others set up camp, I ducked behind a narrow wooden post and swapped clothes. Remi, teasing me, whispered, "So he can be naked in front of you, but you can't be naked in front of him?"

While I changed into dry clothes, Markus began performing a series of photogenic activities for our benefit, a pattern that would repeat over the following days. First, he chopped wood. He positioned the log between his bare feet and swung the axe down between them, inches from his toes, in a way that made me—a person who chops his fair share of firewood—feel a bit uneasy. But he never missed; his accuracy was astonishing. While he chopped, Markus sang a lilting, warbling ditty. I assumed it was a traditional folk song, but I now realize in retrospect it likely was not. (A BBC documentarian named Will Millard, who visited Markus's treehouse a few years before I did, cleverly got one of these songs translated into English. It turned out Markus was making up the words as he went along. At one point, he sang, "We weren't like this before. Nowadays when guests come we do 'activities.'")

The next day, Markus climbed a tree, just so we could watch him do it. The trunk of the tree was about as thick around as my waist, with pale bark coated in a light green algal dust. It was too thick to shin up, so he found a nearby vine and tugged on it to test its strength. Then he clamped it between his big toe and second toe, the way one grasps a cigar. His hands slid up the vine, then his feet; hands, then feet. Within seconds he was fifteen feet off the ground. Then, grabbing hold of two narrow trees that grew parallel to one another, one hand and one foot on each, his body held taut, he climbed another thirty feet up. I would have been happy if he had stopped there, but he then reached out with his toes and grasped another vine, about two feet away, pulled it toward himself, took hold of it with his hand, and then—a terrifying moment, this—swung over into the branches of the big ironwood tree. He stood there for a while, smiling down at us in a posture of utmost ease.

After Markus had returned to earth, I tried to imitate his climbing technique. I shucked my shoes and socks. I grasped the vine with my hands and tried in vain to grip it with my toes. I began to climb, heaving one hand above the next. But the vine was swinging and twisting, and my toes kept slipping on its pollen-dusted bark. It was like climbing that much-hated rope in gym class if it were also coated with Vaseline and cornstarch. In the end I only made it about ten feet before I was completely exhausted. Defeated, I slid back to the ground.

+

Later that day, Markus and Gebil brought us to a nearby sago grove to show us how they harvested their staple food. I was somewhat surprised to learn that, traditionally, the Korowai derived most of their calories from stands of sago trees, pandanus, and bananas, which, though they look wild to our eyes, were the result of intentional planting and tending. Anthropologists have begun to realize that the creation of these "forest gardens" was once common in woodland-dwelling cultures around the world, from the Amazon up to the temperate rainforests of the Pacific Northwest.

We walked down yet more flooded trails. Markus, Gebil, and Muatan led the way, heel-toeing along felled logs, which were as slippery as soaped porcelain, while we clumsy foreigners thrashed and splashed our way forward through the brown water. I noticed that, as they moved about the forest, Markus and Gebil ripped out nearby plants and hacked at the trunks of trees, seemingly at random. Stasch writes that the Korowai believe that the land must be constantly tended, otherwise it will (in their words) "go cold"—a dead place, inhospitable to humans. It was fascinating, and a bit disturbing, to see this ethic in practice. I even heard from one missionary that groups of Korowai people, in moments of great exuberance, will all climb into the branches of a small tree and dance until the tree comes toppling to the ground. Then they walk away, without even harvesting the wood.

Once we reached the sago grove, Markus felled a large sago tree, using a steel axe, and split the trunk open. Then his wife, using a kind of stone sledgehammer, pounded the innards and ran water through them, separating the pulp from the flour. They later cooked the sago for us, wrapped up in sago leaves, along with a whole catfish and some bright red pandanus. (The sago tasted like sawdust; the pandanus like unsalted tomato sauce. The catfish, which had not been gutted, tasted like fish shit.) Other staples of the traditional Korowai diet, we were told, include bushpig, monitor lizard, and a variety of birds and insects. Their most prized food is the sago grub, a fat white maggot-like creature that lives in felled sago trunks, which are said to have a nutty flavor and a custard-like texture.

While his parents felled and processed the sago, their bare backs shining with sweat, little Muatan played idly with a machete. When he grew tired, he curled up on a bed of palm fronds and fell asleep. Vlad craned over him to capture a photo, then checked his viewfinder. "*National Geographic*," he said approvingly.

+

Every Westerner who travels to see the Korowai, myself included, has unconsciously inherited a worldview fashioned by the early anthropologists and their direct antecedents, the writers of so-called travelers' tales like Marco Polo and Ibn Battuta. The early anthropologists sought out the most "untouched" nations they could reach, in the farthest corners of the globe: "darkest Africa," the "green hell" of the Amazon, the "savage wastes" of the Sahara, and the "vanishing paradise" of Polynesia. The only places they avoided were the ones that were familiar and boring. This way of seeing can be summed up in a single word: exoticism. In *Against Exoticism*, Bruce Kapferer and Dimitrios Theodossopoulos argue that exoticism functions by reproducing "a pervasive dualism between the Self and the Other, in which ethnocentric values provide the measure for evaluating difference." In other words, the exotic traveler hungers not for pure novelty, but for a very particular *kind* of novelty, which inverts his own sense of self.

Lovers of the exotic are propelled to the outer edges of the earth by a genuine sense of curiosity, but hidden within that curiosity is always a peculiar attitude of condescension. The writings of early anthropologists like Lewis Morgan and John Wesley Powell were shaped by the belief that all peoples on earth were bent on (in Morgan's phrase) "winning their way to civilization," but that some simply were not up to the task. In this way, argues the historian Peter J. Bowler, Europeans gradually evolved from seeing Indigenous peoples as "savages"—wicked, childlike, and profoundly strange—to seeing them as "primitives," "living fossils preserving the ancient character of the human race."

In exploring and then ranking the world's various cultures, the early anthropologists would invent two grand theories, both rigidly hierarchical, strictly linear, and mutually reinforcing, like the side rails of a ladder. One line of thought, now known as "stadial theory," argued that the "primitive" was a state of being that every race began in and gradually evolved out of—moving on from hunting to herding and then to farming and finally to capitalism. The second line of thought, which would later be called "race science"—and then just "racism"—argued that people don't change at all; instead, the races were arranged in a rigid hierarchy, with white people being positioned on the topmost rung. It was in exploring the various levels of this philosophical ladder that modern anthropology was born.

The oppressive worldview of those early anthropologists began to be dismantled with the arrival of a man named Franz Boas. Boas grew up in northern Germany, where he was repeatedly involved in duels and sword fights, which left his face "scrimshawed like an old walrus tusk," as Charles King writes in his history of anthropology, *Gods of the Upper Air*. Boas, too, was a lover of the exotic. His favorite book growing up was *Robinson Crusoe*, which, he later wrote, gave him "a great longing to see and get acquainted with foreign countries, a longing which has not left me." He dreamed of one day traveling to the humid jungle somewhere, perhaps in Africa. Instead, when he finally got the chance to do fieldwork among a remote Indigenous community in 1883, he ended up in the tropics' polar opposite: studying Inuit migration patterns on Baffin Island in Canada. The longer he stayed with the Inuit, the more he grew to respect their resourcefulness, generosity, and ingenuity. "I often ask myself what advantages our 'good society' possesses over that of the 'savages' and the more I see of their customs, I find that we really have no right to look down upon them contemptuously," Boas wrote in a letter to a friend that year. As Boas's student Ruth Benedict (who popularized the notion of "culture" as a topic of study) once jotted in her notebook, Boas taught that the lesson every good anthropologist must internalize is "Get nowhere unless prejudices first forgotten. Cultures are many; man is one."

Once anthropologists shed the worst of their ethnocentric biases, a world of dazzling diversity was opened up to them: They discovered cultures in which gender and sexuality was fluid, in which women held authority over men, and in which all manner of practices once considered bizarre or wicked, like polyamory or body scarification, were in fact eminently reasonable. Anthropologists began to paint detailed portraits of the norm-exploding diversity of humanity—a people in the Himalayas, for example, where women keep multiple male partners, none of whom have any parental rights, or a group in the Amazon, the Pirahã, who have no words for colors, or any word for numbers higher than two.

Thanks to the work of Boas and his successors, who argued tirelessly that there are countless ways of being human, none of which is inherently superior to the others, the stadial ladder of races at last began to split apart. Instead, they insisted every nation and every people are all merely branch tips on what the anthropologist Ralph Linton called the "Tree of Culture."

+

On our third afternoon, we received an invitation from Markus to join him in his treehouse. It was reached by climbing a long narrow log into which jagged little footholds had been chopped. I was the first to climb the ladder; it swayed, sickeningly, with each step, until I reached the treehouse, which was about thirty feet off the forest floor. Remi and Alena followed. (Vlad, a lifelong acrophobe, stayed behind on the ground.)

The interior of the house was a large, mostly empty room. The floor was made of teak bark and thin wooden rungs; in their gaps, I could see the forest floor far below, which moved, vertiginously, in parallax. The whole structure swayed when I walked, creaking and bending beneath my weight. When Markus walked, somehow it stayed perfectly still.

The room was divided by a small wooden threshold into two halves, one for men and the other for women. One reason for this division is that in Korowai culture, a husband is forbidden from seeing his mother-in-law; if they are both sharing one house, a screen must be erected to hide them from one another's view.

During his studies of the Iatmul people of Papua, the anthropologist Gregory Bateson coined the term "schismogenesis" (literally, the "birth of separation") for the way that boys and girls are culturally encouraged to differentiate themselves. Being placed in distinct genders, boys and girls develop an increasingly elaborate sense of what those genders signify—how one is meant to dress, speak, and act. Later anthropologists would apply the theory of schismogenesis to whole societies. Marshall Sahlins, for example, believed that Athens and Sparta had developed in opposition to one another, growing into "antitypes," or mirror images: "Athens was to Sparta as sea to land, cosmopolitan to xenophobic, commercial to autarkic, luxurious to frugal, democratic to oligarchic" and so on. One sees a similar dynamic at work in the two-party system of many Western democracies, which over time become increasingly—and often irrationally—polarized. Defining ourselves by way of negation, we steadily grow apart.

Looking around, I realized that Markus's house had surprisingly few possessions in it, and I was somewhat dismayed to note that most of them were plastic: empty water bottles, jugs of oil, a sleeping mat rolled up in the corner. One exception was a small arsenal of bamboo arrows, with angry barbed tips, leaning against the wall. I noticed that into the eaves were tucked small bleached bones of animals Markus had killed and eaten over the years. From the number of objects in the room, and the number of bones in the eaves, I surmised that this couldn't be Markus's full-time home. I later confirmed this suspicion with Stasch. He told me that Markus split his time between there and the village; the treehouse was now, in effect, a kind of vacation home. He, who was among the last Korowai to leave behind the old forest-dwelling way of life, already had one foot out the door.

We spent the evening talking to Markus via our translator. In between questions, Markus lay on his side and twanged on a mouth harp made from bamboo. He wore a relaxed smile on his face, which revealed his missing two bottom teeth.

I had read in Stasch's book that Korowai people traditionally do not measure their lives in years, but in treehouses; they can recount each treehouse they have lived in, and since treehouses steadily decay in the hot, humid climate, some people work their way through fifty or more in a lifetime. When a person dies, their body is often left in the last treehouse they inhabited, which becomes their tomb. I wondered—but in the end, not knowing if there were certain sensitivities around discussing death, I was too shy to ask—whether when he died, Markus would be buried here, or in town.

Instead, I asked whether he wanted his son, Muatan, to continue living here in the forest, at least part-time, as Markus did. Markus said that he wanted his son to carry on the old traditions, but he would not command him to do so. He would merely "advise" him. This is a quintessentially Korowai response. After all, if everyone is equal, there is no such thing as parental authority. Here, I had stumbled across another unforeseen quirk of the Korowai's radical egalitarianism. This laissez-faire form of parenting sounds like every teenager's dream, but without the fixing influence of authority—of grandparents and shamans and chieftains and holy books—traditions evanesce. Stories mutate; customs evaporate; opinions blend into a chaotic swirl. Because of this, Stasch writes, the Korowai say that their thinking is "like smoke."

+

During a lull in the interview, I heard someone behind us shout: "I am here!" We turned to see Vlad's smiling, sunburned face. It had taken him the better part of an hour to work up the courage to climb the ladder. "Fucking shit, that was scary," he chuckled.

Vlad sat down near Markus, who twanged out a celebratory tune on his mouth harp.

Vlad pulled out his phone and showed Markus photos of his home in Ukraine.

"This is snow," Vlad said.

Markus's eyes widened.

"Oh!" he said.

Then he shook his head like, *No thanks*.

Vlad wanted to know if, "deep in the jungle," there were any Korowai who had not yet been contacted. Markus replied that there was one "old man" with long dreadlocks, named Libul, who threatened any white person who came near.

"So he's still wild?" Vlad asked. His eyes brightened at this prospect.

He then lowered his voice. "One delicate question: if Markus, or maybe not him, maybe he knows someone who tried . . . man meat?"

Markus shied away from answering this question, as did every other Korowai person I spoke with. It is clearly a highly charged subject. Stasch believes that, due to pressure from missionaries and the Indonesian government, the Korowai stopped eating human flesh sometime in the 1990s. But in 2006, a writer named Paul Raffaele published an article in *Smithsonian* magazine entitled "Sleeping with Cannibals," which described his encounters with Korowai people who claimed to have recently eaten the male witches known as xaxua. Sometimes, the accused xaxua were as young as seven years old. One man Raffaele met, aptly named Kilikili, was said to have killed thirty xaxua. The flesh of humans, Raffaele was told, tasted like the meat of a young cassowary. "I like the taste of all the body parts," one Korowai man told him, "but the brains are my favorite."

When I spoke with Raffaele on the phone from his home in Australia, he said that he had grown up watching movies like *Tarzan* and *Jungle Jim*, and had gone off to Papua seeking "a bloody good adventure." He specifically likened the act of traveling to the Korowai to those old movies in which a scientist steps into a "dinky little capsule," turns a dial back, and then emerges among a clan of troglodytes. The appeal of the Korowai, for him, lay in "seeing what we and others were like ten thousand years ago, and yet understanding that they are humans like us. It's really like time traveling."

Raffaele's article gives off a strong, dark odor of primitive fetishization—a sort of Tarzanic musk—that would have thrilled me as a kid, but which now strikes me as both somewhat artificial and not a little repulsive. (Stasch judges it "probably the low point in the history of travel writing about the Korowai.") But I had to ask myself: Were my reasons for coming to visit the Korowai ultimately all that different from Raffaele's? Didn't I, too, view the Korowai as inheritors—one might even say "living relics"—of an ancient way of life? Wasn't their (for lack of a gentler word) primitiveness, in some sense, why I had come here? These questions pinged through my mind that night as I watched Markus kindle a fire. In the back of his treehouse was a small fireplace, made of clay, which was lashed into the floor so that it could be cut loose in case of emergency. Markus leaned over the firepit, made a small mound of plastic noodle wrappers, and then ignited it with a plastic cigarette lighter. He explained that he still knew how to start fires the old way, using friction, but this way was faster and easier.

I found myself a bit saddened by this sight; I was sad to see the old way dying out, and I was sad to see that the new way involved using disposable plastic. But it was impossible to look at Markus there, amid the smell of petrochemistry, and see him as anything but eminently modern. It was almost as surreal to watch him perform any of his other "activities"—climbing trees, pounding sago, catching fish, and so on—knowing that they were all for show. Markus could leave this forest behind at any time, walk to Mabul, and stare at a cell phone all day if he liked. And yet, he had chosen to be here, in the forest, showing off the skills he'd honed over a lifetime, using knowledge passed down across countless generations.

Over the course of the week, I came to see Markus not as a specimen of Naturvölker, but as a possessor of a specific skill set, a master of what used to be called woodcraft. This is one of those truths that is easy to profess but considerably harder to actually internalize: No people are living fossils, trapped forever in the past. We all live in the present, innovating, adapting, and adopting from one another. The chief difference between me and Markus was that he could (and, in fact, often did) put on a T-shirt, walk into town, and find a way to make a living, but if the global economy collapsed, he could survive back in the forest. Whereas, if left alone in this forest, or any forest, I would likely be dead within a week.

The following night, I returned to the treehouse to conduct a second interview with Markus. I hoped to learn more about his relationship with the forest, and how that in turn shapes his worldview. However, to ask Markus anything, the question had to go through two translators, one who translated it from English into Bahasa Indonesia, and another to translate it into Korowai. I could not imagine asking a question this philosophically unwieldy and having it emerge on the far end of this elaborate game of telephone making the least bit of sense, so instead, I tried to ask smaller, more oblique questions that would angle toward the larger truth I was seeking.

First, I asked Markus if he had any favorite trees. I was expecting, or at least hoping, his answer would touch upon the beauty or spiritual power of a particular tree. But his answer was flatly practical: He said there was one tree, a stout old ironwood with solid roots, where he hoped to one day build a new treehouse.

Next, I asked whether there were any trees in his area that he considered sacred.

He spoke for a moment, softly. My translator said, "There is a tree here, they cannot cut it. They say it's sacred. They cannot touch it either. If they touch it, there will be thunder. You can't walk around the tree either."

I asked if we could visit that tree. He said we could not.

Wanting to steer the conversation in a more philosophical direction, I asked Markus: "What is the most important thing in life?" I was curious to know if he would say it was survival, or duty, or happiness, or having a big family, or stability, or thriving, or enlightenment.

When the question reached Markus, he thought it over for a moment, then bent down, lit a fresh cigarette off the fire, and, with a rascally gleam in his eye, muttered something. My translators started laughing.

"I just want to take a second wife," he said. "I might be old, but if I get a second wife, I will be satisfied."

"What about a white woman?" I asked, playing along. "Could she be your second wife?"

"No," Markus said. "She couldn't pound the sago. It would break her." More laughter.

"And how would you feel if your wife wanted a second husband?" I asked. I was half expecting that, in this highly egalitarian society, there would also be a radical equality between men and women.

Markus waved his hand dismissively. "I would kill her."

The laughter waned, spluttered out, turned into coughs.

Finally, I asked Markus if, while climbing a tree or sitting in his treehouse, he ever says "thank you" to the trees that hold his life in their hands.

When the question was translated, Markus broke into joyous, sighing laughter. He said something in Korowai, and then my translator started laughing as well.

"No, I don't *thank the tree*," he said. "It's not a human!"

They laughed for a good long time at my fuzzy-headed animism.

+

As any journalist knows, the minds of strangers are a wilderness— dark, thorny, and largely impenetrable. Often, one emerges from this wilderness having learned more about one's own mind than about the mind of the other. Michel de Montaigne ruminates upon this troubling fact in a famous essay entitled "Of Cannibals." In it, he describes meeting a member of the Tupinambá tribe, who had been brought over to France from Brazil. He was eager to learn all he could from the man standing before him. The Tupinambá, Montaigne writes, are a "wild" people, "very close to their original naturalness," which, he believed, gave them a deeper, truer understanding of the human condition.

The Tupinambá lived in small, egalitarian clans. Chieftains marched at the head of any war party, incurring the greatest risk. In return, they were granted no more wealth than other members; the only apparent reward for their sacrifice was that, in peacetime, while walking from one village to the next, other members would walk ahead and clear the paths for them. (This, writes Montaigne, is a greater privilege than it might seem, since the Tupinambá "wear no britches.")

At some point in their conversation, the flow of interrogation reverses, and the Tupinamba man begins to critique France. Why, he asks, were there people in France who were so fat with riches, and others "emaciated with hunger and poverty"? Why did the poor "not take the others by the throat, or set fire to their houses"?

The anthropologist David Graeber and the archaeologist David Wengrow write that throughout history, encounters with Indigenous people have often forced Europeans to grapple with the shortcomings of their own society—a phenomenon they call the "indigenous critique." To illustrate this point, Graeber and Wengrow tell the story of a brilliant man named Kondiaronk, from the Huron-Wendat nation of modern-day Canada, whose impressions of Europeans were recorded by a French nobleman. In a tone of mild amusement, the nobleman describes how harsh Kondiaronk and his countrymen were in their assessments of France. "They brand us for slaves, and call us miserable souls, whose life is not worth having, alleging that we degrade ourselves in subjecting ourselves to one man [the king] who possesses all the power, and is bound by no law but his own will," he writes. "They think it unaccountable that one man should have more than another, and that the rich should have more respect than the poor. In short, they say, the name of savages, which we bestow upon them, would fit ourselves better, since there is nothing in our actions that bears an appearance of wisdom."

Something about this argument, its perfect reversal of expectations, its revelation of Europeans' own hypocrisy, rings loudly in us today, just as it did back then. Graeber and Wengrow argue that this critique of European society would help spark the Enlightenment, ushering in the wave of reforms—democracy, progressive taxation, the separation of church and state, and so on—that would lay the foundations of Western modernity.

The one major problem with their argument, as their critics have pointed out, is that there is no way to know that Kondiaronk ever actually said these things. Assuming that the French nobleman is being honest in his representation of what Kondiaronk said—a fairly enormous assumption—how would we know that Kondiaronk was not merely telling his interlocutor what he knew would most pique his interest?

Anthropologists are painfully aware of this pitfall, especially when working within a society like the Korowai, where the culture is "like smoke." Good anthropologists are careful to always temper their grand statements with an acknowledgment that beliefs differ from one individual to the next, and that anthropologists can never have perfect epistemic access to their subjects. They know that we live in a world full of shadows, of gaps, of irresolvable mysteries, and in those dark spaces, it is easy to project our own anxieties, seeing either angels or demons, noble savages or bloodthirsty cannibals.

+

Not far from Markus's house, he had built a second treehouse, which was far more beautiful than the one he lived in. In a nearby clearing stood a single, magnificent ironwood tree, and perched in its uppermost branches, at least a hundred feet off the ground, he'd constructed a small hut. This was the image I had come here expecting to find; it was almost exactly like the one I'd seen in *National Geographic* all those years ago.

One morning, craving some solitude, I decided to climb up into the very tall treehouse. I got out of my sleeping bag at dawn, while everyone else was still asleep, and walked quietly over to the base of the tree. I stared up the length of its one-hundred-foot-long trunk feeling somehow both nervous and numb. Then I grabbed hold of the bamboo ladder and began climbing. The rungs shifted and creaked under my feet with each step; I worried that their rattan lashings would snap. Around halfway up the ladder, I made the mistake of glancing down between my legs; I was faced with the nauseatingly vast distance that had already opened up between my body and the yellow earth. Summoning the voice of Ben Atkinson in my head (*Give up control and let your body do it*), I pressed on, rung by rung.

Finally, after maybe five minutes of slow, steady climbing, I crawled up through a hole in the floor. It consisted of one big room, which was totally empty. Some pig skulls hanging above the fireplace were the room's only decoration.

Remi later climbed up and joined me, and together we sat for the better part of an hour, watching the dawn melt into day. The view from the window was sublime: a choppy green sea of forest canopy, and above it, a flickery, ever-mutating cloud of starlings.

I lingered over the finer points of the treehouse's construction. The uppermost branches rose up through narrow holes in the floor and into the house itself, and then out through the roof. Smaller branches, growing within the treehouse itself, still had little green leaves on them. This flourish was integral to the architecture: The crown of the tree had to be kept alive to preserve the stability of the overall design. It was one of the most spectacular rooms I have ever had the privilege to sit in. It was not just beautiful, but philosophically, aesthetically, and ecologically profound.

It was also, largely, an illusion.

One of the most surprising things I had learned reading Stasch's work was that what he calls "ultra-tall treehouses" are an extreme rarity. Gerrit van Enk, a missionary I later spoke with who lived among the Korowai from 1987 to 1990, told me he had seen hundreds of treehouses over the years, but only two or three that were built at the very tops of trees. Today, virtually all of the very high treehouses in Papua are built for the enjoyment of tourists.

As best I can tell, the boom in building ultra-tall treehouses began with the *National Geographic* article I had seen as a child. George Steinmetz, the photographer who worked on that article, told me that in 1995 he had spent weeks trekking around the area, asking the Korowai where he could find the *rumah tinggi, tinggi tinggi* (high, high treehouse), because he wanted one high enough to photograph from a helicopter. He finally located one and managed to track down its owner, a man named Landi, who had recently been forced to move into the territory of a neighboring clan. To feel safer, he had built a treehouse that was as far from the ground as possible. But it soon proved wildly inconvenient; one major problem, Steinmetz said, is that the Korowai are "ground shitters," so each call of nature required an arduous climb down, then back up the 150-foot ladder—and Landi eventually abandoned it. By the time Steinmetz found it, the house was already decaying.

Thanks to *National Geographic*, that unusual image of a treetop treehouse was fixed in the Western imagination as the iconic Korowai house. Other tourists arrived expecting to see houses that were similarly grand, and were subsequently disappointed with the relatively squat treehouses that Korowai people actually lived in. Film crews and tour guides began requesting that Korowai men build ultrahigh treehouses, for fees of between $300 and $1,000; one Quebecois filmmaker commissioned the construction of an "Ewok village" of six treehouses. (The Korowai built them, but he never returned to pay for them.) This craze reached the peak of absurdity with the making of the BBC documentary *Human Planet*, which purported to document a Korowai family moving into a new, ultra-tall treehouse.

James Hoesterey, an anthropologist who worked on the series, told me that a BBC producer had sent him Steinmetz's photo of an ultra-high treehouse and asked him to procure a treehouse just like it. "The main guiding obsession," Hoesterey recalled, was "We want as tall a treehouse as you can build." So, with the producer's consent, he hired a Korowai family to build precisely that. As the camera dramatically pans up the full height of the tree, the documentary's narrator, John Hurt, declares, "For the Korowai, the higher the house, the greater the prestige." This is false. Traditionally, the higher the treehouse, the greater the fear one had of one's neighbors. Today, the height of a treehouse is seldom more than a measure of a Korowai man's willingness to cater to white people's fantasies about who he is, or should be.

+

After returning home from Papua, I decided to do some reading into the history of the North American treehouse. Because treehouses are so ubiquitous and so plain, I assumed that children everywhere have always built them, but this proved to be incorrect. The American treehouse has a distinct history, and that history, I learned, is intricately bound up with the history of people like the Korowai.

The American treehouse seems to have grown out of the chaos of the Civil War. In 1899, Daniel Carter Beard wrote an article for *Harper's Round Table* entitled "Tree-Top Club-Houses." In it, he describes growing up in Kentucky in the 1860s. Adults back then (understandably) had less time for parenting, so the children began to go somewhat feral. "Gangs of young toughs, under the leadership of local bullies, . . . hunted down, pillaged, and beat every unprotected lad they could catch out of sight of his own home," Beard writes. To protect themselves, Beard and his friends built a "large and strange nest" at the top of a sycamore tree. Beard strongly implies that he and his friends were the first boys in the area—or anywhere in America—to do so.

Beard's article included a photograph of a stunning little treehouse with a zigzagging staircase, as well as the first instructional diagram for how to build a treehouse ever published in the US. This story was widely reprinted, both in other magazines and then in a series of books with titles like *The Fair Weather and Rainy Day Handy Book*, which featured a treehouse on its cover. According to Beard, a treehouse-building boomlet followed; he later recalled driving across the country and seeing, "all along the route, here and there in backyard fruit-trees, shade-trees, and in forest-trees, queer little shanties built by the boys, high up among the boughs."

In this and subsequent writings, Beard takes pains to frame the American treehouse as an Indigenous practice. "Primitive and savage men all over the world for thousands of years have built dwellings in tree tops," he writes. He lists examples in New Guinea, India, and the Philippines, though he could have also mentioned the Solomon Islands, Vanuatu, and the Congo. Beginning in the mid-nineteenth century, as the colonial powers reached their tentacles into more and more remote areas, newspapers regularly carried (often highly exaggerated) accounts of newly "discovered" treehouse-dwelling tribes. A typical newspaper story, published in the *Sandusky Register* in 1892, ran: "Do you know that there are races in the world who build huts and take up their abode in trees? It is no unusual sight for travelers in Africa to come upon whole districts, living like birds in the tree tops." One popular account, by the missionary Robert Moffat, described a single gigantic fig tree in South Africa with seventeen huts built in its branches.

This vision of the "primitive" treehouse neatly overlaid the kinds of treehouses American kids were building, both physically and conceptually. According to the popular pseudoscientific doctrine of racial recapitulation—in which humans pass through each phase of civilization, from caveman to proper English gentleman, as they age—white children were thought to be closer to New Guineans than white adults. Rather than tamping down boys' "savage" impulses, as

Europeans had been doing for centuries, educators and philosophers began arguing that parents should be encouraging them. There was enormous anxiety that white boys—especially middle- and upper-class boys in urban areas—were being "overcivilized," softening into "mollycoddles" and "milksops." To prevent this, they were encouraged to engage in "savage play."

At precisely the same time, Americans were growing fonder of the people they once deemed "savages." The end of the frontier, rampant urbanization, and a belief in the tonic effects of "fresh air"—all contributed to a growing reverence for (at least, certain highly stereotyped aspects of) Indigenous culture. It is no coincidence that Beard, the would-be inventor of the American treehouse, was also a founder of the Boy Scouts of America, which combined Indigenous signifiers (the wearing of feathered headdresses, the building of tepees, the performance of stomp dances) with those of the colonial military. It's a deeply jarring combination of imagery, which only looks normal to us now because of its ubiquity.

These cultural forces reached an apotheosis with the publication of Edgar Rice Burroughs's *Tarzan of the Apes* in 1912, the tale of a highborn British baby raised by primates, who synthesizes the "brawn of the apes" with the "brains of the white man." Upon closer scrutiny, the book is revealed to be little more than a thinly veiled white supremacist fantasy. One often-overlooked detail is that the apes in question are not any known species; they are, instead, a kind of subhuman, or prehuman, ape known as "Mangani." "They have the minds of little children," Tarzan explains. "That is why they remain what they are." Tarzan outwrestles the strongest apes, and wins, using his "superior reason." He also hunts terrified African warriors by hiding in the treetops and quietly slipping a noose around their necks. In doing so, Tarzan balmed the fears of urbanized whites, who felt increasingly soft, increasingly cut off from nature, and increasingly menaced by their slipping grip on racial hegemony. The book was a runaway bestseller. In the subsequent film adaptations, Tarzan was shown living in elaborate treehouses, furnished with turtle-shell sinks, bamboo plumbing, an ape-powered fan, and an elephant-powered elevator. In the introduction to the Penguin edition of *Tarzan of the Apes*, the literary scholar John Seelye recalls that, during his childhood in the 1930s, as a result of the Tarzan films, "the woods behind our neighborhood filled up with partial and remnant treehouses." American kids have been building treehouses ever since—in the trees, and in their minds.

+

I eventually traced the history of the American treehouse as far back as it would go. It led, fittingly enough, to Christopher Columbus. In 1502, Columbus departed on his fourth and final journey to what would soon be known as the New World. He brought along his son Ferdinand, who was then only thirteen years old. Years later, Ferdinand would recount that, while scouring the coasts of modern-day Panama for a strait that would lead them to India, near the Gulf of Urabá, they had run across a group of Native people "dwelling in the tops of the trees, like birds," in huts made of crisscrossing branches. He had no idea why they built them; he guessed it may have been because of their fear of "griffins." (This was likely a reference to the belief, dating back to Homer, that pygmies were at perpetual war with a race of large birds.) Subsequent accounts by Peter Martyr, Sir Walter Raleigh, and Alexander von Humboldt also recorded the existence of tree-dwelling tribes in the region. These accounts likely percolated throughout Europe, seeding the notion that "primitive" people were treehouse dwellers, and that white children, by extension, should be treehouse dwellers too. The rest, it seemed, was history.

However, reading further, I ran across a major flaw in this tidy narrative I'd been piecing together. According to the explorer John Augustine Zahm, these accounts were almost certainly fabrications.

While traveling extensively throughout the region in 1907, he found no evidence of tree-dwelling tribes, and by reading the travelogues of previous explorers more closely, he noted discrepancies that cast doubt on their accounts. Raleigh and Humboldt never visited the areas in question; their reports were secondhand. Zahm chalked up Raleigh's possible deceptions to his wish to "satisfy his reader's desire for the marvelous." (Among other exaggerations, Raleigh claimed to have found evidence of the fabled "great and golden city" of El Dorado.) Zahm concluded that Martyr, writing of Balboa's explorations, "most likely got his information about these strange dwellings from Ferdinand Columbus." And no one else reported seeing treehouses there. To put it another way, Zahm presents the intriguing—and eminently fitting—possibility that the first Indigenous treehouses in the Western imagination, which, centuries later, would go on to change the shape of Korowai treehouses on the other side of the world, sprouted, fantastically and enduringly, from the mind of a teenage boy.

+

When we tourists look at a Korowai treehouse, we are not just looking at a Korowai treehouse. We are also looking at a dream of our own devising. The architecture of the Korowai treehouse has been deliberately refashioned to remind us of our own backyard treehouses, which were (often unconsciously) designed to evoke Indigenous treehouses. In visiting the Korowai, we inevitably project our own preoccupations upon them, like a tree casting shadows upon neighboring trees, which then grow around those shadows. At times this process is so complex that it becomes hard to tell what is real from what is fantasy.

This process also takes place in reverse, when the Korowai look at tourists. Most Korowai people no longer see us as walking corpses, but they continue to refer to us with a slang word, *laleo*, meaning "zombies," because, as Stasch writes, many still view the average Westerner as a "repulsive monstrosity." At the same time, the Korowai have grown to romanticize the material comforts of our lifestyle. As far as the Korowai can tell, our food isn't hunted or gathered; it's "just there." "They are always sitting just eating on and on what's already there," one informant told Stasch, which is why foreigners "all get huge."

I can't help but see a dark humor to all this. We Westerners, hunched over our desks or checkout counters for longer and longer hours, torture ourselves with the thought that hunter-gatherers work only fifteen hours a week, plucking most of their nutrients straight from the earth; the Korowai, meanwhile, tell themselves that our food is just there, effortlessly produced by invisible powers. The same shadowy psychological forces that drew me to Papua also impelled the Korowai to pass their afternoons watching soap operas about the sordid love triangles and dynastic squabbles of wealthy Jakartans. Capitalism is immensely effective at producing and profiting from these kinds of shimmering fantasies, which invert the lives we currently live. We know we cannot really reside in these fantasies, but on some level, that is precisely what makes them so compelling. Some very deep part of us yearns to escape from the harsh light of our earthly life into the shadowland of a dream.

At night there in the forest, as fireflies constellated among the trees, Remi and I would sit around playing cards by the dim light of a candle placed in the center of an old sardine can. Markus often sat up with us, twanging on his mouth harp and singing softly to himself. Now and then, something would make a sound out in the forest, and Markus would look up with wide eyes. Then, he would slip on a headlamp—given to him, Bob said, by some previous group of tourists—and he would stalk off into the trees to investigate. His unease was contagious; soon Remi and I were glancing around nervously at every aberrant night-noise as well. I never figured out what he was so worried about, given that there were no man-eating predators in the forest, and violent attacks by humans are rare.

According to Stasch, a dangerous sense of otherness pervades the Korowai worldview. Xaxua abound, women and men must stay on their respective sides of the treehouse, and mothers-in-law must be avoided at all costs. Even newborn babies begin life "categorized as repulsively demonic," Stasch writes; the challenge of motherhood is "relating to them across this divide." Over time, the newborn—that wrinkly, toothless little banshee—comes to resemble what a mother thinks a human should look like, and she comes to be what the child needs. A sense of monstrousness extends even to the land itself. The Korowai often say that the earth "eats people," which is both a literal reference to how dead bodies decompose in the soil and a metaphorical expression of the basic hostility of wild nature.

I had traveled to Papua assuming that, because of their egalitarian worldview, the Korowai would regard other people and other species without much distinction, like so many enmeshed fibers in a single sheet of paper. But it turns out that I had it exactly backward. The Korowai worldview is defined first by the ways in which they are "strange" to each other, and second, by their efforts to consciously create relationships *across* that divide. I eventually grew to admire the hard honesty of this shadowy Weltanschauung: People are strange, and the earth eats people, but that does not mean one should give up and retreat into solipsism. Markus seemed to spend a good part of each night terrified of what was lurking out there in the darkness. And yet, I noted, he did not shrink from that darkness. He got up, turned on his headlamp, and walked into it.

+

On the night of my final interview with Markus, I was the last of our crew to leave his treehouse. Before I stepped out onto the ladder leading down to the ground—always a queasy moment—I looked back to find Markus seated on his knees beside the fireplace. He was bent forward; his headlamp threw a cold, hard, luminous disc upon the floor. In front of him were two neat stacks of Indonesian rupiah—the money Bob had paid him for hosting us. I watched as he counted the bills before him once, and then again, with a frown of intense concentration.

A black, bilious dread pooled in my gut. I had arrived in Papua looking for a way of life that was free—free from capitalism, free from empire, free from the weight of history. I had long been comforted by the thought that someone, somewhere, still dwelled in a forest, and that if our world should fall apart, we could all return to living in the forest as well. I suspect this sylvan fantasy remains so potent in the West because it helps us go on living the way we do. It is a kind of mirage: As we plod deeper into the desert of our collective future, we comfort ourselves with the knowledge that, should we need to, we can always walk to that shimmery pool on the horizon, dip our hands into it, and slake our burning thirst.

Up close, though, that fantasy had evaporated. The Korowai, like most forest-dwelling peoples on earth, are now moving into villages, and soon, cities. There are a few holdouts, like Libul, the wild man Markus once spoke of, but in the years to come even they will not remain untouched by the steady creep of industry or the chaos of climate change. Our way of life has grown so large that it has grown around them, whether they like it or not. Our gnarls have become their gnarls. There is no escape.

Beneath this fear lay another, deeper one. The great lesson of modern anthropology has been that all cultures are just branches on a grand tree of humanity. There are no monsters out there, only different kinds of humans—densely specific, eternally othery—seeking out the best way to live within the conditions life has given them. But this notion, as liberatory as it has been, also has a dark side. It suggests that, deep down, beneath the superficial differences of culture and tradition, everyone on earth might be as money-hungry, shortsighted, and foolish as we Westerners. After all, they're only human.

Watching Markus count out his earnings, I tried to envision his trajectory in the decades to come. In that dim, dreamy room, sweet with the oil smoke of burnt plastic, a thousand branching futures seemed to proliferate: a thousand Markuses, clothed or bare-chested, coughing or laughing, with two wives or with one; and in some of those futures his son was there, a grown man now, strong in his traditions, and in some he had gone off to the city and never returned; in some, the forest had been set aside as a nature preserve; and in others, the forest was flattened, and cash crops were growing in its place. At every turn in that garden of forking paths, Markus was free to choose which future he wanted to pursue, but all of the paths laid out before him seemed to bend, ineluctably, toward the end of his world, and the end of mine.

6. STEMMING

IMAGINE FOR a moment that there is a race of intelligent beings living on one of the icy moons of Jupiter. These extraterrestrials have been watching Earth for all of its history, as it evolved from a smoldering rock to a stormy water planet and then formed continents and sprouted vegetal life. For millennium after millennium, the Earth went through its slow mutations, icing over and thawing out. Then, something changed: In only a few centuries ("a mere tick in geological time"), the forests began to rapidly recede, being eaten into by some unseen force. Lights appeared: first the warm orange glow of wildfires, more than ever before, then the cold glitter of electric lights, which swept across the darkened planet like plumes of phosphorescence. Something down there on Earth had figured out how to tame the wild planet. Unsurprisingly to the aliens, who have seen all this before on other planets, the Earth's dynamic homeostasis then begins to visibly wobble: Its skies darken with pollution, its glaciers melt, its deserts spread, and its various species vanish by the millions.

"It was all but inevitable, the watchers might tell us if we met them, that from the great diversity of large animals, one species or another would eventually gain intelligent control of Earth," writes the sociobiologist E. O. Wilson in an essay published in 1993, in which he introduces this thought experiment. It was the planet's misfortune to have fallen under the reign of "a carnivorous primate" and not "some more benign form of animal." Alongside meat eating (an ecologically wasteful habit), Wilson enumerates humans' other failings: "Our species retains hereditary traits that add greatly to our destructive impact. We are tribal and aggressively territorial, intent on private space beyond minimal requirements and oriented by selfish sexual and reproductive drives." These innate limitations impel us to overbreed and overconsume. "It is possible that intelligence in the wrong kind of species was foreordained to be a fatal combination for the biosphere."

The philosopher John Gray took Wilson's logic one step further. Humans, he believed, are a "plague animal." Having been born just clever enough to break free from the shackles that limit the growth of other species, we will proliferate, like a virus, until we cause a systemic collapse, killing ourselves off in the process. "The destruction of the natural world is not the result of global capitalism, industrialisation, 'Western civilisation' or any flaw in human institutions," he argues. "It is a consequence of the evolutionary success of an exceptionally rapacious primate." He proposes, rather nastily, that we change our name to *Homo rapiens*.

Around the time our earliest ancestors first dropped down from the trees and began padding across the land on two feet, humanity veered away from our fellow apes and toward a mode of existence unprecedented on Earth. We evolved into unusually powerful, unusually voracious, and, it seems, unusually suicidal creatures. Philosophers and scientists have spent millennia trying to isolate what distinguishes us from all other species. The traditional answers to this question are neat enough to write down on a notecard and tuck into one's shirt pocket: Humans are the rational animal (Aristotle). Humans are the divine animal (Aquinas). Humans, being the only conscious animal, are both free and perfectible (Rousseau). Humans are the only animals who laugh, "because only humans suffer so deeply" (Nietzsche). Humans are the only animals who talk; the only animals who make art; the only animals who use technology; and the only animals who ask questions like "What is human nature?"

Until fairly recently, the topic of human nature (what Antonio Gramsci calls the "main question in philosophy") never interested me much. Being born gay—being told from a young age that your innate desires are unnatural—tends to instill a powerful skepticism about any narrow definition of what a human is or should be. After my trip to Papua, however, as I pondered why people everywhere seem to gravitate to the modern consumer lifestyle, the question of human nature began to take on a new and terrible weight. Perhaps, I thought, there *is* a dark, voracious core to the human species that predestines us for collapse. Can we ever hope to straighten out what Kant calls the "crooked timber of mankind"?

I decided to explore this question by thinking arborescently. Rather than hunting for some divine essence in us, I focused my attention on how humanity grew to be what we are, over the course of millions of years of evolutionary branching, pruning, and gnarling. I traced this crooked story back through the ages and across the Earth, until eventually I found myself in Ethiopia, searching for the very stem of the human family tree.

+

Remi and I arrived in Addis Ababa in the midst of the rainy season, when the city takes on the cool, gray, cement-scented air of a sepulcher. It was considered unsafe to travel outside the city, due to an ongoing civil war, so as we waited for my meeting with the dead woman, Remi and I spent a lot of time in museums, or else in our dreary hotel, where a television in the lobby was forever broadcasting a weeklong track-and-field competition. Ethiopians, it seems, are peculiarly fond of televised long-distance running, a sport that is so crushingly boring to watch that it borders on a kind of meditation. We passed one eternal afternoon watching a fifty-kilometer speed-walking competition from start to finish. Observing the thin figures, with their smooth legs and wriggling, slithery gait, walk for hour after hour after hour, for no particular reason, I found myself once again mulling over the fundamental oddness, and in some sense the greatness, of our species of ape.

The day arrived when I was scheduled to meet the dead woman. We took a taxi to the national museum, but traffic was light and we arrived early. We had a few minutes to kill before our meeting, so Remi and I strolled around the grounds. The museum was a brutalist concrete building, surrounded by gardens composed of huge, lolling tropical plants. Time held a special gravity there; everything seemed to be gently falling apart under the weight of it. Just inside the front door, the red floral carpets were fraying, the marble stairs cracked and stained. Outside, beneath a large gazebo, for no apparent reason, stood a taxidermied baby elephant, its dry gray trunk broken off, two hollow pockets where its eyes had once been.

Strolling along one of those paths, I finally spotted the man who would bring me to the dead woman. He was named Yohannes Haile-Selassie. He was a paleoanthropologist and a fossil hunter of almost mythic renown. We got to know one another as he led me from the museum to the main research building. An elegant figure in a blue wool overcoat, he walked with a slow and careful gait, having recently injured his spine by falling down the stairs. I found it somewhat difficult to imagine this urbane, stiff-backed man marching for miles across the Afar desert with a camel to find new fossils, as he had in his younger days.

We passed through a series of locked gates, up an elevator, down a long hallway, and into what he half jokingly called "the sacred area," which turned out to be a plain white conference room lined with tan-colored, bombproof safes.

"Here," said Yohannes, "is the wonderful Lucy."

Laid out on a long table, in a series of four wooden boxes, was perhaps the world's most famous fossil. Her bones—head, torso, hips, legs—were nested into little spaces cut into a black foam pad. A museum curator, Temesgen Leta, stood nearby, his arms crossed, keeping a close eye on me, perhaps suspecting a heist.

"How often do you pull Lucy out?" I asked.

"Not often," Yohannes said. "Except for, you know, state leaders."

A few years earlier, Barack Obama had been shown the fossil, and had been asked to touch one of her vertebrae, to symbolize his connection to the roots of the human family tree that later branched out across the entire planet. I was not allowed to touch Lucy. Most people are not even allowed to see her. A precise replica of the fossil has been constructed out of plaster and put on display in the museum so that tourists can pose beside it for photos.

With my hands behind my back, I peered more closely at the fragments of her skull. A faint green patina lay over a mottle of yellow and brown, the color of wood left in a garden bed over the winter. It was hard to keep in mind that the bones I was looking at were those of a creature more than *three million* years old.

The skeleton sitting in front of me was discovered in the Afar desert in 1974. Up until that point, very few early hominin fossils had yet been found; the paleoanthropologist Donald Johanson has written that, at that time, all the known remains of those three-million-year-old creatures could "fit into the palm of your hand." After spending a long hot season in the Ethiopian desert searching for hominin bones, one afternoon Johanson and a graduate student named Tom Gray stumbled upon Lucy's skeleton half buried in a dry gully. When they realized what they were looking at, they hugged one another and began howling with joy. The fossil itself was a one-in-a-billion find: both startlingly intact and incredibly old. Johanson decided to name her "Lucy" after the famed Beatles song "Lucy in the Sky with Diamonds." The implication, writes the historian Stefanos Geroulanos, was "that she was so perfect you almost needed to be on drugs to realize she was real."

Lucy was soon classified as a member of *Australopithecus afarensis*, a species that predated the rise of the genus *Homo*, to which we belong. Scientists today shy away from using the phrase "missing link"—because it implies there is a single species that connects apes to humans, when in fact it was a slow and messily branchy process—but in the popular imagination, that is precisely what she was. Amid the malaise of the 1970s, with American napalm still smoldering in Vietnam, the Summer of Love having long ago burned itself to cinders, here was an emissary from an older, simpler, more peaceful time. Lucy—child-sized, arboreal, vegetarian—was often called the "grandmother of humanity."

Scientists like Yohannes have studied each millimeter of her body for clues to our evolutionary past. He enumerated the finer points of her anatomy: She had a brain only a third larger than that of a chimpanzee, and she also had the long, strong arms of an ape. Her rib cage looked more human (less funnel shaped, more round), and her narrow pelvis, curved lower back, and relatively long legs were yet more human still. Her feet were missing, but those of other members of her species indicate that she would have had gently curved toe bones, helpful for climbing trees, but with raised, inflexible arches and no opposable big toe, which were adapted for walking upright.

If she were standing in front of me, she would have been about three and a half feet tall and, at the ripe old age of seventeen, would have been densely muscled. Her life would have likely been spent wandering through sparse forests and meadows, walking upright;

then, reaching a tree, she would have scampered up into its branches with an ease I can only dream about. She would have subsisted primarily on leaves, flowers, fruits, seeds, and tubers, perhaps mixing in insects and meat from small animals when she could catch them. At night, she likely slept in a nest. Her world was partly terrestrial and partly arboreal. It sounded, to me, at the easy distance of deep time, to be the very epitome of the sylvan fantasy; it was as if she had stepped out of Eden into the human realm but had left the back gate unlocked so she could return whenever she liked.

The planet that Lucy inhabited would have been unrecognizable to us; hers was a global warm period, when the poles were bare of ice and a race of extinct giant camels roamed what are now the tundras of northern Canada. In another way, though, it would have been eerily familiar: Her era, the Pliocene, was the last time in all of human history when atmospheric carbon levels were as high as they are now. (The difference is that back then, the Earth tended to go through temperature shifts at a slow, geologic rhythm; now the warming is happening at the frenzied pace of human industry.) Her species flourished for more than a million years before dying off. Our species, *Homo sapiens*, has been around for less than a third of that time, and already we have begun to ponder our own doom.

In *The Songlines*, Bruce Chatwin describes holding the skull of the Taung child, which belonged to *Australopithecus africanus*, a more apelike hominin that lived in southern Africa about a half-million years after Lucy. He stared deeply into the skull's empty eye sockets. "You had the impression of a very wise little person staring at you down the ages through a pair of binoculars," he writes. Looking down at Lucy, I caught myself imagining her staring back up at us, standing in this plain room full of strange antiseptic light. I wondered: What would she have thought of what she saw?

+

Following Charles Darwin's world-splintering insight that all living beings are connected in a tree of life, writers began developing a new vision of human nature, founded upon evolutionary theory. Human nature, they argued, was not reducible to any one thing, such as a rational soul. Instead, it was a complex biological system, a meat-machine made up of interlocking traits allowing us to better survive and reproduce. As our ancestors evolved, older traits gave rise to newer ones, much like how a tree grows outward from earlier versions of itself. The key to divining human nature, the evolutionists suggested, was to drill down into that history, inspecting its innermost layers. In their view, the earliest adaptations—the things that first set humans apart from our apelike predecessors—were the most central to our being, and thus would be the hardest for us to slough off. How did humans become human? Did we do so by fighting and undercutting one another, or did we achieve it by more peaceful and cooperative means? Did we win by learning to wield tools? By outbreeding our competitors? By killing more animals? By gathering more tubers? If we could answer these questions conclusively, the thinking went, then we might be able to isolate the key variables that would delimit our abilities—to carve out our future along the grain of our nature, rather than against it.

Beginning in the 1930s, the anthropologist Raymond Dart, the discoverer of the Taung child, put forward a bold new theory of human history, based on his research. This theory consisted of two controversial claims. The first was that humans evolved out of apes living in Africa, rather than in Asia, as was then commonly believed based on the scant number of extant fossils. The second was that these australopithecines ("southern apes") split from their fellow apes by becoming predatory carnivores. To secure their dinner, the earliest humans fashioned weapons out of the bones and antlers of other dead animals, turning death itself into an implement of death. (This image would later be immortalized in the rousing opening scene of Stanley Kubrick's *2001: A Space Odyssey*.)

In the 1960s, a playwright turned pop-science writer named Robert Ardrey built on Dart's theory to argue that hunting big game had shaped the course of humanity—what came to be known as the hunting hypothesis. Ardrey folded these evolutionary findings into the emerging science of animal behavior and the Freudian concept of a rapacious id to create a chilling portrait of humanity. If humans were acting largely on genetic "instinct" (or, as ethologists liked to say, "fixed action patterns"), then much of our behavior must have been shaped by our long, bloody evolution. Hence, Ardrey concludes, the core of human nature is a "killer ape." He opens his book *African Genesis* with an image drawn from his childhood growing up on the South Side of Chicago. Every Wednesday, he and his family would attend prayer meetings at a Presbyterian church. While the adults upstairs were praying, he and his friends would play-fight in the darkened basement below, smashing chairs over each other's backs. Whatever lofty aspirations and starchy sanctimonies we may profess, Ardrey argued, the substrate of humanity is one of bestial violence.

Over the course of a bestselling series of four books, his Nature of Man tetralogy, Ardrey built up a vision of human nature that was rooted in animal nature. Humans, he insisted, had evolved to live in territorial, male-dominated, carnivorous, violent clans. Attempts to change or stifle that basic nature, such as communism, were doomed to failure. The effect of these books was twofold: It threw cold water on left-leaning idealists (or "neo-romantics," as Ardrey called them), who believed that human nature was endlessly malleable and world peace attainable; and it provided refreshment to a new breed of reactionaries who could use it to bolster their underlying beliefs that men should dominate women, social classes should scrap for economic resources, and nations should from time to time march heroically into war. William S. Burroughs accurately dubbed Ardrey's thesis the "spirit of true conservatism." The primordial was, suddenly, political.

When one reads Ardrey's tetralogy today, the predominant fears of his time shine through, namely: feminists, Bolsheviks, and hoodlums. Hovering above everything, though, was the horrible specter of a mushroom cloud. The invention of the atom bomb had introduced a mutant strain into human consciousness, wholly unseen until this point: the possibility that we (and not God) could engineer the destruction of humanity. Seven years after the appearance of *African Genesis* came an equally explosive, and equally frightening, threat: In *The Population Bomb*, the biologist Paul Ehrlich runs the Malthusian math on human reproduction and concludes that, having now freed ourselves through medicine and technology from the constraints of nature, we are all but destined to overbreed until we exhaust the Earth's natural resources. Attempts at humanitarian aid, like famine relief, only worsen this problem, by swelling the population further. If Ardrey's theory indicted the right wing of human nature, then Ehrlich accused the left. We would either fight to death or fuck to death.

+

Happily for us, and for life on Earth, both of these stark portraits of humanity turned out to be deeply flawed. Ehrlich's predictions failed to account for how drastically humans around the world would curtail their reproduction once they attained a middle-class lifestyle, and how successful modern farming would become at eking more and more food from the soil. (Indeed, among certain intellectual circles, the current fear is that the planet will suffer a catastrophic population crash, rather than an explosion.)

Ardrey, too, was disproved with time, in part because he grossly undervalued women's evolutionary contributions as food-providers, and in part because his work was based on Dart's now-defunct "killer ape" theory. *Australopithecus africanus*, it turns out, likely relied on plants, not big game, for the bulk of their diet, and there is little to no evidence that they fashioned bones into spears or clubs. They lost their long, sharp canine teeth because smaller dog teeth allowed them to better chew tough roots and tubers they dug up out of the ground. And in any case, *Australopithecus africanus* very likely was not our direct ancestor, but rather an evolutionary offshoot that went extinct. Lucy's kind, *Australopithecus afarensis*, came to be seen as our earliest hominin ancestor instead. (Whether that, too, will one day prove false is currently a point of heated debate in the world of paleontology.)

Indeed, the more we learn about human evolution, the more we realize how little we actually know. Some of our most basic assumptions may well have been wrong all along. Since the time of Darwin it has generally been assumed that early humans evolved from knuckle-walking apes. Any grade school student would be familiar with the image, known as "The March of Progress," of a line of figures slowly straightening up: an ape, a caveman, then a modern human. (One popular spoof of this graphic shows the last figure in the line slumping back down again—this time in front of a computer screen.) But many evolutionary scientists now believe this image of human evolution is either oversimplified or wholly incorrect. The fossil record indicates that our early primate ancestors may have *already* evolved to be bipedal in the treetops, walking along branches on two legs with our hands grasping higher branches as modern orangutans sometimes do. Strange as it sounds, rather than evolving from walking on all fours to walking upright, it seems increasingly likely that the other species of great apes, like chimpanzees, evolved *downward*: As their upper bodies grew to be evermore elongated and muscular, they hunched forward until they were forced to move on all fours. (Indeed, certain elite rock climbers I have met, with their hypertrophied backs, their spindly legs, and their deeply hunched posture, seem to be halfway there.)

Likewise, even after half a century of studying Lucy, one of the most complete hominin fossils ever found, there are still basic questions about her kind that we have not yet answered. For example, Yohannes told me that day at the museum, we still aren't sure what her shoulders looked like. This seems like a minor detail, but this one tiny mutation would eventually change the very face of the Earth. To illustrate this point, he reached down and gingerly picked up Lucy's shoulder joint, holding it before my eyes with two fingers. For decades, he explained, scientists had been debating whether it was oriented upward—he tilted the socket so that it faced the ceiling—like an ape's, allowing her to hang comfortably from tree limbs, or whether it was oriented sideways—he now tilted it ninety degrees, so it was facing the wall—like a modern human's, which would allow her to throw objects with enormous speed and accuracy, as only humans can. This simple shift in orientation would have had profound implications for human evolution, setting hard limits to how well we could hunt and how easily we could retreat to the treetops.

+

The more we learn about our earliest ancestors, the clearer it has become that the distance between today and the prehistoric past is simply too great, and the fossil record too incomplete, for paleontologists to be able to construct Big Theories about human nature. It is like trying to build a house using only petrified wood; there simply isn't enough material to work with.

The paleontologist Louis Leakey learned this fact the hard way; his career was largely spent constructing elaborate theories, based on thin evidence, and then launching them into the world like so many paper boats, only for most of them to be destroyed. Frustrated, he made a bold swerve. He decided that the best way to decipher our evolutionary past would be to begin observing our great ape relatives in the wild. As one of his colleagues later wrote, "He wanted to superimpose the current over the ancient, the living flesh over the decayed bone."

Beginning in the 1950s, Leakey recruited three remarkable women and dispatched them to the forested homelands of the chimpanzees, gorillas, and orangutans. These researchers came to be known as the Trimates: Jane Goodall, Dian Fossey, and Biruté Galdikas. Leakey believed women were generally more patient and observant than men, and that they were less likely to incite the apes to violence. Knowing the work would be grueling, he made extreme demands of them to assure himself of their dedication. Famously, he asked Fossey to have her appendix surgically removed, lest it become infected in the field; only once she had done so did he inform her that this request was merely a test, and that the procedure was unnecessary. Less famously, he asked Galdikas, apparently in all earnestness, to undergo a clitoridectomy, so that she would be less likely to have sex with her husband and become pregnant. (Galdikas, horrified, refused.)

The lives of the three women mirror one another, in that all conducted landmark field studies of elusive species over the course of many years, all ended up on the cover of *National Geographic*, and all later campaigned passionately for wildlife preservation. Of the three women, Goodall, who studied chimpanzees, is the most widely known and the most beloved; willowy, silver-haired, and soft-spoken, today she is regarded less as a scientist than something of a modern-day saint. Fossey, owing to her violent temper, alcoholism, open racism, and the mysterious circumstances of her eventual murder, is the most controversial. But Galdikas, while the most obscure, is in some ways the most impressive. Orangutans are solitary and elusive creatures, and the swampy, buggy, rashy jungle environment in which they live makes researching them both hideously unpleasant and nightmarishly difficult. Goodall once remarked that she witnessed as much social activity among chimpanzees in two hours as Galdikas saw among orangutans in two years.

The grueling enterprise of a prolonged field study is worth the time and effort it requires, Galdikas argues, because it gives us a "partial glimpse into what we were before we became fully human." Such a glimpse, Galdikas writes, "is the best we can hope for until time machines are invented that will actually take us back to face our ancestors in the flesh, to smell their sweat and hear their voices."

+

From Ethiopia, Remi and I flew to Tanzania, the home of our nearest evolutionary relatives, the chimpanzees, and the strange subspecies of humans, primatologists, who spend their lives studying them. At a tiny airport in the city of Mpanda, we met up with a group of bedraggled scientists, piled our gear into a convoy of Land Cruisers, and sped out along red-dirt roads to a remote camp in the dry scrubland of the Issa Valley, home to the Greater Mahale Ecosystem Research Centre.

We emerged from the jeeps at the research center coated in red dust, which gave our hair the stiff, sticky-outy texture of bad wigs. The camp consisted of a series of metal-roofed huts, one of which housed computers and other electronics powered by rooftop solar panels; a small library with locking mesh doors to keep rodents from chewing on the books; an open-air kitchen; and a freshwater spring, where we gathered our drinking water and, a bit farther downstream, bathed each day to cool down and wash away the dust.

We were shown around the camp by a pair of primatologists: Fiona Stewart, a tawny-haired Scot with happy-sad green eyes, and her husband, a lean, amiable Californian named Alex Piel. In tow was their trio of tan, dirt-stained, poshly accented children—two young boys and a baby girl—who would spend much of the summer living here at the research camp. (That week, the boys mainly entertained themselves by carving, stringing, and then inexpertly wielding a wooden bow and a quiver of arrows.)

Fiona and Alex had chosen this part of Tanzania because of its mix of open savanna and arid woodland habitats, conditions that closely approximate those that early humans evolved in. They knew from the outset their work wouldn't be easy; the density of chimps was about a tenth as high here as it was in Gombe, where Jane Goodall conducted her studies. Alex referred to their work in those early years as "chasing ghosts." They each took different approaches. Alex began setting up microphones throughout the area, using them to remotely locate the chimps' movements, a trick he picked up from whale researchers. Fiona focused on gathering genetic samples from what the chimps left behind in their nests (mainly feces and hair). Gradually, a picture of how the apes manage to live in this harsh landscape began to emerge. One of the most startling findings was that chimps, who are usually highly territorial, can be surprisingly tolerant of other unrelated groups. "These guys share like 40 percent of their territory with other chimps," Alex told me. "It's crazy, you would never see that anywhere else." The "fixed action patterns" of chimpanzees may not be as fixed as it once seemed. In any case, it is clear that our understanding of chimpanzees—and by extension, our understanding of early humans—has been far too narrow for far too long.

The next afternoon, Remi and I went in search of wild apes. To avoid spreading any pathogens to the chimps, we changed into a fresh pair of clothes, dipped our shoes in an antiseptic bath, and donned medical masks. Then we followed Alex and Simon Sungura, a senior field assistant, as they walked at a quick clip out of camp, through a wavering, almost liquid heat.

We hiked across a prairie-like expanse of straw-yellow grass and through occasional stands of elegantly crooked, three-story-tall hardwood trees. Across this gold-and-green landscape stretched great swaths of bare, black-burned earth; Alex said that local pastoralists routinely set wildfires to keep tick populations low, clear away woody shrubs, and produce flushes of new green grass, which their cows prefer. This tactical use of fire is, of course, another quintessentially human trait, which may well predate the rise of *Homo sapiens*. In *Catching Fire*, the primatologist Richard Wrangham makes a convincing case that mastering the art of cooking—which allowed us to digest meat more easily, while also reducing our risk from parasites—led to the explosive increase in human brain size that occurred some two million years ago with the emergence of *Homo erectus*.

Chimpanzees, too, seem to have a surprisingly sophisticated understanding of the workings of fire. Studies show that, far from being panicked by approaching wildfire, they tend to regard the blaze calmly. They can usually predict the movement of where the fires will spread and skirt around them accordingly. Chimps also spend more time grazing in areas that have previously been burned than those that haven't. The authors of one study, Jill D. Pruetz and Nicole M. Herzog, suggest that even the earliest humans would have recognized that fire is "a force shaping their local ecology," and would have incorporated it into their survival strategy. (Indeed, it makes perfect sense that the earliest mouthfuls of cooked meat that we as humans enjoyed would have been plucked from a carcass left behind in the aftermath of a wildfire, rather than one deliberately roasted over a campfire.) We learned to live *with* fire long before we grew brains big enough to master it.

After about thirty minutes, Simon, who was in the lead, stopped, turned around, and whispered something in Swahili. Alex translated: "There's a chimp right there. Can you see it?" In the distance we saw a dark figure scaling a tree trunk.

"It's so tiny," Remi said.

"Yeah, from this distance," Alex replied.

For most of European history, primate studies were conducted in the artificial confines of captivity. Expeditions into the habitat of wild apes were made primarily either to kill animals or to capture them for zoos and the pet trade. Darwin's collaborator, Alfred Russel Wallace, wrote some of the most detailed descriptions of the behavior of wild orangutans then on record, all while chasing them with rifle in hand. His bullet-riddled victims had a heartbreaking tendency to build nests as their final act, in effect preparing their own deathbeds. In pursuit of the fleeing specimens, Wallace sometimes hired men to fell the tree. He would then gather up the dead orangutan, skin it, boil its bones, and ship its remains home to be displayed in a museum. These two methods of observation, both artificial in their own ways, long hampered our understanding of the intelligence and ingenuity of the great apes.

The full range of primate behavior began to be illuminated by the tireless work of the Trimates, who repeatedly recorded wild apes behaving in a startlingly human fashion: Goodall famously witnessed chimpanzees using broken twigs to "fish" for termites and ants, a form of tool use; Fossey saw mature gorillas tickling youngsters, provoking laughter; and Galdikas witnessed an orangutan (who had been spying on her kitchen staff) try, and fail, to start a fire with kerosene. Some of their observations make for painful reading. Galdikas once witnessed an orangutan mother care for her deceased infant daughter—pressing her lips to the child's eyes, picking the maggots from her fur—before laying her to rest in a nest atop a tree, where the infant gradually became mummified.

However, primate researchers also discovered seemingly hard biological limits to what the great apes can achieve. They can all walk upright, but only for short distances. They can wade through shallow water on two legs, but they cannot swim. They can throw objects, but not very accurately. They sometimes drum on tree trunks and can even keep a steady beat, but they produce no other form of what we recognize as music. They can plan ahead, but seldom do so more than a few hours in advance. (It seems Bertrand Russell may have been right when he proclaimed, "Forethought is the most important of all the causes that make human life different from that of animals.")

Similarly, though apes can speak—or, as scientists prefer to put it, they "make vocalizations"—they do not possess anything as intricately patterned as true language. For one thing, chimpanzees' tongues are firmer and flatter than ours, which allows them to lap up water like dogs do, but it makes spitting out tongue twisters a tad bit trickier. The power of speech also requires key neural components, some of which apes appear to lack. For example, all four of the great apes can be taught human sign language, and they can ask for objects, learn names, and solve puzzles. But beyond that, their use of words has so far proved rather depressingly unimaginative. Apes seldom ask questions, and they have never been seen asking abstract questions, which human children begin doing (sometimes ad nauseam) by about the age of four. Moreover, apes have never been seen to use what linguists call "recursion," the ability to embed ever more meaning into a single sentence, which would allow them to express increasingly complex ideas. One gorilla who was taught sign language appeared to be able to convey the notion that cats eat birds by calling a bird a "cat-eat" but, when asked to form a long sentence with the word "meat" in it, replied, simply: "Meat meat meat meat meat meat meat meat meat."

When read with a cold eye, many of these apes' statements sound suspiciously like either trained responses, random utterances, or simple requests for things like food, water, or physical touch. For example, Koko the gorilla frequently asked to be tickled. One can't help but wonder: Did she truly understand the notion of *asking* to be tickled, or did she merely associate making the sign for tickling with a pleasurable outcome? Either way, even in this rudimentary form of conversation—in "cat-eat" and "meat meat meat"—we can detect the kinds of shard-like phrases that may have been spoken by one early human to another, before the mortar of grammar and syntax allowed them to be assembled into ever more ornate mosaics, enabling us to portray the shadowy, luminous contents of our own minds.

+

We slowly approached the chimpanzee in the tree. Simon went first, making a *tlock-tlock* sound with his tongue, which the scientists had habituated the chimps to recognize. (Since poachers don't make this sound when they approach, the chimps can more easily distinguish friend from foe.) One by one we followed, creeping up to the tree. I crouched down in the grass about twenty feet away. The chimp, a young female with an elfin, leathery brown face, was reclining in a bend in the trunk, her arm draped over her head. She stared at me with an impassive expression, like a sun-pruned retiree watching a slow tennis match on television.

It is jarring—no, the precise word is "uncanny"—to gaze into the face of a nonhuman animal whose features are so distinctly human, who is clearly scrutinizing you, running little internal calculations about what your appearance might suggest. Sensing I was not a threat, the old she-chimp grew bored and turned her attention elsewhere. I continued studying her for many minutes, amazed by her every gesture: the way she brushed the flies from her brow with the back of her index finger; the way she toyed idly with her toes; the way she squinted smokily at the horizon, as if pondering something imponderable.

Finally, glancing around, I noticed that there was another chimp atop a nearby tree.

Then I noticed another, and another.

"Oh my god," I whispered.

I counted ten apes in the trees around us.

For the next four hours, as the land baked to dust, we sat watching the chimps. Every time they did something interesting, Alex and Simon made a note of it on their phones, and at five-minute intervals, even when nothing happened, they made note of that too.

At one point, Alex waved me over. He pointed out a female chimpanzee in the branches directly above him who, with an expression of studious absorption, was inserting a twig into an ant nest. After a few seconds, she extracted the twig and ran it between her lips horizontally, licking up the ants the way a child eats the last piece of an ice pop.

This nifty trick, Alex explained, is in truth a rather sophisticated form of tool use; chimps gauge the depth of the nest and then tailor the length of these sticks to match. Until Goodall first witnessed this behavior back in 1960, it had been widely assumed that only humans used tools. "Now we must redefine tool, redefine man, or accept chimpanzees as human," Leakey famously quipped. Primatologists have since witnessed chimps using stones to smash termite nests, using leaves to sponge up water, using chunks of wood to dig up edible roots, and using sharpened sticks to skewer the adorable little saucer-eyed primates called bush babies, who sleep in the hollows of tree trunks. (Contrary to their reputation as prelapsarian frugivores, chimpanzees often hunt for small game. Later that week, I personally witnessed a chimp snacking on the carcass of an unidentifiable mammal, chewing on its stretchy hide like a Fruit Roll-Up.)

While moving about in a tree, chimpanzees are a study in nimbleness. I felt a twinge of envy watching their dense, dark bodies swing, dangle, leap, and nap forty feet in the air. Most of the time, though, they just sat around, calmly grooming one another's fur for lice, or sitting alone, watching the world down below with a cool, monastic serenity. In *The Silence of Animals*, John Gray argues that this state of existential quietude is one that humans have lost, which is the source of much of our unhappiness. "Only humans want to silence the clamour in their minds," he writes. He believes we go looking for that silence in all the wrong places—churches, temples, monasteries—when all we need to do is fully open our senses to the world, as every animal does, for every waking hour of every day, by sheer necessity.

I thought again of the forest monk Bhaddiya, the one with "a mind like a wild creature's." Anxiousness, boredom, unease: Are these distinctly human flaws? Is ennui the divine spark that drives our species to such outlandish feats of invention? Then I recalled a chimpanzee I'd once seen living in a cage in a roadside zoo, who had grown obese on a diet of banana-flavored Twinkies. Never in my life have I seen a creature more visibly bored and anxious than that poor soul. An unnerving thought: Perhaps what Buddhists call *dukkha* (a kind of existential unsatisfactoriness) is a disease of human culture, not human nature. It is a symptom of having imprisoned ourselves (and many other species) in unnatural and unsettling conditions. Nietzsche memorably wrote that man is the animal that rubs itself raw on the bars of his cage. What he meant was that we chafe against the constraints of morality, decency, self-denial—a mental prison that we have constructed for ourselves, which, it seems to me, is mirrored by our built environment. The Buddha, like the ancient Stoics, taught that the only way to escape this prison is to achieve nirvana from within it. The sutras often liken enlightened beings to lotus flowers, which, though rooted in the mud of society, remain unstained by it. But then, the Buddha lived in the forest, without a job, never so much as touching a coin. Clearly he recognized the role the outside world plays in shaping our inner peace.

Around and around my mind turned like a flywheel, mulling the inward and outward sources of our malaise. The solution suddenly seemed so simple. Once again, I felt a vision of sylvan freedom tugging at my soul, albeit in a new form. *Look at the chimpanzees!* I thought. *Why can't we all live like them, happy, lazy, and free?*

Then, a commotion broke out. For no apparent reason, a hulking male chimp hooted loudly, leaping with terrifying speed from one branch to another, and began chasing after a mother with an infant clinging to her chest. To avoid him, the mother leapt into the branches of an adjacent tree, clearing a gap of perhaps fifteen feet. She landed on a dead branch, which snapped. For one awful moment, it seemed she would come crashing to the ground, but as she fell, she managed to grab another, lower branch and swing to safety.

Variations on this scene repeated throughout the afternoon: A seemingly minor transgression would lead one chimp to begin shrieking in rage at another, followed by a brief clash. I never saw them inflict any serious wounds, but Alex said it happens from time to time. (When male chimps from different clans fight, he said, they have a disturbing tendency to rip off one another's testicles.) I later read that some 30 percent of dead chimps contain fractures in their skulls "consistent with falls from trees." Idyllic though it may appear at first glance, life up in the treetops is a never-ending battle fought over an abyss.

+

While teaching classes to undergrads at Harvard, Richard Wrangham likes to point out a fundamental difference between apes and humans: "If you trapped three hundred chimpanzees who did not know each other in a plane for eight hours, many of them probably wouldn't leave it alive. People, on the other hand, barely touch each other on a long-haul flight." He estimates that the level of violence among any average group of humans (whether city dwellers or hunter-gatherers), on any given day, is roughly one thousand times lower than among chimpanzees.

Wrangham theorizes that our relative lack of what he calls "reactive aggression"—the knee-jerk leap to violence—is a direct result of our evolutionary past. Noting humans' and other domesticated animals' strange tendency to retain certain childlike traits (smaller teeth; frailer bodies; friendlier, more curious dispositions) deep into adulthood, he argues that about three hundred thousand years ago, humans, by continually teaming up against bullies and psychopaths, weeded those antisocial tendencies from the gene pool to a much greater degree than any other great ape. Taming ourselves—not fully, but partially—gave humans an unprecedented ability to coordinate our behavior and minimize needless conflict. But species-wide self-discipline is not the unalloyed good that it seems. Because, Wrangham believes, even as we were breeding hotheaded aggression out of ourselves, we bred a different kind of violence *into* ourselves: what he calls "cold" violence—the ability to launch a premeditated, delayed, and coordinated attack. Cold violence, Wrangham writes, is what allows humans to commit any number of atrocities, including "massacre, slavery, hazing, ritual sacrifice, torture, lynchings, gang wars, political purges, and similar abuses of power." Chimps might rip one another apart on a flight from New York to London, but an ape would never think to firebomb a city to rubble.*

---

* One interesting complication to Wrangham's theory, which he highlights, is the behavior of the bonobo, the smaller genetic cousin of the chimpanzee. Bonobos are often called the "hippie apes" because they live in matriarchal societies, they share their food, and they often resolve their conflicts with sex (even, notably, homosexual sex) rather than fighting. However, scientists have recently discovered a wrinkle that threatens to ruin their cuddly reputation: A study conducted by Maud Mouginot of Boston University found that male

It occurs to me that "cold" violence is also a perfect description of the acts that humans—and, especially, members of the industrialized world—routinely commit against the Earth itself. Our species has an unparalleled ability to transform, torture, and even massacre whole ecosystems. To a certain degree, we cannot help *but* do so; we must, at the very least, slaughter plants to keep ourselves fed. The question then becomes: How do we choose to inflict this cold violence? How widely, how deeply, how wisely?

When I went looking for answers to this question, I was disturbed by what I found. In the minds of many scientists and historians, the outdated image of "Man the Hunter" has gradually evolved into something far more horrifying: "Man the Exterminator." In 1982, Jared Diamond, drawing upon the work of the geoscientist Paul Martin, argued that nearly every major pulse of *Homo sapiens*'s spread across the planet has been met by a subsequent mass die-off of the regions' large game animals. The flightless moa birds in New Zealand, giant tortoises and giant kangaroos in Australia, the giant ground sloth in South America—all happened to disappear from the fossil record right around the arrival of human beings in the area.* In many parts of the world, this ecological holocaust extends to the present day. The current extinction rate of vertebrates is hundreds of times

---

bonobos are three times more likely to engage in aggressive behavior than male chimps. The key is that this aggression almost never leads to the death of a fellow bonobo, as it does among chimps, because coalitions of dominant females (violently) discourage deadly violence. "The root of everything," Wrangham told one reporter, "seems to be female power."

*Some readers might take heart in the fact that many scientists believe that it was a shifting climate, not humans, that killed off the great slow beasts of each newly peopled continent, or else it was some combination of the two. But, considering that we are also currently warming the climate at a nearly unprecedented rate, this reassurance seems like cold comfort.

higher than the global historical average. More alarmingly, a recent study found that humans are also eliminating entire genera—imagine not only all the world's gray wolves dying off, but also all the dogs, jackals, and dingoes too—at a rate thirty-five times higher than normal. The authors of the study described it as an ongoing "mutilation of the tree of life."

Looking back over the whole of human history, Diamond concluded that humans have often been clever enough to eradicate other species, without being wise enough to stop ourselves. If, indeed, this blind lethality is a core aspect of human nature, the implications are chilling. It suggests that we can devise new systems of government, new social arrangements, find new forms of renewable energy, but at every turn, when it is required of us (and it *will* be required of us), we will fail to make the sacrifices necessary to prevent the ongoing death of the nonhuman world.

To me, one of the most haunting trajectories for humankind is not the one where we cause our own extinction—which, according to all the evidence I've read, seems unlikely*—but rather one in which some number of humans survive, but we do so on a planet increasingly emptied of other species. Life on Earth would be much like life today in Midtown Manhattan, where humans subsist only on the plants and animals we manipulate, and practically the only other

---

*The most helpful book I've read on this topic is the philosopher Toby Ord's eminently levelheaded *The Precipice: Existential Risk and the Future of Humanity*. He calculates that, because human settlements are so spread out across the globe, the current nuclear arsenal couldn't annihilate all human life on Earth, nor would the resulting "nuclear winter" wipe out humanity, even if that was humanity's desired result. As for climate change, he deems the risk of total human extinction "very small." This does not rule out the (very high) chance that a nuclear war or runaway climate change would cause death and suffering on a scale never before seen in human history; it is simply to say that it will not kill *all* humans everywhere. Once again, if this is any consolation at all, it is the coldest of comforts.

living things one encounters are the plethora of pests and parasites (rats, pigeons, roaches, flies) that have adapted to feed on our waste. E. O. Wilson writes that the arrival of such a future would mark a new geological era, which he calls "the Eremozoic," the Age of Loneliness. It would be an especially cruel fate for a species who, murderous as we may be, also takes such an unusual pleasure in looking at, studying, and living alongside other animals.

+

Two hours before dusk, Simon turned to me and said, "They'll leave now." I had no idea how he knew this, since I could detect no change in their behavior. But, shortly afterward, the chimpanzees began to stir. Within a few minutes, one by one, all ten of them had dropped to the ground and scampered downhill. We jogged after them, pushing through vines and thorny branches as they made their way down to a stony riverbed—the cool, damp air smelling of a cellar—then up the far bank and out into a meadow, where they climbed up into another tree and helped themselves to a *spuntino* of yet more fruit, leaves, and insects. Finally, they settled down in a nearby stand of trees. We stood below in the viridian twilight listening to the sounds of rustling as they deftly wove their nests, rapidly bending and tucking the springy branches—a flurry of random-looking movement that somehow resulted, within minutes, in something startlingly intricate, much as a magician's frantic gestures give birth (*et voilà!*) to a balloon animal.

Watching the chimpanzees bunk down for the evening, I felt a sudden, powerful urge to join them. This notion was not quite as outlandish as it might sound. I knew that Fiona had done just that on multiple occasions. Once, in Senegal, while studying the evolutionary advantages of arboreality, she famously spent five nights sleeping in various chimpanzee nests. (To ensure she wouldn't fall out in her sleep, she wore a climbing harness and kept herself securely roped up all night.)

When I first spoke with Fiona, months earlier, I'd asked her, somewhat offhandedly, if I could sleep in a chimpanzee nest as well. "I don't see why not," she'd replied. After all, chimpanzees abandon their nests after only one night. (Making a new nest each evening, Fiona informed me, is only a little bit more onerous to them than making the bed each morning is for us. They prefer these new nests, which, being made of fresh green branches, are stronger, safer and, presumably, more comfortable to sleep in.) She'd assured me I wouldn't be bothering them, only inconveniencing myself.

Watching the chimps build their nests there in Mahale only intensified my curiosity. What, I wondered, would it feel like to return to the literal cradle of humankind? Would it be the best sleep of my life, or the worst?

+

The following evening, I packed my gear and hiked with Remi down to a nearby river, about thirty minutes outside of camp, where there was a *Brachystegia* tree with a big, fresh, comfortable-looking nest that an adult male chimp had built the night before. With relatively little effort, I managed to anchor a climbing rope to a branch just above the nest, which meant that all I needed to do was to climb up the rope, using my mechanical ascenders, and then lower myself into it.

With us that day was Pascal Gagneux, a leathery, alert-eyed, voluminously talkative evolutionary biologist. During one phase of his research he had climbed into more than three hundred chimp nests to collect samples of their DNA. Pascal gave me three warnings: First, he suggested that, as I ascended, I should take care not to jostle the nest too hard, or else it could "explode" in my face. Second, he pointed out that chimpanzees frequently soil their nests in the morning, so I should be sure to check it for droppings. Third, he said that while I was up there, I should be ready to come down at a moment's notice. It was not likely, but it was possible that a chimp might not be happy to see me up there, in their domain. He said that one time while he was climbing into a nest, he had encountered a female chimpanzee carrying the corpse of her recently deceased baby. The mother, in a fit of grief and rage, screamed, threw the baby at him, and then fled.

While I prepared my climbing gear, Remi began unpacking the rest of our stuff. He was acting as my support crew for the night and was armed with a walkie-talkie should anything go wrong. Pascal warned Remi that the area was frequented by lions, leopards, and hyenas. Before leaving, he told us a story about a local man, the grandfather of a staff member at the research camp, who had been attacked by a hyena and had half of his face ripped off. "So all his life, to eat, he had to hold one hand against the missing half, to keep the food in," he said.

Never in all of our years traveling together have I seen Remi set up our tent so quickly.

As the daylight began to dim, I attached my ascenders and inchwormed up the rope. The nest sat about thirty-five feet off the ground. I paused for a moment just below it to admire its construction. It resembled a small green cloud. The branches had been woven into an ovoid shape, then lined with an extra layer of fresh leaves. I was somewhat humbled to realize that, if asked to, I, with all of my human intelligence, would have no idea how to replicate it.

Once I was above the nest, I switched over to my rappel device and lowered myself down into it. It sank beneath my weight, with a sickening softness. For a moment, I worried I would fall right through the bottom. But then the layers of branches compressed into a kind of net, gained tension, and held me. I slacked out my rope completely, so that all of my weight was resting on the nest. It was comfortable, in a tenuous kind of way. The only problem was that my legs—those wonderful, quintessentially human appendages—are much longer than a chimp's legs. When chimps sleep, they tend to lie on their backs and fold their short legs up, frog-like, with their heels near their crotch. I was too tall and too inflexible to do that, so my legs dangled in the open air. The blood began to pool in my feet. After only a few minutes, it was clear that this would be a very uncomfortable night.

Down below, in the tent, I could hear Remi inventorying all of his cozy accoutrements.

"Okay, I've got my pillow, I've got my sleeping mat, I've got my sleeping bag . . ." he muttered to himself. A few minutes later, I heard him sighing contentedly as he settled into his soft, crinkly, synthetic little nest. Then he went quiet.

Night spread; the sky turned lilac, then indigo, and a single fiery orange star appeared through the branches. More stars soon joined it. Ovid said that man alone can raise his face to heaven. It occurred to me that chimps, who tend to sleep on their backs, look up at the stars every night as they drift off to sleep. I wondered what they thought those pale, distant dots were.

Down below, I heard Remi gasp.

"Oh my god," he said. "The ground is *alive*." He'd unzipped the door to his tent for a moment, to adjust something, and within that brief window of time, dozens of bugs had gotten in; I could hear him down there, hunting down the infiltrators. "They're everywhere!" he yelled, slapping the sides of the tent.

Fiona had told me that, on the nights she slept in chimp nests, she was woken up far less often than on nights when she slept on the bare earth without a tent, because down on the ground, roaming animals and creeping insects frequently startled her. She also discovered that she was bitten by fewer mosquitoes in the nest, which is somewhat odd, since they're perfectly capable of flying that high. (She theorized that the broken branches might emit a natural insect repellent.)

Fifteen minutes later, Remi, having evicted the last remaining insects, was softly snoring. For the next few hours, I lay there in the dark, growing increasingly bored and miserable. My dangling legs caused my lower back to arch, which caused it to cramp up, so I tried propping them up on a branch, but each time I drifted off to sleep, they would slip off and I would jolt awake with a terrible plummeting sensation. This phenomenon, known as a "hypnic jerk," is surprisingly common; it is estimated that 70 percent of people experience it at some point. It occurred to me that it might well be an ancient holdover from our arboreal past, a time when the act of sleeping and a fear of falling were deeply intertwined.

Hours passed, a small eternity. I fished out my phone to check the time, thinking it must be only a few hours from dawn, at which point I could climb down and stretch out on the ground.

The clock read 11:04 p.m.

By this point, I had been aloft for five hours. My lower back was already so badly cramped that I was afraid I would soon become trapped in the nest. (I thought of my great-aunt Helen, who, according to family lore, once excused herself from Thanksgiving dinner to use the bathroom and then somehow fell backward into an empty bathtub, with her pants still around her ankles, and was forced to wait there until someone could haul her out.) What's more, every time I shifted my weight or moved my legs in an attempt to find a more comfortable position, I could feel the twigs below me sproinging loose, which meant that my sleeping platform was gradually disintegrating; I recalled Pascal's warning that with too much jostling, the nest could simply explode.

Utterly defeated, I heaved myself upright, crawled out, rappelled down to the ground, and, glancing about warily for hyenas, slipped into the tent beside Remi. My camp bed—nothing more than a stinky old sleeping bag and a mouse-chewed foam pad—suddenly felt like the pinnacle of human innovation.

+

One of the great mysteries of human evolution resides in a dark, amnesiac realm: the enigma of sleep. Studies show that getting a better night's sleep improves our memory, creativity, immune response, metabolism, and emotional regulation. And yet, spending eight hours or so each night in a state of bodily paralysis and mental hallucination leaves us open to attack, both from predators and from other humans. And the deeper we sleep, the deeper the risk.

Curiously, humans sleep for fewer hours overall than any other primate, but we spend more time in the phase of deep sleep known as REM, when the body is immobilized. This is odd, since it would seem that our early ground-sleeping ancestors would have been more vulnerable than their arboreal cousins. Sleeping in a chimpanzee nest, as I learned, is not comfortable, but it is safe. This is in part because it lifts you above any ground-dwelling predators, and in part because the tree itself serves as a kind of natural alarm system; any large predator that attempts to sneak up on you will jostle the branch, startling you awake. On solid ground, this alarm system is disabled. So how did humans come to feel safe enough to sleep so deeply on the ground, surrounded by predators?

The anthropologist David Samson has dedicated much of his life to solving this riddle. He began his career by studying the sleeping habits of chimpanzees; his fieldwork included climbing into seventy-two nests to study their construction. He then moved on to orangutans, and then human hunter-gatherers, namely the Hadza people of Tanzania. In his papers, he highlights the fact that building nests was a major step in the evolution of apes (compared with, say, monkeys, who sleep on bare branches and who, perhaps not coincidentally, exhibit the skittery irritability of the perpetually sleep-deprived). But early humans, by abandoning nests and learning to sleep on solid ground, made an even greater breakthrough.

The most common explanation for the origins of human ground sleeping is that by that point in our evolutionary history we had already mastered fire, which would have provided heat and deterred predators. But this theory faces a major challenge: Wielding fire undoubtedly allowed us to become a smarter species, but how did humans become smart enough to master fire? Anthropologists sometimes refer to this catch-22 as the "gray ceiling," a reference to the brain's gray matter. Samson suggests an elegant solution: It could be that mastering the art of sleeping on the ground, over the course of many generations, gave us the increased cognition necessary to master fire—among a thousand other innovations unique to our species of ape.

Fire, it turns out, is not as essential to sleeping comfortably outdoors as it might seem. Samson's research among the Hadza has shown that the presence of fire, while pleasant, does not actually improve sleep quality. Likewise, it is common knowledge among safari operators that fires do not ward off lions; in fact, in certain cases, it draws their attention. Studies of modern hunter-gatherers show that what seems to most reliably ward off lions are large numbers of humans in a tight formation, ideally in a hut or fenced-in area, with at least one individual serving as a sentinel in shifts throughout the night. Samson believes our early ancestors learned to sleep in precisely this manner around 1.8 million years ago. If true, this would make literal the maxim, put forward by Martin Nowak and Roger Highfield, that life was not simply a "struggle for existence"; it was also a "snuggle for existence."

Perhaps, Samson's research suggests, what distinguished early humans from the other apes was the ability to be *humane*. Other scientists seem inclined to agree. In 2021, the paleoanthropologist Jeremy DeSilva published a book entitled *First Steps*. While studying various hominin fossils around the world, he had noticed that they often showed signs of injury. This was not surprising; when sprinting away from predators on two spindly legs, accidents are inevitable. What surprised DeSilva was how often those same injured bones—which in many cases should have been life-ending injuries—had healed. To survive, DeSilva surmises, our early ancestors would have often needed friends and family members to help care for them when injured. We could not afford to be lone wolves or petty tyrants. "Bipedalism in an overly aggressive ape with purely selfish tendencies and a low tolerance for other group members would have been a recipe for extinction," he writes. If true, this theory could push back the start date of Wrangham's self-domestication process by millions of years, to the dimmest dawn of humankind.

Cooperation functions as a kind of evolutionary skeleton key, unlocking many of the constraints on the growth of human intelligence. Social sleeping may have given us that key. It would have created a feedback loop between increased group cohesion, increased emotional regulation, and increased cognitive capacity: In other words, we got calmer, kinder, and smarter, the one feeding into the next in a virtuous circle. It also would have created a negative selective pressure against psychopathically dominant individuals, who couldn't be trusted to watch one another's backs. Nestled together like a pack of dogs, dreaming alongside one another, early humans would have quickly become tightly bonded in ways no other apes are.

Once individuals or families cohere into tribes, their collective abilities mushroom. The invention of cooperative parenting, for example—where extended family and community members occasionally pitch in to help with the burden of child-rearing, a practice human communities almost universally share, but chimpanzees altogether lack—allowed mothers to participate in more aspects of social life and be more productive while still nursing their infants. It also allowed those infants to explore, play, and learn from various adults before finally setting about the hard work of gathering food for themselves. Indeed, one of my favorite theories of the origin of language is that it emerged not among adults, but among children, who had both flexible minds and ample free time, allowing them to play around with sounds until they began to formulate humanity's first words. Once language was invented—once our thoughts and dreams could be shared to create entire conceptual worlds—humanity acquired a power to coordinate our actions and achieve complex tasks no other ape could even imagine. We became, in the words of the anthropologist Loren Eiseley, "a dream animal."

+

After spending a week at Mahale, trailing the chimpanzees as they roamed about the sere land, we said goodbye to Fiona and her team and rode off in a Land Cruiser to the city of Kigoma. Remi and I then hired a blue wooden motorboat to ferry us across Lake Tanganyika, up near the border of Burundi, to a place called Gombe Stream—the famed research camp of Jane Goodall.

We arrived to find the pier ruined by storms, which forced us to jump out onto the pebbly shore instead, splashing in nippy, knee-deep water. For a surprisingly low price, we were able to rent a canvas tent, complete with a shower, solar electricity, and locking screen doors to keep out the area's baboons, who, we were warned, would "tear the room to shreds" if they got half the chance. We dropped our bags, took a dip in the lake, and then shared a big brown bottle of Kilimanjaro beer. This was an idyllic corner of the Earth; I could see why Goodall kept returning to it throughout her life.

Afterward, we hiked to a nearby waterfall, which, unlike the surrounding forest, was wonderfully misty, mossy, and cool. Here, Goodall repeatedly witnessed chimps performing a strange ritual she called their "waterfall dance." She had noticed that chimpanzees had a tendency to stand in front of it and sway from side to side. Sometimes they would climb vines and swing out into the waterfall's spray. "Afterward, you'll see them sitting on a rock, actually in the stream, looking up, watching the water with their eyes as it falls down, and then watching it go away," she recalled. "I can't help but feel that this waterfall display, or dance, is perhaps triggered by the feelings of awe and wonder that we feel." If Goodall was right, that means our capacity for sublime self-transcendence is a gift older than humanity itself.

+

The following morning, we embarked on a guided trek to see the area's famed chimpanzees. We were warned that it might take hours to find even a single group of chimps, but our guide managed to locate them within less than ten minutes. We crept up on a large family huddled together right in the middle of the trail. I counted nine of them in total. Our guide told us they were led by a wizened matriarch named Gremlin. They sat with their backs to us, grooming one another in a meticulous, unhurried manner. It struck me as absurd, and not a little comical, how profoundly interested we were in them, and how profoundly uninterested they were in us.

We ended up spending the better part of two hours watching the chimps, snapping hundreds of photos, and cooing over an infant taking what appeared to be its first shaky steps. I marveled as a mother lifted up her infant's legs to pick the nits from his inner thighs, holding his little pink foot with the precise mix of tenderness and firmness that human parents use when changing a diaper. The baby's ears looked as if they'd been made of Silly Putty, and I wanted, suddenly, very badly and somewhat inexplicably, to bite down gently on one.

Some of the chimps lay sprawled on their sides in the dirt, one arm folded under the head, like a pillow, and the other extended into the air, a sort of recumbent taxi-hailing gesture, which allowed them to air out their armpits. I was concerned that these chimps looked somewhat lethargic, almost weak. But our guide explained that it was the dry season, so they were saving their energy by waiting for another chimpanzee group to locate some ripe fruit trees and call out, at which point this group would join them.

When Goodall first arrived here in 1960, one of the ways she habituated the area's chimpanzees to her presence was by feeding them bananas, which turned out to be a grave mistake. Over time, the apes came to rely on Goodall's largesse, visiting her camp every day for their haul. As the population pressure and competition around the bananas grew ever more intense, it eventually led to a war among two rival factions of chimps that lasted for four years, until all of the males in one group had been killed. (It is often said that scarcity is the ultimate source of violence. But a sudden flush of affluence—be it in the form of bananas, gold, or petroleum—can often prove just as destabilizing.)

At first many scientists assumed that the conflict, which came to be known as the Four Year War, was artificially induced by Goodall's feeding program, rather than by any innate warlike tendencies in chimpanzees. But in subsequent decades, numerous other chimpanzee wars have been witnessed elsewhere in the wild, especially in times of ecological disturbance.

Those hard times, sadly, appear to be increasing, and again we humans are largely to blame. Scientists have found that the warming climate is changing chimpanzee behavior in disturbing ways. On sweltering afternoons, chimpanzees have recently been seen sitting in pools of water to cool off, even though chimps are normally hydrophobic. In drier areas, like Mahale, they have been observed digging wells, a cultural practice that appears to be spreading as water grows more scarce. In Gabon, chimpanzees have even been seen killing baby gorillas for the first time in recorded history; the two species, which are normally peaceful and even playful with one another, appear to have begun battling over scarce resources.

+

The heart of the modern environmental crisis is what philosophers call a collective-action problem. The most famous example of this type of problem is commonly known as the "tragedy of the commons": When a group shares a resource—like, say, a communal well with a limited amount of water in it—it is in the *group's* best interest to conserve that resource, but it is in each *individual's* best interest to use up as much as they can, because if they don't, someone else might.

Chimpanzees navigate this kind of collective-action problem all the time. When a troop of chimps reaches a tree that has fruited earlier than all the others in the forest, it is in the group's best interest to graze lightly, allowing the rest of the fruit to ripen, but it is in each individual's best interest to simply gobble up as much as they can as quickly as they can. By running experiments in controlled conditions, researchers have found that chimpanzees resolve this kind of problem by fairly brutal, Hobbesian means: One chimpanzee tends to dominate another, forcing them to back down rather than continue ratcheting up their intake of food (in this case, a container of mango juice with two straws leading from it, which is specially designed to shut off the flow of juice if either participant drinks too quickly). However, when pairs of human children (all around the age of six) were asked to solve a similar puzzle, without any instruction, they tended to solve it by the opposite method: Nearly half of the children agreed to share the resource equally between both members. Not one child resorted to simply terrorizing their partner into consuming less.*

Diamond, riffing on the Nobel Prize–winning work of the political economist Elinor Ostrom, writes that out in the real world, there are three typical solutions to the tragedy of the commons. The first

---

* As the primatologist Christine Webb astutely points out in *The Arrogant Ape*—her rigorous, well-intentioned, but, to my mind, not entirely convincing attempt to dismantle the notion of "human exceptionalism"—studies of chimpanzee behavior that take place in captivity must always be regarded with some skepticism. For instance, who is to say whether human children, if held in captivity for years, in a state of perpetual boredom and hunger, wouldn't also resort to unusually aggressive or even psychopathic methods when asked to share a jug of mango juice.

is rigid government oversight, which is effective but expensive and oppressive. The second is privatization, which is cheaper but far less effective, because, in a market economy, the owner of a given resource is forever tempted to plunder it. The third solution, which Diamond terms the "ground up" method, is "for the consumers to recognize their common interests and to design, obey, and enforce prudent harvesting quotas themselves." This method is clearly preferable, because it doesn't involve any elaborate bureaucracies or draconian punishments. The problem with this system, he notes, is that it requires a high level of trust among the members of the group in question, all of whom understand that they "share a common future" and all of whom wish to "pass on the resource to their heirs."

When facing a collective-action problem on a global scale—like overfishing in international waters or the pollution of our shared atmosphere—meeting these conditions can seem like an insurmountable challenge. To do so, people everywhere on Earth (but especially in the world's most powerful countries) would have to become more tightly bonded, more aware of the limits of the land on which they live, and more devoted to the needs of future generations. Most political debates can be pared down to this one simple question: Can humans ever hope to care deeply about beings outside of their own families and communities? Is it human nature to care about humanity itself?

The long, branching arc of human history seems to provide an answer. One of the most notable changes in human societies over the past thousand years has been the formation of nations, "tribes" containing millions or even billions of people. This radical expansion of tribal bounds—from clans to villages, villages to cities, cities to nations—seems normal to us now only because it is so familiar. Beginning with the European Enlightenment and reaching a crescendo following the Second World War, cosmopolitan philosophers began arguing that humanity must transcend even those enormous categories, learning to instead see oneself as, in Kant's words, a member of a "universal community." These thinkers do not argue that this transcendence of national identity is inevitable, or easy. But they insist there is no compelling reason why it isn't possible. At its heart, politics is the creation of a community of strangers, strung together with lines of communication and bonded by systems of mutual aid. If that community can be as large as Canada, why can't it be as large as the world itself?

When Wilson charges that humans are "tribal and aggressively territorial," he is cropping out at least half of the picture: We are that, but we are not *just* that. Philosophers like Peter Singer frequently liken the human capacity for compassion to a circle that can be widened or narrowed, much like the circle of light thrown off by a campfire. Build a bigger fire, and the circle will widen; tamp down the fire, and the circle will shrink. The Mahayana ideal of the celestial bodhisattva—a being possessed of infinite compassion, caring equally for every living thing in the cosmos—is probably unattainable, at least by most mortals. But history shows that widening the circle of compassion beyond the self, the nuclear family, or even the nation is within every person's grasp. Indeed, refusing to expand that circle is, in some very real sense, profoundly inhuman. After all, what other species is capable of feeling isaak—the respect born of recognizing the deep kinship of all living things? What other beings have uncovered the essential unity of the evolutionary Tree of Life?

Humans are, as philosophers like to say, naturally "porous" beings: We empathize with our friends; we intuit the desires of strangers; we can even journey into the minds of other species. (We may never be able to know precisely what it's like to be a bat, but it is a small miracle, too often overlooked, that we can even try.) Beginning with the domestication of dogs tens of thousands of years ago, humans have been forging especially tight emotional bonds with what the posthumanist philosopher Donna J. Haraway calls "companion species"—dogs and cats, pigs and cows, horses and llamas, the birds that lead us to honey and the microbes that live in our guts. I remember once, while in Borneo, watching a group of Penan hunter-gatherer children pass the afternoon toying lovingly with their pet—an orphaned pangolin, with two wet black ink-dots for eyes and an imbricated armor of dust-brown scales—just as I had played with my pet iguana as a child. Neither animal was particularly cuddly, but our innate biophilia easily bridged the species divide. Even John Gray, caustic misanthropist that he is, has said that a life "denuded" of encounters with other species is "not worth living."

The most memorable animal encounter of my life occurred when Remi and I traveled to the Virunga Mountains of Rwanda, where we trekked to see a troop of mountain gorillas. One young female had a habit of gazing directly at us in the most human way imaginable. Staring into those sharp-cut dark eyes, I felt a sweet, almost sad welling in my chest, accompanied by a desire to protect this creature at all costs. "There is more meaning and mutual understanding with a gorilla than with any other animal I know," proclaimed David Attenborough as he stood within inches of a troop of mountain gorillas in Rwanda back in 1978. In the presence of a gorilla, he felt himself "escaping the human condition and living imaginatively in another creature's world." Humans experience this sensation all the time, if not always this powerfully. Peering deeply into the eyes of a chimpanzee, or a dog, or a whale, or an octopus, or a dragonfly—or, for that matter, pressing our fingers into the whorled bark of a giant sequoia—we can feel the boundaries of our own humanity momentarily dissolve and through those porous borders flows a wild auntish love.

If there is a flaw in human nature that has fated us to eradicate other species, I quite simply cannot believe that it resides in either the human soul or the human genome. We can be cold-blooded killers, but most of us are not born sociopaths. Rather, I suspect that the flaw lies outside the body altogether, in that dark space *between* humans, an invisible meshwork of cultural structures—politics, economics, law—that are meant to keep humanity alive but that, over time, have taken on a life of their own. It's one of the great and terrible wonders of human existence: how ideas can gnarl into social arrangements and then go on shaping lives for centuries. Our notions become our nature.

+

By the time we'd returned from our trek, it was a blinding, shadowless equatorial noon. Our canvas tent had turned into a sweat lodge, so Remi and I put on our bathing suits and dove into the lake to wash off the day's grime. As I was exiting the cool, limpid water, I turned my head to find that the same troop of chimpanzees we'd visited earlier that morning was now marching down the beach, the babies clinging to the fur of their mothers like tiny jockeys. The chimps passed directly through the camp, in a straight line, unhurried and apparently unconcerned with the humans all around. Eventually they found their way to an array of solar panels near the kitchen; then they all stopped and sprawled out in their shade. The employees at the camp later told me that this peculiar siesta had become a fairly routine occurrence.

Looking out over that futuristic tableau—solar panels glinting up above, apes lolling down below—I began thinking about how almost all of our energy ultimately comes from the sun. Energy either flows from the sun down to the earth, where it is absorbed by plants, which convert it into sugars, which we then eat; or it gets absorbed by trees and locked up in the form of wood, which we burn; or it gets absorbed by plants and compressed down over the course of eons into fossil fuels; or it creates perturbations in the atmosphere, which turn windmills, or it evaporates water, which rains down again elsewhere, turning hydroelectric turbines; or else it gets harvested directly by solar panels and converted into electricity. What had been missing from my exploration of human evolution thus far, I realized, was the question of where we as humans procure our power as a species. Unlocking the power of fire, we now know, helped our ancient ancestors take an enormous evolutionary leap forward. Mastering fire allowed us to feed bigger brains, to warm our furless bodies, and to alter entire ecologies. But the story too often ends there, leaving out the last million years of human history.

In *The Evolution of Power*, the paleoecologist and evolutionary biologist Geerat Vermeij argues that power is the prime mover of natural selection. Vermeij defines power, simply, as "energy expenditure over time." A being's power, in other words, is defined by how much it can do and for how long it can do it. Trees expend power to grow upward and defend themselves from pests, albatross expend power to cross oceans, and so on. One of the peculiarities of biological power is that it naturally self-perpetuates. Whales and sequoias grow larger for the same reason that fish collect into schools and bees into colonies: It allows them to amass, and then expend, greater power, forming a virtuous circle. By exerting that power, organisms also go on to alter the local ecology—termites erect towers; elephants fell trees; trees seed clouds—bending it in such a way that their power can flow more smoothly. The flow of power shapes worlds, just as the flow of water carves out canyons.

By this definition, humans are the most powerful organisms who have ever lived. Our power, ultimately, stems not from our size or our speed, but from our adaptability; humans evolved to survive in every ecosystem on earth, and then we began bending them to our needs. The Korowai have adapted to survive in the forest, just as the San have adapted to survive in the desert, and my teenage neighbor has adapted to survive in a small-town high school. This is why Marxist scholars so frequently, and not wholly incorrectly, assert that there is no such thing as human nature, only human nature *under* a particular system, like capitalism or feudalism. In pursuit of power, we create new power structures, which act upon us even as we act within them.

From a certain angle, it might appear that humanity is everywhere following a bleak trajectory from forest idyll to strip-mall hell, but this is only one part of a larger, more complicated picture. Some aspects of modernity—steel axes, gas engines, synthetic medicine, "Baby Shark"—are too powerful to resist. If humans have access to these tools, we will probably avail ourselves of them. However, human history shows that we are not fated to do any one thing with these tools. We are fated to do many different things. Our destiny is to follow what Wilson calls "branching pathways," which we explore simultaneously, like so many army ants fanning across the forest floor, following, and reshaping, the runnels carved out by the flow of power.

+

"Humankind has no nature, only history," declared the philosopher José Ortega y Gasset. After reviewing all of the theories of human nature I could find, I've come to believe this definition is truer than most. Our "nature" is simply our past—a past that shapes, but does not dictate, our future. But the story we tell ourselves about that past has often been much too narrow. It has been the story of a single linear progression of apes, gradually rising up from a crouch, learning first to hunt and gather, and then to farm, and then to invent money and drill for oil and synthesize nitrogen and genetically engineer crops and create computers and fly to the moon, even as people starved to death down below and other species went extinct. Seen in this unilinear framing, John Gray seems to be right: Humans are nothing more than clever but equally selfish and shortsighted animals, who are fated to overpopulate the planet, exhaust its resources, and die off en masse.

Science has begun to uncover our own early history in greater detail than ever before, and what it has revealed is a messy, ramous process. These findings suggest that a more honest way to tell the story of humankind might sound something like this: One species of apes came down out of the treetops. They could still climb trees (indeed, they still can), but now they could also do new things: Their free hands were magically adaptable, all-purpose tools, capable of carrying food, throwing rocks, and helping friends. These new apes were unusually willing to help one another when they were injured, an impulse that would only grow as time went on. They slept together, watching out for one another's safety; they learned to hunt together; they figured out how to parent communally. They shunned or killed malicious individuals, rather than kowtowing to them. Living in cooperative communities allowed some members to take risks, to be weird, to experiment. That enabled them to devise yet more ways of thriving within a given landscape, information they passed along in grunts and gestures, which grew into words, and then increasingly complex forms of symbolic communication. They made strategic partnerships with certain species. They bent stone, and then metal, to their ends. They tamed fire. They clad themselves in other plants and animals. They reshaped ecosystems. They wove their lives into that of the land.

Using all these skills, humans spread across every ecosystem on earth—adapting to icy tundras and searing deserts and foggy rainforest and even the open sea—for century after century, millennium after millennium, while the other great apes continued living back in the treetops, steadily growing ever more adapted to a very narrow mode of life. Humans shared many things in common with their hominin cousins, but our socially oriented experimental impulse—an eternally fracturing-and-forging fire of the mind—was not one of them. From our first wobbly steps, the nature of humans has always been to branch out, to diversify. We are the apes who gave up arboreality to become arborescent.

The question worth asking, then, is not: Could such a branchy species ever change their ways to prevent planetary collapse? The question is: How could we not? What force on earth—what industry, what system, what tyrant—is powerful enough to stop us?

7. RESISTING

A FEW YEARS ago, a group of people who loved trees did something a bit odd: They snuck into an urban forest and built a treehouse. The forest was not a particularly nice place to build a treehouse. It was wedged between a rail line and a highway; the air reeked of car exhaust, and the branches shook with the clatter of passing freight trains. The forest also lay in the path of an oil pipeline that the government wanted to build, which meant the trees would need to be cut down. That was exactly why the tree lovers had chosen to live there: By stopping the pipeline, they would save the trees, and by saving the trees, they would stop the pipeline.

Soon, the police showed up and ordered the tree lovers to leave, but they refused. Some of them were arrested and sent to jail. More showed up, and more were arrested. Still, they managed to remain there in the treehouse for more than a year, thwarting the advance of the nation's largest industry. They had nothing personal to gain from this action, and much to lose. They did it merely for their love of trees and people and other living things.

I tried to tell this story to my two young nieces recently, because I thought it might give them hope for the future of humanity. But it isn't an easy story to tell, especially when you have two inquisitive grade-schoolers, deep into their why phase, asking probing follow-ups.

One simple way to explain all this to kids, I discovered, is by telling the story from the perspective of trees. For a long time, I explained, humans burned trees to cook food and keep ourselves warm, which was an elegant arrangement, because new trees continually sprouted up, soaking up the smoke that the old trees released as they burned. (I was, admittedly, oversimplifying somewhat.) Then humans discovered pockets of ancient plants and plankton buried under the soil, and they learned to pull those up to the surface and burn them for energy. Because these plants and plankton had been compressed by the slow crush of centuries—turning them into coal and oil—they contained far more energy than living trees. So more and more humans began burning coal and oil for energy instead of trees. The problem was they were now releasing the smoke that had been soaked up by those ancient plants and plankton over the course of millions of years, all in a tiny fraction of that time.

Even back when I was a kid, no older than my nieces are now, the result of all this burning was easy to foresee: The smoke went up into the sky and began trapping heat. The world grew warmer, the weather cycles more chaotic. This led to a rash of changes down on earth, including a cycle of ever-worsening wildfires, killing off ever more trees.

Fortunately, while all this was going on, humans had been inventing other ways of gathering energy directly from the sun and wind and water. This was a beautiful idea: Now, we could begin living *like* trees, drinking in the sunlight and eating the wind. The skies would grow cleaner, the weather more stable, and people and other living things would be able to flourish.

Many individuals did everything they could to bring this bright future into reality. They voted; they marched. They bought less stuff, or different, better stuff. They invented; they invested. They rode the subway or they walked instead of driving, and they skipped trips they didn't need to take. Shiny solar panels began cropping up in deserts, in grasslands, on the roofs of homes; the hills sprouted giant windmills, like so many metal daisies. New cars were invented, new trucks, new trains, new boats, new leaf blowers and lawn mowers and chainsaws, even new airplanes, which ran on sunlight and wind, rather than dead plants and plankton.

And yet, the system had evolved to run on the old types of fuel, so for a long time coal and oil remained cheaper, more reliable forms of energy. Making matters worse, governments spent trillions of dollars supporting those old forms of energy. Even though they said they wanted to stop burning oil and begin using renewable energy, politicians kept approving the construction of new oil pipelines, which were designed to last for fifty or one hundred years. It was like hearing someone with a serious heart problem vow to quit drinking coffee, and then, five minutes later, watching him go out and buy an expensive new espresso machine.

Some people believed the problem was human nature: We were too greedy, too shortsighted, and too callous to change our ways. But that, I assured my nieces, was wrong. Humans are innately clever, inventive, and adaptable. They are social and forward-looking. When they need to, they *can* change, and quite quickly. But the structure of modern civilization could not. Humanity had gnarled around the needs of its industries, not its people.

The grand tree of human innovation had branched out to find new, cleaner sources of energy, but the older branches were infected with a kind of blight—the black rot of coal and oil—that was slowly sickening the tree as a whole. The only option left, many people felt, was to forcibly prune away the blackened branches of fossil fuels. So a group of people in Canada decided to stop the construction of a new pipeline designed to carry tar sands oil, the world's dirtiest form of fuel. They wanted to do so peacefully, without hurting anyone. And they felt that, in this fight, trees would be their best allies, because people loved trees, and trees had been at the center of this story all along.

That is how a group of people who cared about trees ended up living in a smoggy, unlovely little forest, blockading an oil pipeline.

+

For years, I had been following the news about a plan to build this new pipeline, which would send an armada of oil tankers sailing across the sea that I swim in each morning, with a mixture of dread and cold rage. The pipeline was called the Trans Mountain Expansion, or TMX. It was designed to carry bitumen—a heavy, sticky form of oil, the extraction of which requires massive amounts of energy (and, thus, creates massive amounts of carbon pollution)—from Alberta to just outside Vancouver, and from there to foreign markets. In 2018, the company that had been trying to build the pipeline had decided it would be too difficult and expensive to finish. Rather than allowing the project to die, the nation's Liberal prime minister, Justin Trudeau, announced that he would use taxpayer money to purchase it so that the government could force it through, cost be damned. This announcement occurred less than twenty-four hours after his party had declared that the nation was facing a "climate emergency." The oil, Trudeau argued, was simply too valuable to leave in the ground; the market *demanded* that it be extracted. It was the kind of decision that, when one is enmeshed in the perverse logic of carbon capitalism, seems to make sense, but when one takes a step back and views it through the eyes of future generations, begins to look like sheer madness.

So when, in 2021, I found out that a group of protesters had built a treehouse to blockade the pipeline, I reached out to them, thinking

I might write an article about their unlikely crusade. After some initial hesitancy (they were, understandably, paranoid about government spies infiltrating their tight-knit cohort), they agreed to let me visit the treehouse and talk with them.

One April day, I crossed the Salish Sea and then pushed through traffic amid the gleaming cyan towers of Vancouver to reach a fast-growing, unlovely satellite city called Burnaby. I parked outside a massive Korean grocery store, grabbed my backpack full of climbing equipment, and walked along the shoulder of the highway. I could feel the eyes of each passing motorist scrutinizing me, skeptical of this strange human particle amid the machinescape.

After a few minutes, I spotted a small trail leading through a stand of cottonwood trees. The trail was blocked off with a yellow rope and a sign warning that I was now entering "a Trans Mountain project/operations site," which I ignored. I passed a pair of portly, aging security guards wearing yellow reflective safety vests. I was worried they would try to stop me, but they were content to merely film me with their phones. Up above, in the branches of a large maple tree, sat the treehouse, which was shambolically festooned with protest banners, mirrors, wooden crates, and homemade art. A rope was lowered to me. I pulled on my climbing harness, clipped a pair of ascenders onto the rope, climbed up, and then swung over into a cargo net beneath the treehouse.

At that time, the treehouse was inhabited by a bearded, bespectacled man in his sixties named Tim Takaro, who acted as a spokesman for the blockade. I ended up spending the better part of three hours up in the tree, talking with him.

It was a mild, pleasant spring afternoon; sunlight slivered through branches hung with green catkins, like tiny chandeliers. Tim opened a can of beer one of his supporters had brought him and sipped it while we talked. His manner of speech was punctiliously (even fussily) intellectual, which should not have surprised me, given that he was a Yale graduate, a medical doctor, and a tenured professor of environmental health at one of the nation's best universities, but which nevertheless struck me as incongruous, given the fact that he was, currently, an unwashed, barefoot eco-radical living in a tree.

Tim explained to me how the blockade worked: The treehouse needed to be occupied at all times, otherwise the police would swoop in and quickly demolish it. (This had happened once before, to a different treehouse nearby.) However, it was impractical for any one person to stay up in the tree for long. So, once every few days, a new treesitter arrived to swap out for the previous one, in a rotating roster. Since many people were not suited to the task of hanging out, all day and all night, on a six-foot-wide ledge in a tree, risking arrest, one of Tim's chief tasks was to recruit and train new treesitters. (The movement ultimately managed to attract about a hundred volunteers—treesitters, organizers, and supporters—although being a loose, informal coalition, people continually drifted in and out; its core was made up of only about twenty individuals, who did most of the work.)

"We always need new people," he said.

While talking with Tim, I realized that, in some ways, I was ideally suited to the odd task of sitting in a tree and doing nothing all day. I did not need to show up to work at an office, I had no kids to tend to, and my husband was accustomed to my being away on reporting trips, sometimes for weeks at a time. My tree-climbing training had taught me how to be comfortable high above the ground, my meditation practice had taught me how to sit still, and my years spent in the journalism world had taught me how to shape a narrative and how to get that story into the public eye. It was as if the many branches of my life had all prepared me for this single task.

A decade earlier, when I was reporting on the Occupy Wall Street movement, amid the panoply of signs people held, one in particular pierced me. It read, simply: "Stop Gawking. Join!"

Why, I wondered, had I for so long been content to merely observe while others fought for the things I believed in?

Why wasn't I sitting where Tim was sitting?

+

I had my reasons. The most obvious of these was the fact that I wasn't yet a Canadian citizen; I only had "permanent residency" status, a misnomer, since it had to be renewed every five years. This meant that if I was arrested, I would risk being kicked out of the country that had become my home, a country I'd come to love. Tim assured me that there were ways of minimizing my chances of running afoul of the law. If arrests were imminent, he said, the police were obligated to read a legal document known as an "injunction" and then give me time (about ten minutes) to vacate the tree. So there would always be an opportunity for me to simply run away, if need be. Ideally for the movement, of course, I wouldn't run; I would chain myself to the tree and slow down the loggers for as long as I humanly could. But Tim explained that my very presence in the tree would suggest that I was a person willing to chain myself to it, which would force the police to assemble a special unit to extract me. That would take time. And time—taking time from them, buying time for ourselves and other living things—was what this protest was all about.

+

Three days later, I embarked on my first treesitting stint. At a prearranged hour, I snuck up through the surrounding woods to the base of the tree and texted the current resident of the treehouse, who dropped down a rope. I climbed up and hauled up all of my gear, and he rappelled down. From that point onward, I was alone, day and night, for the better part of a week.

On the inside, the treehouse itself was rather squalid; it was more a tree shanty, really. The floor was made of a large sheet of graffitied plywood, and the roof was covered with a pair of heavy plastic tarps. Inside was a small camping tent, in theory to keep out mosquitoes and mice, although mice soon chewed a hole through the tent, allowing mosquitoes to sneak through as well. Outside the tent were a few Tupperware tubs containing dried and canned food, a small library, and a collection of goofy wigs and disguises. Underneath the treehouse was a large cargo net. On hot afternoons I would swing down onto that cargo net and spend hours lying on my back, feeling the warm wind move beneath me and musing about how to save the world. It didn't seem quite so far-fetched up there. With the cosmos above and death below, lofty thoughts seem to naturally sprout to fill the empty space.

The treehouse was located in a strip of forest only about a few hundred yards wide, which was squeezed, sickeningly, between a six-lane highway and a freight rail line. Cars flowed by at all hours of the day and night, creating a raging, riverine wash of noise that was broken now and then by the metallic din of passing freight trains. At times, when the air temperature and wind conspired against me, the smell of car exhaust wafted so thickly into the treehouse that I would resort to sleeping with an N95 mask clamped over my face, for fear of all those particulates. I would awake to find that, in the cold night air, a slime of dew had formed on the inside of my mask, as upon a cave wall.

Meals were sometimes brought to me by volunteers, who would deliver them to the base of the tree and clip them to the end of my haul rope. On days when no one brought food, I fended for myself, heating up cans of lentil soup or packets of vegetable curry over a camping stove. When it came time to use the bathroom, I peed into an old milk jug, which would later be emptied into a nearby stream; solid waste went into a garbage bag filled with sawdust and baking soda to kill the smell, which I hauled away at the end of each stint.

I eventually put in six shifts in the treehouse, totaling about a month, though up there it felt like much longer. At first, I struggled to find ways to fill the empty hours, then I learned to luxuriate in them. I finally read *Middlemarch*, one of those classics I'd always intended to get around to once I found the time. I also started meditating again. There was a small balcony built out on one side of the treehouse, and two or three times a day I would sit cross-legged there for the better part of an hour, with my eyes loosely focused on the young maple leaves that grew from the branches at my eye line. At times those leaves would melt together, and I would feel myself on the cusp of an Emersonian dissolution into the wild green multiplicity—and then a train horn would blast or a motorcycle engine would roar, and my concentration would be shattered, and I would be, once again, just a weird guy living in a tree.

+

A few days into my first treesit, a pair of young people arrived in the forest wearing face masks and dark clothing. They began constructing a treehouse in a nearby cottonwood. I watched as they lashed four long pine beams to the cottonwood, crosswise, like a tic-tac-toe board, then began installing a floor made out of plywood. They worked tirelessly for about six hours, moving from one branch to the next, sixty or so feet off the ground, with the angelic ease of riveters atop a skyscraper.

At one point, the male climber called down to the security guards below, advising them that they should be wearing helmets, in case anything accidentally fell on them. In bemusement, one of the security guards said to the other, "*He's* telling *me* to be careful?"

There was a long rope attaching the top of their tree to the top of mine—not a climbing rope, but the cheap, braided-plastic kind that crab fishermen use. At the end of the day, the two climbers attached mechanical ascenders to that rope and, hanging upside down like tree sloths, made the long, slow traverse over to my platform. It gave me the willies to watch. At that angle and under that amount of strain, it seemed to me the teeth of their ascenders could easily saw through the rope at any moment. But they made it safely across and seemed totally unfazed by the ordeal.

These two lithe, blithe creatures joined me on the cargo net and introduced themselves. Her name was Amanda Hehner, though here at the blockade she went by the code name "Cauliflower." He, for reasons both legal and personal, has asked me to refer to him in writing only as "Emerald." They made a dashing pair; Amanda was feline and fair-haired, while Emerald had the large eyes, thick black eyebrows, and neotonous features of an anime hero. Together, they gave off an aura of dikost and moral urgency, which made me instinctively want to join their efforts, even if it meant risking my life to do so. In an interview with a local reporter, Emerald once summarized the philosophy behind this blockade with perfect succinctness. "Treehouses are an analogy for humanity's interdependence with nature," he'd said. "Tree falls, human falls."

+

Over the coming months, when I wasn't living in the treehouse, Emerald enlisted me to act as his sidekick on various "missions." I helped him complete the construction of the second treehouse, about fifty feet from the first one. Then we built a rickety, Indiana Jones–style rope bridge between the two, so that a treesitter could walk from one treehouse to the other to evade the police. Finally, we began tying ropes to the tops of surrounding trees in the area so that a climber could, theoretically, move from treetop to treetop, like a spider. The notion of actually doing this—climbing from tree to tree, forty or fifty feet off the ground, on a length of plastic fishing rope—was so terrifying that I never even for a moment considered doing it. But Emerald was made of sterner stuff than I. He would routinely descend from the second treehouse on a rope that was about ten feet too short to reach the ground; while rappelling out of the tree, he would speed down the rope and then, at the moment when the rope ran out, he would enter a free fall, grab the tree trunk like a fireman's pole, and slide the rest of the way down, all in one unbroken motion. "The guy is a maniac," Tim once told me. "But in a good way."

Once the trees leafed out, our treehouse became invisible to passing cars, so I had the idea that we should hang a long banner reading "TMX PIPELINE STOPS HERE" from a goliath Douglas fir beside the highway. The rest of the blockaders agreed. We planned it all out for weeks: how we would climb the tree, how the banner could be designed so it wouldn't twist in the wind. Remi and I bought a long roll of teal fabric, laid it out in our friend's backyard, stenciled out the giant letters, and then filled them in with white and red paint. It dredged up fossilized memories of doing arts and crafts projects as a kid; I imagined what my kindergarten teachers would think, seeing the skills they'd taught me put to this use.

Then one evening, beneath the pale, weirdly illumined sky one finds only on a cloudy night in a very big city—the *aurora urbanus*, as it were—Emerald and I set out for the Doug fir. Ducking down so that passing cars would not spot us, we crept along the roadside until we reached the base of the tree. We used a large slingshot to fire a beanbag attached to a length of thin cord over the lowest branch in the tree, then we secured a rope to that branch. Emerald and I both tugged on it to test the branch's strength.

"I don't know," I told him. "I'd prefer the rope be on a higher branch, so that if one branch fails, the next branch will catch you."

"I think it'll be fine," Emerald said.

I watched from the shadows as he climbed the rope. When he was partway up the trunk, it began to rain lightly. Off in the distance, a white vein of lightning appeared in the lilac sky. Emerald, laughingly, called down, "What a time for lightning!"

Undeterred, he kept climbing. When he reached the lowest branch, about eighty feet off the ground, he secured himself to the trunk, before hauling up the banner, unfurling it, and fixing it in place. All this took the better part of an hour; I was amazed none of the passing cars called the police. Back on the ground, Emerald was wild-eyed with adrenaline. He explained that when he reached the branch that his rope was hanging from, he had realized that it was completely dead. This meant that while he was climbing up, it could have snapped at any moment, sending him hurtling to the ground.

We paused briefly to take some photos of the banner, billowing triumphantly in the predawn breeze. Then, whooping, we dashed off into the forest.

+

When I wasn't occupying the treehouse or hanging up protest banners, I began lending my support in other ways: attending strategy meetings, helping with social media, and using my connections in the journalism world to try to publicize our story. On this last front, I ran into more resistance than I had expected; writers and editors didn't seem as interested in our pipeline battle as I thought they would be. We had managed to get a few stories in the national media, but then interest had largely dried up. We were forced to continually ask ourselves: How do we make sure our protest—what appeared to many to be a lost cause, in an unglamorous corner of the province, organized by a small group of data-obsessed nerds, aging hippies, and penniless rock climbers—garners the attention it needs to succeed?

In a curious twist of fate, not far away, another protest movement was growing—slowly at first, and then explosively—which provided an enlightening counterpoint to our own. Over on Vancouver Island, less than a hundred miles away, a group of blockaders had been fighting to stop the felling of an old-growth forest. This battle was taking place in a grove called Fairy Creek, on the land of the Pacheedaht First Nation. The protesters, led by a charismatic Pacheedaht elder named Bill Jones, had built little utopian encampments throughout the forest, which drew in people from all over Canada. Treesits were erected and roads blocked off. An eruption of violent police crackdowns followed: The blockades were dismantled, many protesters were brutally beaten and pepper-sprayed, and the treesitters were dramatically arrested and airlifted out of the treetops in helicopters. These arrests, which were highly publicized, led to more protesters showing up, and more being arrested, which led to more crackdowns, the kind of feedback loop that every direct action protest movement seeks to achieve. By the end of the summer, it would become the largest act of civil unrest in Canadian history; one could feel it, already, being inscribed into the national mythos. Its scale and media visibility placed enormous political pressure on the provincial government to ban old-growth logging outright. In short, they were winning in precisely the ways we were not.

+

Why, I wondered, does one protest movement continually gain energy, grab attention, and achieve its aims, while another remains small, local, and doomed? Wanting to answer this riddle, I assigned myself a kind of intellectual side mission: I decided to research the history of previous treesits. I hoped that my odd skill set (the ability to tirelessly dig through archival material and shamelessly bug strangers with an endless barrage of questions) might allow me to figure out what was hampering our pipeline protest, as well as the climate movement more broadly.

I began by getting in touch with other treesitters, past and present, from all over the world. I spoke with people who had used their treesits to prevent the desecration of a sacred Native site in Humboldt County; the expansion of highways in England and Los Angeles; the widening of a parking lot in New York; and the construction of a new natural gas pipeline in West Virginia. Some of these efforts succeeded; most failed. What these protesters invariably impressed upon me was the fact that the treesit was not just about saving trees. "I'm not some tree-hugging fucking hippie," an Australian activist named Erik Hayward, who had campaigned to save old-growth forests in Tasmania, told me. "It's not necessarily about the individual trees. It's about a culture change."

One of the world's most successful treesits took place in Germany's Hambach Forest, where a group of land defenders built an aerial village of treehouses to block the expansion of a coal mine. At its height, the encampment had consisted of eighty-six treehouses, many of which were connected with rope bridges. In 2018, police swept through the area, destroying most of the treehouses, but afterward the activists immediately began rebuilding. Their aerial blockade lasted for eight years, until, in 2020, the government finally relented, declaring that the remaining forest would be preserved. More importantly, the forest had become a symbol for the larger fight against the coal industry; in July of that same year, the government, under mounting public pressure, announced a plan to phase out coal by 2038.

I spoke with a Hambach protester named Floki, a full-time blockader who scavenged his food from dumpsters and shoplifted his meager possessions. He was an anarcho-communist, an autodidact, and happily unemployed. Some of his beliefs sounded a bit naive or paranoid, but he also struck me as being wild and free in a way most people are not. I imagined that the average German citizen, visiting his forest on a weekend protest march or watching it on TV, would feel similarly.

Near the end of our conversation, I asked Floki why he thought the Hambach movement had proved so successful, compared with other blockades.

"The forest is standing more for the people as a logo," he said.

He explained that the protesters actively reached out to the public, leading tours through the forest every Sunday. Visitors, looking up at the treehouses, were reminded of childhood stories like *Peter Pan* and *Die Rote Zora und ihre Bande*, the tale of a group of children who take over an abandoned castle. By evoking these childhood memories, protesters encouraged the public to imagine a different world, a world more closely aligned with their actual desires, which gave them the courage to make political change. I thought, once again, of the image of the Korowai treehouse—how it tugged on half-forgotten yearnings from my childhood, vestigial romances, ancestral fantasies. "The treehouse is symbolic," Floki said. "It stands for more than this world."

+

My life in the treehouse was for the most part uneventful, at times eerily so. Just after my first stint as a treesitter, logging in the area was halted, because members of our group had successfully argued to regulators that it would affect the nesting season of the Anna's hummingbird, an otherworldly creature with an iridescent pink head. When the announcement was made that logging would not resume until the end of the summer, we celebrated by festooning the treehouse with paintings of hummingbirds. I found it inspiring that a tiny bird could temporarily subdue something as colossal as heavy industry. Others were less amused. One writer for the conservative-leaning *Calgary Herald* newspaper criticized the decision in an op-ed entitled "A $100-Million Hummingbird Nest and Other Trans Mountain Absurdities."

One of the strange side effects of this hiatus was that we were now protecting a forest that, for the next five months, was no longer under any direct threat. Most of the time, our tree was left unguarded by pipeline employees, so we were free to come and go at will. Stealing a page from the Hambach playbook, we organized tours so the public could visit the treehouses every Sunday, and we urged parents to bring their children along. For the average person, our thinking went, climate change and carbon capitalism seem too huge and diffuse to tackle. But if we could get children and their parents to care about our treehouse, we might be able to get them to care about the surrounding forest, and if we could get them to care about the forest, we might be able to get them to care about stopping the pipeline.

When these tours arrived, I always made a point of putting on a show for them, climbing nimbly from one part of the tree to another. When the visitors lifted their phones to take photos, I found myself assuming the same posture that Markus Nguali, the Korowai man I'd spent time with in Papua, had struck at the top of his treehouse: one hand resting ever so lightly on a higher branch, my bare toes curled prehensilely around the one beneath me. A pose, I realized, meant to convey nonchalance, comfort, and stability. *This is our true home,* it seemed to say. *Join me.*

+

Treesitters are secretive and clannish, both by nature and by necessity, which leaves them oddly invisible to the gaze of history. The most helpful information I found was in old issues of the *Earth First! Journal,* a newsletter written by activists for activists. Earth First! was founded in 1980 as a self-described "pure, hard-line, radical" environmental action group. Their logo was a raised fist; their motto: "No compromise in defense of Mother Earth." A decade prior, Greenpeace—by blocking whaling ships and nuclear test sites—had offered the public a fiercer, more confrontational alternative to the patrician inside-the-Beltway dealmakers of the Sierra Club and Save the Redwoods League. Now, Earth First! promised a yet-more-feral alternative to Greenpeace. One of the group's founders, Dave Foreman, declared, "It is time for women and men, individually and in small groups, to act heroically and admittedly illegally in defense of the wild, to put a monkey-wrench into the gears of the machine destroying natural diversity."

One of the core tenets of Earth First! was the philosophy of biocentrism, which holds that other species have the same basic right to live that we do. From the hard-line biocentric point of view, the life of a tree is worth as much as that of a human. ("Whether a tree dies or whether a man dies, in either case a living being dies and returns to the earth," wrote the biocentrist philosopher Klaus Michael Meyer-Abich.) It was not uncommon to hear biocentrists speaking of trees as having been "massacred," "slaughtered," or "butchered." This was not hyperbole; to many biocentrists, deforestation felt akin to mass murder. Of course, logically speaking, the same was true of all plants—even the weeding of a garden was, technically, a minor holocaust—but trees were special. Earth Firsters believed that the environmental crisis was synonymous with the destruction of wilderness and the spread of civilization, and deforestation was the most symbolically resonant form of that devastation.

To protect old-growth forests, Earth First! evolved a wide array of tactics, but among them, treesitting proved the most successful in drawing media attention. In large part, this was because treesitting looked so dangerous. As the essayist Olivia Laing (drawing from the work of the civil rights leader Bayard Rustin) notes, "The power of this kind of civil disobedience is directly indexed to the body's physical vulnerability. . . . The more dangerous or precarious a position the protester took, the more powerful its effect, both in terms of the publicity it generated and the cost of their removal." That danger was frighteningly real. In 1987, a man named Randy Prince, who had been living in a tree for forty-two days, was forced to descend when a logger began cutting into the trunk of the tree he was sitting in, threatening his life. In 1991, a group of treesitters in Australia were nearly killed when loggers showered the forest with napalm. In Texas, police officers chopped down a tree that an Earth Firster was perched in, severely injuring his leg. And on two occasions, treesitters have accidentally fallen to their deaths—a man named Naya in California, and a woman named Beth O'Brien in Oregon.

Dangerous, beautiful, wild: Treesitting, unlike many other forms of protest, felt like an adventurous, even spiritual, undertaking. In an issue of the *Earth First! Journal* from 1985, the writer Stephanie Mills argued that a treesit "burns in brilliant contrast to the dreary monoculture, the life of quiet desperation that is the culmination of the post-Paleolithic era." An unsigned article in a later issue of the journal framed treesitting as an extension of an ancient Indigenous way of life: "When you look into the roots of treesitting, you see natural ties between the direct action tree villages of today and the aboriginal tree peoples of New Guinea, Africa, and Indonesia."

The earliest Earth First! treesit occurred in the Millennium Grove, an old-growth forest in Oregon, in 1985, when an experienced rock climber named Mikal Jakubal decided to climb into a thousand-year-old Douglas fir after a road blockade failed. He ascended it by hammering pins into the trunk every few feet to attach a rudimentary ladder, called an etrier, and then, at around sixty feet up, he unfolded a platform called a portaledge. His attempt ultimately ended in failure—the loggers simply cut down all of the surrounding trees, and when Jakubal descended to go to the bathroom that evening, he was arrested by a pair of Forest Service officers who had been hiding nearby—but he and his fellow Earth Firsters nevertheless saw potential in the tactic.

Throughout the late 1980s and into the 1990s, as timber companies (increasingly supercharged with Wall Street money and beholden to Wall Street profit margins) scaled up their operations, treesits proliferated and evolved. By the end of 1985, treesitters in Oregon had begun to build tree "villages," clusters of five or six treesits, which could be traversed one to the other, allowing treesitters to avoid arrest and (perhaps more importantly) to ward off loneliness. By 1987, the tactic had spread to Northern California, where treesitters took up residence in the tops of towering redwoods, hundreds of feet off the ground.

At first, the appeal of treesitting was a simple equation of time and money: While a group of protesters blocking a road could be swept away in minutes by riot police wielding pepper spray, it could take hours or even days to remove a treesitter, and if the removal involved the use of a crane, it could cost up to $100,000. Treesits could also buy time for advocacy groups to file a lawsuit, for legislators to pass a new law to halt logging operations, or for private groups like Save the Redwoods League to raise money to buy the land. In response, timber companies would sometimes engage in "spite cutting," the preemptive logging of an area's most valuable trees, before a court could declare them off-limits, a tactic that further enraged activists and much of the general public.

Soon, another tactical benefit of treesitting became clear: Whether a given treesit succeeded or failed (and most failed), it nevertheless served as a powerful tool to garner media attention. Realizing this, treesitters began to haul up typewriters and, later, cell phones, so that they could communicate with the outside world. However, news outlets were fickle, and their attention span was short. Some of the treesits that gained the most attention were of the least consequence. In 1989, a group of women in California staged the world's first "all-women treesit." One of the climbers, who went by the name of Hellen Woods, later expressed disappointment with the action because it was situated in an area of second-growth forest that was under no threat of being cut down. It was purely performative. However, the stunt nevertheless drew a number of television reporters, including one from the *Today* show, who lobbed inane questions at the women, like "What are you wearing?" and "Where do you go to the bathroom up there?"

This staging was part of a larger event, orchestrated by the Earth

Firsters Darryl Cherney, Judi Bari, and Greg King, which they called a "nationwide treesit": Protesters took to the treetops in at least six states, stretching from Massachusetts to Washington. The protesters, cleverly, did not choose to only climb trees that qualified as pristine and ancient. They selected all kinds of trees, including those in third-growth forests; one of these treesits was even located in a black walnut tree in the yard of a California state assemblyman. The event was featured in *Time* magazine, then one of the nation's largest print news outlets. The story included an interview with a former logger turned environmentalist named George Atiyeh. "The forest is my church," Atiyeh told the reporter. "No one has the right to defile it, any more than I would have the right to desecrate anyone else's church." Such sentiments, rooted in an American romantic tradition dating back to Thoreau and Muir, enraptured the public, spawning more treesits, and more coverage, year after year, throughout the 1990s. The seeds of ideas planted in a prior century, patiently watered for generation after generation, were beginning to bloom.

+

As an environmental activist, the ability to become invisible—slinking through the night dressed in black, obscuring one's identity, leaving no evidence behind—is a useful talent. But the ability to become visible is a far more useful, and far more difficult, skill. In the decades-long history of treesitting, one person perfected this skill above all others: a young woman called Julia "Butterfly" Hill—a name that, in the intervening decades, has attained a kind of beatific glow.

Hill grew up mostly in Arkansas, the child of a traveling Baptist preacher. In her memoir, *The Legacy of Luna*, she describes her upbringing as strictly religious and somewhat hardscrabble, but otherwise normal. When she was twenty-two, Hill was involved in a high-speed car crash, which drove her right eye back into her skull and left her with temporary brain damage. "Having survived such a horrible accident, I resolved to change my life, and I wanted to follow a more spiritual path," Hill writes.

After ten months of rehabilitation, some friends invited her along on a road trip to the West Coast. While there, she walked through a redwood forest for the first time and experienced a kind of religious epiphany. First she burst into tears, then she began to laugh. "Surrounded by these huge, ancient giants, I felt the film covering my senses from the imbalance of our fast-paced, technologically dependent society melt away," she recalls. "I walked out of the forest a different woman."

Hill returned to California the following year and, having made up her mind to dedicate her life to forest protection, soon became involved with Earth First! One day, a protest organizer announced that they needed someone willing to stage a treesit in a one-thousand-year-old redwood they'd nicknamed Luna, which was slated to be cut.

Hill volunteered.

"I need somebody for at least five days," the man said.

That sounded like a long time to Hill, but she nevertheless agreed.

Hill hiked all day over muddy, mountainous terrain to reach Luna. She spent that night huddled under a tarp, "wet to the bone and freezing cold." Then, at dawn, she slipped on a tattered rock-climbing harness ("which had *duct tape* on it!") and climbed the 180-foot-long rope up to her new home. Tentative at first, she soon grew comfortable living high above the ground; she learned to move around the tree freely, without any rope to catch her, climbing all the way to its topmost spire. She preferred to climb barefoot, she writes, because it allowed her to feel which branches could support her weight. To purify her spirit, she fasted and prayed for days at a time. In the end, she spent more than two straight years living in the top of Luna, braving savage winter storms, frigid nights, and hostile police, who buzzed her tree with helicopters and tried to cut off her access to food and water.

In Hill, the news media had found its ideal hero, someone possessed of a pure heart, a sharp intellect, and a dark, sylphlike beauty. She was often photographed clinging barefoot to the side of Luna, dressed all in black, like some strange hybrid of arboreal mammal and dendrite monk. Perhaps just as importantly, journalists had found their ideal villain in Hill's chief adversary, Charles Hurwitz—the Texan "junk bond king" who had acquired the family-owned Pacific Lumber Company, slashed the employees' pensions, and began ruthlessly clear-cutting their holdings of ancient forests. It was a story the world could immediately grasp: the gentle girl who lived in a tree standing firm against the cold-blooded forces of corporate greed.

By the end of her first year living in Luna, Hill had become a national celebrity. She sometimes spent ten hours a day on a radio telephone hooked up to solar panels, talking with reporters and other members of the public, and she wrote more than one hundred letters each week. She was visited in the treehouse by celebrities like Woody Harrelson and Joan Baez. She was named one of *People* magazine's "25 Most Intriguing People of the Year," and the *New York Post* (derisively) dubbed her the "queen of the tree-huggers." Though she loathed consumer culture, she possessed an innate genius for marketing. That year, she proposed that instead of celebrating Independence Day on July 4, people should begin celebrating Interdependence Day on July 3, to highlight the deep connection between humans and other species. The event spread as far as the Philippines, and in some places is still celebrated today.

By the end of her second year in the tree, Hill had successfully brokered a deal with the logging company to save Luna, including a two-hundred-foot buffer zone of forest. She had won, but more importantly, she had served as a figurehead for the efforts of thousands of dedicated volunteers—treesitters and monkey wrenchers, but also organizers and lawyers and policy wonks—who fought in quieter ways. In 1999, Hurwitz agreed to sell the Headwaters Forest, which included large swaths of intact old-growth redwoods, to the government so it could be set aside as a reserve. In the ensuing years, a combination of new federal and state regulations, court rulings, and public pressure would make the clear-cutting of ancient redwoods (mostly) a thing of the past.

In the course of her protest, Hill had also brought the topic of old-growth logging—and the environmental crisis, more broadly—to the attention of people in suburbs and cities with no old trees worth saving, including into my own home, in suburban Illinois. One night, when I was in my mid-teens, my mother and I watched a special global warming–themed episode of the news program *20/20* filmed for Earth Day—I had tuned in mostly because I thought Leonardo DiCaprio, who was guest-hosting the episode, was cute—when a segment came on about Hill's protest. "This is the story of the woman who lived in a tree . . ." the segment began, precisely like a children's storybook.

I was rapt.

+

Years before I became a treesitter, I had reached out to Hill for an interview for this book, but she declined, saying that she had suffered a string of tragic accidents (the loss of her partner, another terrible car crash, the onset of a chronic illness), and she did not have the emotional energy to talk with me. I waited for a year and then wrote to her again. This time, she responded by asking me what the recycled paper content of my book was. I told her that I had no idea. "If you are able to get a contractual obligation from the publisher that they will do better than 30% recycled content, then i would do an interview with you," she wrote. "Otherwise, i would have to pass, as being a part of a book that needlessly cuts down trees to talk about the importance of trees is not in alignment with my heart's values."

I wrote to my publisher, asking if they'd grant this request. It took yet another year for them to say yes. By this point, I had begun treesitting, and I was brimming over with questions to ask her.

Finally, one sunny day, I met Hill for coffee at a cute little sidewalk café in Sausalito, California. She had driven there in a solar-powered van, which she lived out of. She had a head of bright silver hair, and she walked stiffly, because she was wearing a back brace, which she called her "exoskeleton." Only by squinting could I recognize her as the nimble girl who once routinely climbed to the topmost spire of a redwood tree to pose for photographers in passing helicopters.

Her personality, too, did not quite align with the image I had of her in my head—she was bawdier, for one thing, and darker, and weirder. She said she hears this often. "I'm a wild human being," she said. "I'm very goofy. I'm very intense. I curse like a sailor and I pray to trees."

She confided in me that much of the image people had of her was not entirely true. For one thing, her upbringing was considerably rougher than she'd previously let on. At the age of seven, she was sexually assaulted by a neighbor boy. (She recalled that when she informed her parents about the attack, her mother scolded her for being "lascivious.") Hill began suffering from depression, which at one point became so severe that she attempted suicide. By the time she was sixteen, she was living on her own and self-medicating with various drugs, including methamphetamine. "The fact that I'm still on the planet is kind of remarkable," she said.

Hill told me she intentionally left these darker aspects of her personality out of her book because she wanted to maintain a relatable image for the public. As a figurehead for the environmental movement, she felt the need to be above reproach; any wrinkle or stain in her otherwise angelic image was perceived to be a flaw in the movement itself. But in the intervening decades, the media's gaze, like the roving eye of Sauron, had moved on—at that moment, it had settled on a young woman in Sweden named Greta Thunberg—so Hill no longer felt compelled to hide the more painful aspects of her past or her present. "Whenever I do question-and-answer periods, I always tell people, you can ask me anything you like and I won't get offended, because getting offended is a personal choice and I choose not to make it," she said.

Her treesit, too, had not been as idyllic as it had been portrayed in the press. She believes she has lasting emotional scars from the experience. While she was in Luna, the loggers began felling the surrounding trees, and Hill was forced to witness their demise. Her abnormally strong sense of empathy, which had driven her to environmental action in the first place, now became a liability; she said that, watching chainsaws cutting into the trunks of those ancient trees, she could feel them ripping into her own body.

Her life after the treesit had been almost as difficult as her life before it. Immediately after descending from the branches of Luna, Hill embarked on a yearslong public advocacy campaign in support of various environmental causes, which she found exhausting and disenchanting. Then, the following year, she learned that someone, in an act of extreme malice, had taken a chainsaw and attempted to cut down Luna—perhaps the living entity that Hill loved more than any other. Thankfully, the tree was eventually doctored back to health. My friend Steen visited Luna once and texted me photos of its gashed trunk, which had been bolted together with a steel plate. It, like Hill, now has its own exoskeleton.

Today, Hill runs a nonprofit environmental outreach organization called Circle of Life, and she offers life-coaching services. But much of her time appeared to be spent managing the pain resulting from multiple car accidents and a rare disorder called Ehlers-Danlos syndrome, which causes connective tissues to loosen and deteriorate. Her body, which had once taken her to the top of a two-hundred-foot-tall redwood, could now barely walk for ten minutes at a time. (We had originally planned to go for a hike through the redwoods of Muir Woods that day, but she was in too much pain.)

Though I should have come away from this meeting depressed, the darkness in Hill's present circumstances was offset by the brightness and warmth of her intellect. I ended our conversation by asking whether she has any hope for our collective future. Are humans doomed to continue overconsuming until we kill ourselves off, and much of the rest of the planet? Does human nature leave any hope for nature?

"I don't like to talk about hope," she said. "Because when people hear there is hope, they use that as an excuse to not get off their asses and do something. And when they're told there is no hope, that's an excuse to not get off their asses and do something!"

She paused, staring at a copse of stone pines down by the sea, bent over by the wind.

"Hope exists only in this moment," she went on. "*Am I creating hope in this moment or am I not?* That's all there is. Everything else is just a myth we make up to try to manage being alive."

+

My time living in the treetops was both less sublime and less arduous than Hill's. It passed in discrete increments, broken up by trips back home, where I would swim in the sea and go for long trail runs through the forest, relishing my newfound freedom.

When I was stationed in the treehouse, I tried my best to ignore the roaring highway and instead appreciate the forest for its beauty, corrupted as it was. On my hikes in, I stopped to admire bumblebees drunkenly lolling in the purple, vulval blooms of invasive Himalayan balsam. From my treetop platform, I watched as the maple's leaves unfurled, grew to dinosaurian proportions, and then, during the later months, yellowed, crinkled, and desiccated. It was an unusually hot summer. I watched in awe and alarm as the moss that covered the branches came to resemble the rough side of a kitchen sponge, while the detritus on the forest floor attained the antiheft of dried corn husks.

Halfway through the summer, a cloud of wildfire smoke wafted up from California and settled over Vancouver. I happened to be occupying the treehouse that week, a bad piece of luck. It was one hundred degrees for a number of days, and the smoke was so thick that the air-quality app on my phone informed me that the simple act of breathing had become "dangerously unhealthy"; the little cartoon icon, which normally wore a cloth mask when the air was bad, now bore a gas mask. Wearing two soggy N95 masks, one atop the other, I lay on my back most of the day, sweating and shooing flies. In the west: a Beijing sun. Despite the heat, our list of volunteers grew; people brought me ice packs and thermoses of chilled mint tea. The public seemed to intuitively understand that the combination of smoke and heat we were suffering was a foretaste of exactly the future we were fighting to prevent.

During this Tartarian fug, I plucked a book out of our little treehouse library called *How to Blow Up a Pipeline*, by Andreas Malm. Its title was so incendiary that I felt uncomfortable even speaking it aloud, and I worried that I would be discreetly photographed holding it and later prosecuted as a terrorist. But in truth, once I began reading it, I discovered that the title was something of a coy misdirect. The book provides no concrete instructions for ecotage; rather, it is a philosophical examination into whether such acts should be committed. Malm is openly in support of property destruction (which he doesn't view as violence, since property is not alive). "At what point do we escalate?" he asks. "When do we start physically attacking the things that consume our planet and destroy them with our own hands? Is there a good reason we have waited this long?"

Malm believes that the time for destruction (of pipelines, of coal mines, of private jets and helicopters and luxury SUVs) is long past due. I came away unconvinced. My understanding of social movements, like so many things, is arborescent: I believe that radicals have a place in the movement just like mainstream and even conservative environmentalists, and that the movement is well served by a wide diversity of tactics. The problem with property destruction, it seems to me, is not that it is inherently unethical. (Even the most ardent pacifist would not feel guilty for, say, destroying the weapons depot of an invading army.) The problem is that in adopting tactics of destruction, a social movement—which is wholly unlike a guerrilla army, a distinction Malm largely fails to make—loses the moral and symbolic high ground. Instead, protesters enter a battle based solely upon physical force, which the armies of industry, who have both money and the police state on their side, will almost invariably win. This is precisely what happened, beginning in the 1990s, when a yet-more-radical group, known as the Earth Liberation Front, began blowing up car dealerships and ski resorts. The car dealerships and ski resorts were rebuilt, likely using insurance money, whereas some of the activists responsible for the bombings were sent to prison for decades. To my knowledge, no people were ever hurt in these bombings, and yet the use of explosives and the specter of violence allowed the Right to paint anyone halting the expansion of heavy industry as "ecoterrorists." This same pattern repeated itself in 2022, when a group of masked radicals broke into a pipeline facility in northern BC and used axes to smash machinery, including two dump trucks; the activists (who, having escaped arrest, remain unidentified) were subsequently branded by the premier of Alberta as "foreign funded eco-terrorists."

Earlier that spring, we had experienced a taste of this kind of smear campaign, albeit in miniature. One day, someone in our group noticed that a laminated sign had been quietly attached to one of the trees near the treehouse. The text read: "Many of these trees are inoculated to protect them from greed." It went on to explain that galvanized steel spikes had been inserted into the trees to prevent them from being cut down. It was signed "Dr. Anonymous."

The "spiking" of trees, a tactic dating back to the early days of

Earth First!, involves pounding a nail or metal rod into the tree's trunk so that, when the tree is cut down and run through a sawmill, there is a high risk of the nail destroying the saw. Unfortunately, the nail could also destroy the person using the saw, which is why this tactic has since largely been abandoned in the intervening decades.

Though everyone in our movement vehemently denied putting up this sign, I knew it was not outside the realm of possibility that some roving eco-punk had decided to spike the trees in our forest without our knowledge. But I found the sign itself highly suspicious. For one thing, it didn't even sound like something we would write, because it didn't criticize the pipeline or mention climate change. In fact, the text read like it had been written by someone whose understanding of the environmental movement had fossilized back in the '90s. The text was eerily similar to a line attributed to Paul Watson, the famed eco-radical, in *Earth First! Journal* in 1990: "In a biocentric context, tree-spiking is simply a form of preventive medicine. It is the inoculation of a tree against the disease of logging."

Among our cohort, it was widely agreed upon that the sign was posted by someone attempting to discredit our movement, and that, in all likelihood, no trees had been spiked at all. It made sense why our opponents would choose this tactic. Our conflict was largely one of images and ideas, a semiotic war played out in the mirrored hall of mass media, and in that realm, tree spiking was an almost perfect symbolic inversion of treesitting. Tree spiking was an act of sabotage, committed in darkness; treesitting was a peaceful protest, carried out in the daylight. Tree spiking summoned images of guerrilla warfare; treesitting was reminiscent of the sit-ins of the civil rights era. Tree spiking damaged the tree and potentially killed one's enemies; treesitting involved risking one's own life to save that of the tree. And, as a rule, tree spiking alienated members of the general public, while treesitting inspired them. In short, the treesitter takes the high road; the tree spiker, the low.

One day in August, a news crew arrived from the CBC to celebrate the one-year anniversary of the treehouse occupation. They shot photos of me from the ground, wearing a black medical mask to hide my face, standing on the branches of the tree. My photo later appeared on the CBC website, referring to me as "an unnamed protester." The longer I stared at this photograph, the more I felt the uncomfortable weight of my own symbolism, as a person. I scrutinized my face, my body, my unremarkable clothes, my nondescript haircut, and wondered whether I would inspire me to climb a tree, the way Julia Butterfly Hill had inspired me as a young person.

To be truly effective, the treesitter must be someone the public can incorporate into their private dreams and public debates, someone who stands for something. This elevated stature invites enormous scrutiny, and it inevitably results in ad hominem attacks that seek to discredit the movement as a whole. But this strange semiotic aspect to treesitting, and of the environmental struggle more broadly, ultimately works to our advantage. The beauty of wild landscapes intertwine with the bodies of those trying to save them, creating something mythic. And beauty, I came to understand, was the one arrow in our quiver that our enemies wholly lacked.

+

Eventually, my excavations into the history of treesitting led me to a foundational figure who'd been largely forgotten to environmental history, for reasons that I would only later come to understand.

As best I could tell, the origins of the modern act of treesitting could be traced back to a man named Stephen Tamatea King, also known as the "Barefoot Botanist." (He's unrelated to the famed horror writer.) In 1978, when faced with the imminent logging of the Pureora Forest on the North Island of New Zealand, King, then in his mid-twenties, climbed up a vine to reach high into the branches of a giant totara tree and strung up a wooden pallet to sit on. Five of his allies, including his nineteen-year-old brother, Bernard, and his twelve-year-old brother, Sam, did likewise. They camped out in the Pureora Forest for about a week, climbing back up and down whenever they felt the trees were threatened. Normally, treesitters strive to make themselves highly visible, both to loggers and to the media, but King and his allies ingeniously inverted this tactic: When they were in the treetops, they revealed their location only to reporters, but remained hidden whenever loggers were nearby, so the loggers never knew which tree they were in and therefore couldn't cut down any trees without fear of killing someone. At one point, the loggers, believing that the protesters were bluffing, felled a tree that stood within ten yards of the one that King's little brother, Bernard, was hiding in. Bernard stuck his head out of the branches and called down to the loggers, letting them know they could have killed him. The loggers, horrified, halted all cutting for the day. A public outcry ensued, and the logging was called off a week later. That forest was later made part of a national park and is now preserved in perpetuity.

One winter, on our way home from Australia, Remi and I flew to New Zealand to visit that forest with King. We drove with him down from his home in Dargaville, five and a half hours south, to the Pureora Forest, where we found stands of giant trees, their bark painted electric green with tiny mosses and lichens, as well as huge tree ferns, which, rising high above our heads, fragmented into trippy fractals. We hiked to the base of the tree King had first climbed, a towering totara, which he called the TV Tree (because it was easily accessible to television crews). This one was as wide as a one-car garage, with a flaky, rippling trunk and, at the ends of each outstretched limb, sprays of tiny needles—a pale antipodean cousin to the coast redwood.

King's friend, a professional arborist, rigged up a rope, and King and I climbed it together. We settled on a large crook between the main branches, atop a plush carpet of moss, amid a spiky aerial garden of epiphytic ferns, a hundred or so feet off the ground. Leaning out over the branches at perilous angles, King took dozens of photos of the forest floor below, pausing now and then to wipe his smudged camera lens with the hem of his red Hawaiian shirt, until his battery died. Then (and only then), he set aside his camera and commenced to answer my endless questions, charting the course of a life devoted wholly to the task of wilderness preservation.

During the course of our interview, which eventually stretched out over a week, King revealed himself to be in some ways the prototypical environmental activist, and in other ways an unusual, even grotesque, character. He had long hair, a scraggly beard, a sun-reddened face, and the large, flat, splayed, deeply calloused feet of someone who has gone barefoot his entire life, which he had. He drank copious amounts of raw milk, which he filched from a dairy near his house. He talked volubly and somewhat self-aggrandizingly, and every ten seconds or so, he let out a honking, asthmatic wheeze. On our drive south to Pureora, for luggage, he had brought along only a small black garbage bag full of clothes, a whole watermelon, and a rusty carving knife. We stopped intermittently along our drive so he could collect wild foods and show us some of his favorite plants. He knew the English and Maori names for them, as well as their uses: flax (for making rope), plantain (for making bandages), a tree called the tutu (for treating arthritis). He had a strong preference for native plants, which he called "real." Species from elsewhere he referred to as "rubbish."

Following his victory in Pureora, King had waged successful campaigns to preserve other old-growth forests. In 2001, he helped secure a nationwide ban on old-growth logging. He subsequently turned his attention to two related missions: restoring disturbed areas like farms and ranches to native forest, and winning land rights back for the Maori people. One of his most creative ventures was something called the Millennium Forest. In the year 2000, he climbed a number of two-thousand-year-old kauri trees to collect their seeds, then he planted them on land he was attempting to restore. Those trees, he said, would reach full maturity by the year 4000—a mind-bending prospect. Oddly, as a staunch if unorthodox Christian, he also believed in the prophecy of the end-times. "Some people say to me, 'Why the heck are you interested in conservation when the world is going to end tomorrow? Why are you interested in growing trees that will take a thousand years to grow—doesn't that seem like a paradox?'" he said. "But you also live today, the same as you would a thousand years ago. It's the boss's land; we need to respect his place and his space."

King was full of these kinds of paradoxes. He was fluent in the latest ecological science, but he cherry-picked the findings he liked and discarded the parts that he didn't (such as the overwhelming evidence of anthropogenic climate change, which he distrusted).

Part of me was charmed by this complex, mischievous, hirsute little man, who had spent his life trying to save trees and secure land for the region's Indigenous people. But after spending a week with him, driving all over the North Island, I began to notice that King's natural philosophy bled over into his political philosophy in disturbing ways. For example, his preference for pristine, ancient landscapes made up of native species led him to support radically restricting immigration, to protect the "native" New Zealand culture from outsiders, like Asians, who he believed contributed little to the country. He defined "native" New Zealanders, rather self-servingly, as both Maori and white people. (King himself was a white, fifth-generation New Zealander whose father, a Christian missionary, had given him a Maori middle name and taught him the Maori language as a child.) Likewise, as a strong proponent of biodiversity, he argued that the best way to maintain human diversity was through ethnonationalism. "There's a need for ordinary Western

Europeans to stand up and say actually this is our culture, and we're proud of this," he said. At the same time, he supported Christian missionaries, despite their tendency to homogenize local belief systems. And though he was skeptical of strong government oversight (which he believed inevitably devolved into useless bureaucracy), he expressed warm sentiments for right-wing authoritarian leaders like Vladimir Putin. (When King voiced his admiration for Putin during our drive, Remi acidly replied that if King tried to live in Russia as he had in New Zealand—thwarting industrialists and mocking the nation's leaders—he'd likely end up in the trunk of a car with a bullet in his head.)

King's overarching philosophical approach was to filter the world through a polarized lens, sorting everything into the dual categories of the natural and the unnatural. When faced with a tricky decision about whether something was the one or the other, he defaulted to his Christian worldview. He also viewed people (and all other living things) as "naturally" belonging in one place or another, except for white Christians, whom he seemed to tacitly view as the rightful custodians of the whole earth. This made for a strange new ideology, one that I expect to see more of in the decades to come: the perverse offspring of ethnonationalism and ecological purity, what is sometimes (rather blurrily) called "ecofascism."

Looking at King's generation of environmental protesters, one sees how a "love of the earth," that most innocuous of phrases, can turn sinister. The Earth First!–era biocentrists were notorious for their misanthropy, which could often shade into open racism. Foreman famously advocated allowing people in Ethiopia to starve, while Chris Manes (writing under the pen name "Miss Ann Thropy") wrote, "As radical environmentalists, we can see AIDS not as a problem, but a necessary solution." Echoing these sentiments, the biologist Wayne H. Davis proclaimed, "Blessed be the starving blacks of Mississippi with their outdoor privies, for they are ecologically sound." To lift their standard of living, he suggested "fertility control"—an ominous term, given the history of forced sterilizations of Black people in America.

The rot of racial oppression extends down into the very roots of the conservationist movement. As Greg King discusses in his book *The Ghost Forest*, among the board members of the Save the Redwoods League in the first half of the twentieth century were a shocking number of eugenicists, racists, and Nazi sympathizers. King shows how the eugenicists' understanding of plant heredity—the way that, say, an apple tree could be tweaked into a hundred new varieties—informed their views of the perfectibility of human genetics and the immutability of racial categories. The status of certain "apex" species, like redwoods, was equated with the status of the white race, which was seen as similarly noble, towering, and endangered. The most notorious figure among the founders of the Save the Redwoods League was a man named Madison Grant, the author of *The Passing of the Great Race*, who defended the logic of slavery and argued in favor of eugenics. Adolf Hitler once called Grant's book his "Bible," and the Norwegian ecofascist terrorist Anders Breivik cited it as one of his inspirations to commit mass murder. Breivik, in turn, went on to inspire another ecofascist named Brenton Tarrant, to enter a pair of mosques in Christchurch, New Zealand, and slaughter fifty people. In a manifesto he published online, Tarrant bemoaned "rampant urbanization and industrialization, ever expanding cities and shrinking forests, a complete removal of man from nature, with the obvious results." He went on to declare: "The Europe of the future is not one of concrete and steel, smog and wires but a place of forests, lakes, mountains and meadows. Not a place where english [sic] is the defacto [sic] language but a place where every European language, belief and tradition is valued. Each nation and each ethnicity was melded [sic] by their own environment and if they are to be protected so must their own environments." What is most disturbing about these parts of his manifesto is how reasonable they sound, when divorced from the larger context. It is chilling to consider how easily a sincere environmentalist with a purist cast of mind can slide into genocidal thinking.

One afternoon, while we drove south along the highway, King began sharing his thoughts on homosexuality, which, like many of his beliefs, were rooted in a muddy mixture of ancient scripture, modern ecology, and personal eccentricity. He didn't know that Remi and I were married to one another (he thought Remi was merely my photographer), so he felt free to express his true feelings on the matter, which was that homosexuality was "an aberration" and that gay parents adopting children was a form of "child abuse."

At the mention of child abuse, Remi's hands tightened around the steering wheel until his knuckles glowed white. I knew exactly what he was thinking. King's choice of words was supremely ironic, since a few years earlier, we both knew, the police had raided King's home and found child pornography on his computer. When I later asked King about the details of his arrest, he did not deny having downloaded the abusive material, but he initially chalked it up to nothing more than "curiosity." Then, he attempted to contextualize it within biblical history. "Joseph would be in court these days, because he married a girl of fourteen," he said. He found it absurd that homosexuality was now condoned, but child marriage was condemned, when the norms had once been exactly reversed. Ours, he said, is a "strange society."

Following his arrest, King was largely shunned by his former allies in the environmental and Maori communities, which had further isolated and embittered him. "Somehow I've gone from being King David to a leper," he sighed.

Compassionate people tend to care about the welfare of trees. But, as King demonstrates, caring about trees does not automatically make a person compassionate. Indeed, precisely because trees are such powerful symbols, they can also serve as powerful tools of obfuscation and division. The Nazis loved trees of all kinds, especially the hearty Germanic oak. Their "eternal forestry" system was the most progressive silviculture program in the world and, at the same time, a razor-clear metaphor for their homicidal view of humanity: It fostered the natural regrowth of native species, which were then meticulously cleansed of weaklings and invasives, all with an eye to improving the fitness of the forest as a whole. Proclaimed one prominent Nazi, "Ask the trees, they will teach you how to become National Socialists!"

Trees are beautiful things, but not all who love forests have beautiful souls. What I learned from my time with King is that loving wilderness but hating humans will, in the end, leave a man withered and cruel. Hard though it can be sometimes, one must learn to love both.

+

For months, a strange sense of calm had pervaded the forest. Even after they were legally allowed to begin cutting the trees again, the pipeline company held off. We could tell that the treehouse was being surveilled, both by the police and by a special unit known as C-IRG—whom we called "the green men," because they dressed in military fatigues rather than police uniforms—which the province had put together specifically to combat environmental protesters. It was clear that a plan was being formulated, but whatever it was, it was slow to materialize.

Finally, one day in September, the siege began. They started by erecting a blue steel fence around all of the areas in the forest where they planned to cut, including around our treehouse. Then they rolled in a massive white "bucket truck" with a long mechanical arm—picture the mythic offspring of an army tank and a fire truck—which they used to lift men with chainsaws high above the ground so they could fell trees from the top down.

We called this machine the Tank.

Once the Tank had cleared a path to within a few hundred feet of our treehouses, we mobilized our supporters to show up the following morning and march in protest. A seventy-nine-year-old woman named Catherine slipped through a gap in the fence and sat down in front of the Tank, before being hauled away on a stretcher by police. (When the pipeline workers discovered her impeding their work, I overheard one of them snark, "Are we calling the cops or the bus to the old folks' home?") Then a few of us created a diversion so that a young protester named Zain could sneak in and lock himself to a concrete block we'd secretly buried, days earlier, deep in the ground. That night, we erected two hammocks high in the trees, where we stationed protesters, with their safety lines attached to fallen logs. Because their lives would be put at risk by any machines moving through the area, it took the police days to carefully extricate them.

What was baffling (and, indeed, perversely frustrating) was how gently the police were handling these arrests. At the old-growth logging protests in Fairy Creek, the police had been notoriously brutal, often pepper-spraying protesters directly in their eyes and mouths. Those abuses caused outrage, which inspired more protesters to show up. But here, the police had adopted the calm, slightly imperious demeanor of Nurse Ratched dealing with a mental patient. As Gandhi and Martin Luther King Jr. both argued, part of the logic behind nonviolent protest is to reveal the violent nature of one's enemy. Our opponents, apparently, knew this all too well. There was something deeply creepy about the feeling of the State slowly, gently surrounding us, like an enormous and very soft hand, and slowly, gently beginning to squeeze the life out of us, so slowly and so gently that almost no one outside our movement realized it was happening.

Nevertheless, by the third day of the siege we had managed to assemble perhaps two dozen people on the far side of the steel fence to chant, sing, beat drums, and taunt the tree fellers. The tone was heated but surprisingly civil. "Oil is war!" shouted one protester. "This is unceded Indigenous land," said another. An older man showed up and began blaring out a tune on a bagpipe. "This is a song from my seventh grandson, who will have to live with your shit!" he shouted. The pipeline workers, who were visibly agitated by our taunts, occasionally shouted back. One of them told us to get a job, or, at the very least, to let them do theirs. "You're all a bunch of hypocrites," said another. "How did you get here today? Did you drive?"

Some of them made fair points. The oil would go to market on a train if not in a pipeline, they argued, and if it didn't come from us, it would come from Russia. These arguments tended to combine frugality with futility; it was the familiar logic of scarcity, of zero-sum. Our arguments, by contrast, hinged on hope and outrage, in terms that sometimes felt a bit nebulous or simplistic to me. It was impossible to explain the totalizing nature of carbon capitalism while shouting through a fence, so instead we shouted, "No new pipelines!"

At one point, I watched as a First Nations woman named Kelilah made an impassioned speech to a pipeline worker about the ways that the oil industry hurt Indigenous women in particular—the rapes and murders that result from man camps, the miscarriages and cancer that result from poisoned water, the ongoing loss of cultural heritage. It seemed to move him more than any of our bumper sticker microdiatribes about destroying the earth.

"What do you think I should do?" the worker asked her.

"Hop the fence!" she replied. "Quit your job! Implore other people to quit their jobs!"

It was clear from the expression on his face that this was not an option for him. He remained on his side of the fence.

Justin Trudeau once justified the continuation of tar sands extraction with the remark that "no country would find 173 billion barrels of oil in the ground and leave them there." And yet, climate scientists were telling us, leaving that oil in the ground was precisely what needed to happen. In an influential essay entitled "The New Abolitionism," the political commentator Chris Hayes calculates that when slavery was abolished, Southern plantation owners lost around $10 trillion worth of wealth (adjusted for inflation). That was the price they were forced to pay to achieve a more equal, less monstrous society. The current value of Canada's untapped oil wealth, meanwhile, totals around $7 trillion. That is the sacrifice we blockaders were asking the nation to make in order to ensure the stability of the earth.

Sacrifice is an easy thing to demand. Where it becomes difficult is in deciding who must make that sacrifice. The pipeline worker on the other side of the fence evidently didn't want to sacrifice his job any more than I wanted to sacrifice my residency. But to demand that sacrifice of any one individual is to miss the point of collective struggle. The sacrifice required is too enormous for any one person to bear. One could live a life of saintly ecological purity, eating only wild nettles until one's skin turned green, as the Buddhist saint Milarepa is said to have done, and still the world would continue to warm. One could even douse oneself in gasoline and set oneself on fire—as two men have done, on two separate occasions, in recent years—and the public would merely gawk in horror for a moment, and then move on. The overarching goal of the climate movement, in other words, is not to demand acts of martyrdom from everyday people. The goal is to sacrifice carbon capitalism itself, and to supplant it with something wiser, so that, at long last, ecological action will not be synonymous with sacrifice.

+

By day four, I was beginning to feel cautiously hopeful that our blockade might actually succeed; each day, we managed to recruit more volunteers, and the news media was beginning to take notice. That morning, the Tank had reached within a few yards of the westernmost of our two treehouses, where Emerald was stationed. Before the Tank could reach the base of the tree, Emerald clipped on to a plastic rope attached to another nearby tree and swung himself out into open space, then pulled himself across. The Tank could not fell that tree as long as Emerald was in it, but the police knew that as soon as they attempted to arrest him, he could simply traverse back to the treehouse, playing a game of cat and mouse eighty feet in the air. The Tank eventually retreated, and a cheer went up through our supporters.

The following day, the turnout on our side was even higher; it seemed that the final showdown was imminent. Around noon, the Tank once again attempted to advance to the base of our treehouse, and once again Emerald valiantly traversed into a neighboring tree. Only this time, by a terrible stroke of luck, his movements jostled loose a dead branch that had been suspended in the canopy (what loggers call a widow-maker), which fell, landing directly on the head of a pipeline worker down below. The worker, who was fortunately wearing a helmet, was briefly knocked unconscious. Within an hour, a police officer was announcing through a bullhorn that Emerald was being charged with assault and that if he didn't come down willingly, they would add a charge of resisting arrest. Emerald, with few options left, rappelled down to earth. The police cuffed his hands behind his back and dragged him off to jail.

In the aftermath of this arrest, the energy left our movement, like a sail that begins to luff and then goes slack. Most of our supporters drifted home, dejected. A core group of us gathered in an attic apartment in Vancouver, and held a strategy meeting. We had run out of volunteers who were willing to be arrested, and we had no other way of stopping the Tank from felling the rest of the trees. Our only hope was to station someone in both treehouses, on the off chance that it would buy enough time for us to regroup. It was decided that Tim would occupy the newer treehouse. I reluctantly volunteered to occupy the older one. No one else was free to do so—some had jobs to work; others had previous arrests. The arrangement was less than ideal. Tim didn't want to be arrested because it would ruin his plans to perform another treesit farther along the pipeline's proposed route. I didn't want to be arrested, for fear that I would get kicked out of the country. So we agreed that we would hold off the police as long as we could, and then, at the last possible moment, we would simply run away. It was not the most courageous plan, but it was the only one we had.

The following day, Tim and I took our places in the treehouses. Expecting the police to arrive within hours, we readied ourselves to summon volunteers to rally around the treehouses once more. But the police didn't make a move that day. The same thing happened on the second day. It was a clever tactic: Since we didn't know what day our opponents would show up, we couldn't organize a rally, and since we couldn't organize a rally, we couldn't inspire the kind of feedback loop of violent repression that would get media attention and swell our ranks. They were killing us with kindness.

The next day was a Monday. We figured they would come then, since most of our supporters would have to be back at work, but again they didn't arrive. It rained hard for most of that day, the kind of cold, ferrous rain that squeezes your temples and makes your teeth ache. I hid in the treehouse, in my sleeping bag, in a grim, gray mood. Around five, the sun broke through the clouds, a beery-yellow light that made the leaves glint like glass. Tim called me and invited me to cross the rope bridge that connected our two treehouses so that I could join him for a drink.

"Who knows, this might be our last night up here," he said.

I reluctantly agreed.

I slipped on my harness, put on a climbing helmet, then swung out onto the rope bridge. It was terrifying: The rungs were slick with rain and the bridge wobbled sickeningly with each step. I remained clipped into the rope handrail as I made my way forward so there was no chance of me dying, but that was cold comfort to my lizard brain. As I made my way awkwardly across, some forty feet in the air, a pair of security guards down below pointed high-powered flashlights at me and filmed me with their phones, hoping, I assumed, that I would fall, get tangled in the rope bridge, and require a humiliating rescue operation.

Eventually I made it to the other side, slick with a mix of rain and sweat.

"Welcome!" Tim said, giving me a hug.

I sat on a plastic bucket Tim had set out for me, while he sat on the far side of the platform in his sleeping bag, heating up a can of lentil soup. I sipped bourbon from a blue tin cup as the adrenaline in my veins dissipated. To the west of the treehouse, I could now look out over the progress the pipeline workers had made so far. A corridor of felled trees had been cleared from here all the way to the nearest highway overpass. The Tank now had a straight route to us from where it was parked, just beyond.

"So what do you think?" I asked Tim. "Will tomorrow be the end?"

"Who knows," he said. "I've thought it was the end so many times now, and I've been wrong."

The sun sank back into the clouds, like a white stone falling through silt. I wanted to stay longer, drink more whiskey, and ponder the coming days (What would we do once the treehouses were torn down? How could we possibly manage to regain any sense of forward momentum?), but I was afraid of crossing the bridge in the dark, so I roped back up and slowly, carefully made my way back. I collapsed into my sleeping bag as the rain began to fall again, and slipped into a caliginous, dreamless sleep.

I awoke at 7:30 a.m. to the insistent vibration of my cell phone. In a state of instantaneous, almost clairvoyant alertness—part of me already knew what was happening before I consciously knew it was happening—I squirmed out of my sleeping bag and retrieved it.

I opened the Signal app to find a cascade of recent messages.

"A big black cube van . . . just went in gate . . ."

"I think that is the tactical team . . ."

"Big machine moving . . ."

"Green men are here."

"Tactical team on site."

I called Tim.

"What are you going to do?" I asked.

"What we planned. I'm going to bail out," he said. "I suggest you do the same."

I hung up and began packing frantically. My heartbeat was clearly audible in my head, as rapid and insistent as the subwoofer of a passing car. *Hurry up, hurry up, hurry up . . .*

Once I'd finished packing, I poked my head out of the treehouse and watched as Tim rappelled to the ground and walked quickly away. No police officers chased him. I looked down to find three men in camouflage vests and helmets gathered under my tree, craning their necks to look up. They were soon joined by two more officers, who set up a loudspeaker to play a prerecorded recitation of the injunction. I hastily rigged a rope up so that I could rappel down outside the steel fence they had erected around my tree. With the police watching from below, I tugged my mask higher on my face, clipped into the rope, and awkwardly rappelled over the edge of the balcony. As I lowered myself down, I heard one of the police call out, "The safest way might be to come down inside the fence. We'll let you go freely!" Unfooled by this ploy (if that's what it was), I rappelled outside the fence, unclipped from the rope, crossed a nearby creek, and then dashed off into the woods.

I looked over my shoulder.

No one had followed me.

My first impulse was simply to keep running until I reached the nearest train station, go home, and sleep for a week, but I realized that someone needed to record the destruction of the treehouses and relay the footage to the news media. So I changed all of my clothes, put on a baseball cap, buried my backpack under some brush, snuck out to the highway, and then reentered the injunction zone from the far side. On my walk in, I ran into a first-time protester who was wearing a thick camel hair coat. I asked if I could borrow it, to complete my disguise. He graciously handed it over. Thus, mere minutes after running away as a masked blockader, I returned, in new garb, as a journalist, to document the destruction of the treehouse I had just been defending. I felt like Spider-Man transforming back into Peter Parker.

By this point, the Tank had reached the base of my tree. I watched as a long mechanical arm with a man-sized bucket at the end (known as a cherry picker) lifted up three C-IRG officers, who cut down the rope bridge, sliced away all of the connecting ropes, and tore through the tent. They began tossing our possessions down to earth. Books, food, ropes, mirrors, the collection of silly wigs: It all came raining down, landing in a giant heap. The very last thing they dropped was the jug of my urine, which landed on top of the pile, soaking it through.

Oddly, the one item that fell outside the fence line was a copy of *How to Blow Up a Pipeline*. I couldn't tell whether this was a warning, a taunt, or a cosmic joke.

+

I found Tim sitting on the banks of the muddy creek that ran beside the treehouse, his cheeks flushed with anger, watching the arboreal carnage unfold. As officers began dismantling the platform itself—the platform where he had lived, sweated, and shat for so many days—he shouted up at them through a megaphone.

"Hundreds died this summer in the heat waves," he said. "If this pipeline is built, millions more will die! You are killing Canadians!"

After his speech was finished, an older protester in a puffy orange jacket chided him for being too anthropocentric. "I would have liked to hear you advocate on behalf of the millions of other species who will go extinct from climate change," he said.

Tim smiled apologetically. "I'm a doctor," he replied. "I have to talk about what I know."

I sidled up next to Tim and put a hand on his shoulder.

I asked how he was feeling.

"Rough," he said. "But we're both here. We lived to fight another day." (A few weeks later, Tim would stage another treesit, in a churchyard farther along the pipeline route. He was arrested, convicted, and served a month in jail. Though his arrest garnered media attention around the country, it was not nearly enough to halt the completion of the pipeline.)

As the light faded and our few remaining supporters dispersed, I found myself wondering what this protest had all been for. I comforted myself with the thought that most blockades fail, even the most famous ones, but their effect can reverberate for decades. Given the resistance that the TMX pipeline faced, and the enormous cost it required, the desire to build new pipelines was rapidly waning. This was true in the United States as well. That year, the *Financial Post* warned that North America was becoming a "graveyard of mega pipeline projects." Resistance grows upon itself, arborescently, over time. I once spoke to a treesitter who had been arrested attempting to stop a natural gas pipeline in West Virginia. He told me he'd first become active in the climate movement by showing up to the Standing Rock blockade in North Dakota. But then again, he added, half the young blockaders he knew got their start at Standing Rock. Once you begin acting on your beliefs, it is hard to stop. And so, from the stem of a single blockade, new forms of resistance can branch out in all directions: resistance to the next pipeline, the next oil well or tar sands pit or fracking project, the next coal mine, the next attempt by myopic men to enrich themselves by plundering the past and poisoning the future.

One day, we will at last outgrow the gnarled world carbon capitalism has built. The key question is how that transformation will take place—and how fast. My time at the TMX blockade made it clear to me that direct action campaigns will never succeed in changing laws unless that action is backed up with a story powerful enough to win the public's imagination and overwhelm the brute logic of profit seeking. It does not suffice to simply be *opposed* to climate change; one must also propose a life that is better, deeper, more meaningful than the one we currently live. To change laws, one must first change people's minds—not just their opinions, but their *philosophies*. The treesitters of the Redwood Wars succeeded in drawing upon a deep well of secular nature worship, which had been accruing for centuries. But in the hotter, harsher, more chaotic climate of the new millennium, those dark green waters have grown stagnant. Something else must take its place to nourish the climate movement. Something new. Or, perhaps, something very old.

8. ROOTING

THE DAY our pipeline blockade was crushed by the police, I lingered for a long while, staring at the wreckage of our treehouse. It lay in a pile on the ground—a year of work, reduced to a chimera of plywood and plastic tarps and almost cartoonishly random objects (wigs, canned food, metal chains, climbing ropes, electronics, a bag of feces and sawdust) in a matter of hours. It was painful to look at it like that. Within a few years, the pipeline would be finished, and tankers filled with tar sands oil would begin hauling it overseas, furthering our nation's addiction to oil revenues and the world's addiction to fossil fuels.

I walked down the highway to a restaurant called House of Tofu Soup, where I balmed my melancholia with a spicy bowl of *sundubu jjigae*. I sat with a pixie-haired activist nicknamed Firestarter, who had come to the pipeline blockade from Fairy Creek, where people were still thwarting the logging of an old-growth forest.

While we ate, Firestarter scrolled through the news on their phone.

"Oh shit!" Firestarter said, suddenly brightening.

A British Columbia Supreme Court judge had just lifted an injunction against the protests at Fairy Creek, due to "serious and substantial infringement of civil liberties" by the police. The protesters could now remain in the forest without fear of arrest, so long as they weren't breaking any other laws. Videos popping up online already showed the protesters beating drums and singing in celebration. A bearded, long-haired blockader dressed in army green told a reporter he was "absolutely euphoric."

Deep in my own sense of loss, their joy was especially stark. There was a weird, almost cosmic symmetry to the fact that on the same day our blockade had suffered a great loss, theirs had enjoyed a great victory.

I mentioned to Firestarter that I would love to visit Fairy Creek, to find out what had made their movement so successful, but also just to see all of those beautiful old trees.

"I'm headed back there next week," Firestarter replied. "You should come!"

+

Around the time I started writing this book, I began noticing photos appearing on social media of clear-cut hillsides and surreally gigantic logs and stumps in British Columbia. A fury began to steadily grow—in me, and in people like me—that the province was still allowing the logging of ancient trees. As in other parts of Canada, the vast majority of the logging in BC takes place on public land, under the auspices of permits (revealingly) called "tree farm licenses"—a fact that, at least in theory, should have made it relatively easy for the government to protect most of those ancient trees with little more than the swipe of a pen. To most environmental advocates, the logic for doing so seemed equally clear: It was estimated that of the iconic, towering old-growth forests that once grew throughout the province, there was only a tiny percentage still standing.

Unbeknownst to me at the time, an American teen named Joshua Wright had begun using satellite images to monitor all the new clear-cuts appearing in the Pacific Northwest. By tracking the approval of new logging permits online, he realized that an intact old-growth forest in the Fairy Creek watershed area—a deep, damp, thickly wooded cleft between two ridges, which was reputed to be the last unlogged, unprotected old-growth valley on southern Vancouver Island—was slated to be razed next. In July 2020, he relayed what he was seeing to a group of local activists, who would later call themselves the Rainforest Flying Squad, and seventeen days later, a road blockade was formed.

The centerpiece of the blockade was a gigantic cross section of an old-growth tree that had been logged in a nearby valley, which the land defenders dropped into the center of the road. It was a perfect symbol: at once an impediment, an elegy, and a prophecy.

Before long, an unofficial leader of the Fairy Creek movement had emerged: a genial white-haired man named Bill Jones. Elder Bill, as he was known, was a member of the Pacheedaht Nation, upon whose ancestral territory the old-growth forest of Fairy Creek lay. In the symbols game being played out in the news and on social media, he became an ideal figurehead. As a former logger, he understood the intricacies of the industry, and as a Pacheedaht who had survived the residential school system, he could never be accused of being a clueless, idealistic outsider. He also spoke in a way that resonated intensely with environmentalists: projecting a broad, holistic vision of a healing earth, grounded upon Indigenous ideals. Videos posted on social media showed him standing on the front lines of the protests, dressed in a traditional red cedar bark hat. In one video he makes an impassioned speech to unblinking, masked police officers. "We have to find a better and more wholesome solution to our thing we call civilization," he declares. "That is why we are here."

With the road blocked by two dozen protesters and negative

attention beginning to grow, the logging company retreated. More blockades sprang up, like mushrooms, on the other roads leading to the top of the mountain. Then in April 2021, a judge ruled in favor of the logging companies and declared an injunction for the entire region surrounding Fairy Creek. Round after round of violent arrests ensued, and images of young protesters being showered with pepper spray and dragged by police down gravel roads proliferated on social media. A familiar pattern: The protest swelled; more arrests followed. By the time I showed up, nearly 1,200 arrests had been made. The blockade had already become the largest act of civil disobedience in Canadian history, and if what I was seeing on the news was any indication, it was thrillingly close to securing one of the greatest victories in environmental history: a sweeping ban on logging old trees, in one of the world's most heavily forested regions.

+

One week after the fall of the TMX treehouse, my husband and I loaded up our hatchback with some camping gear and took a ferry over to Vancouver Island. Along the way, we picked up Firestarter, as well as a bleach-headed, vibratingly energetic rascal named Monkey, who showed up carrying a backpack loaded with tree-climbing gear. His goal, he explained, was to disappear into the forest and set up some new treesits.

We drove for about two hours, through stupefyingly long stretches of second-growth conifer forest. The cool air streaming through my open window brought back a nostalgic scent memory of Christmas morning. These tree farms, when viewed through the gentle blur of a car windshield—which, it occurred to me, was the only way that most people in Canada ever interact with them—looked rather pleasant. All one saw (and smelled) was a sea of deep green.

We arrived an hour before dusk, at an encampment people simply called Roadside. Vans and cars were parked bumper to bumper. Some of the vans had clearly been there a long time; they were equipped with custom woodstoves, little metal chimneys, and jerry-rigged vestibules made of old rain tarps. Beside the road were various tents, a campfire, and a kitchen area. A hand-painted sign read: "Respect Your Elders!" I recalled that Julia Butterfly Hill had hung a sign bearing the same message from the top of Luna. But here, the message acquired a double meaning. It was a call to respect the ancient trees, but also to respect the ancestral owners of this land.

Firestarter and Monkey, both of whom had been here before, jogged off on their separate missions. Remi and I stood in the parking lot, feeling like the new kids in school. We wandered into the "intake area," an open-air tent with a small fire at the center. People in raincoats, young and old, milled around, performing various chores. Many covered their faces with scarves or medical masks, for fear of police surveillance. An older woman with a constellation of small blue dots tattooed across her cheeks greeted us brusquely, then asked us to hang up some red dresses—a symbol for the thousands of missing and murdered First Nations women and two-spirited people in Canada—on a nearby tree. This was the ethos at Fairy Creek: You got there, and then you got to work.

Within a few minutes of our arrival, one of the blockaders pulled up to the encampment in a pickup truck and announced some bad news. A judge, he said, had just reinstated the injunction in this area.

The information spread through the camp like a hard wind across a flat lake. Suddenly everyone was in motion.

Remi looked at me.

"What does that mean, exactly?" he asked.

"It means we can be arrested just for being here," I said.

"What do you want to do?" Remi asked.

I thought about it for a moment.

"Help out, I guess," I said. "We've come this far."

The blockade was already mobilizing. Decisions rippled invisibly across the camp, amassing into waves of organized action, which swept us up in turn. Remi, who had arrived intending just to drop me off and then head home, volunteered to help retrieve a cache of blockading hardware (chains, locks, PVC pipes, and the like) that had been hidden in a distant corner of the forest. I was conscripted to fill in a ditch that was preventing our own trucks from getting where they needed to go. I shoveled for about two hours, while Nas's *Illmatic* thumped from a nearby pickup. My hands blistered; the blisters burst, and then the little ovoid wounds grew black with dirt.

By the time the ditch was filled in, night had fallen. Remi came back, adrenalized, from his covert mission. Moments later, we were told that a crew was forming to construct a blockade higher up the road, which would slow the advance of the police. I decided to tag along, while Remi set up the tent.

A small group of us hiked up the road, through dark woods, about a mile or so, until we ran across a cluster of protesters who were lounging around on the ground, painting one another's fingernails with sparkly pink nail polish, waiting for a critical mass of people to arrive.

While we waited, a blockader I'll call Chan told me about the various tactics used at Fairy Creek to obstruct roads. They were as creative as they were courageous: One tactic, known as a "Lorax," involved chaining oneself to a fallen tree laid across the road. Another, called a "Flying Dragon," involved dangling oneself from the end of a log that was hanging over the edge of a cliff, so that any attempt to move the log might cause the protester to fall to their death.

Talking with Chan, I began to worry that I might be of little use here. I still couldn't get arrested without risking losing my residency. They didn't seem to need my help with media outreach either. So for most of my time on the mountain, all I could offer was a pair of—soft, writerly, blistered—helping hands.

The blockade we were building that night was called a double tripod. It involved felling a number of trees to build two twenty-foot-tall tripods, and then suspending another, longer trunk horizontally between the two, like a giant rotisserie, so that a land defender could sit, airborne, atop the horizontal log. (In certain extreme instances, Chan said, the protester would affix a noose around their neck, increasing the potential danger of the extraction process and making for more dramatic photos.)

A trio of the most experienced people climbed up the hillside beside the road and began cutting down some alders, using chainsaws. The energy was frantic. Trees went slicing quietly through the darkness as they fell. We below did our best to dodge them. At one point an alder crashed down squarely on the head of a young man with floppy hair and round spectacles. Looking concussed, he was evacuated by truck to a nearby hospital.

When enough trees were felled, we lashed them together, and then all pulling in unison on a single long rope, we heave-hoed them upright. As the tripods rose, the three legs splayed and then sank into place. We dropped heavy rocks around the base of each leg, then a guy wielding a hammer began studding the legs with nails so they couldn't easily be dismantled by loggers or police.

Some consider these types of blockades hypocritical, since they require felling trees to save other trees. I heard similar complaints during our pipeline blockade. Our opponents used to tease us for the hypocrisy of driving cars (which run on oil) to blockade a pipeline (which will carry oil). One also frequently hears this accusation lobbed at politicians, who fly on airplanes to reach global climate change conferences. It seems to me that such complaints are, at best, naive, and, at worst, deliberately obtuse. The hard truth is that one must work within the confines of the present to build a different future. I'm certain that the forces of industrial extraction would prefer for environmentalists to start living in caves and traveling everywhere on foot for the sake of ideological purity. What better way to neutralize one's opponents?

Once the blockade was erected, I took a moment to admire it, standing there in the pale, eldritch light of our headlamps. It resembled some kind of ancient statue, a monument to unknown gods. In my exhausted, slightly delirious state, I couldn't imagine anything more beautiful: the product of grassroots collective action, the plain stuff of the earth elevated to the task of protecting the earth.

+

After we'd finished constructing the blockade, I walked down the logging road back to our tent, the skin on my hands burning, a light rain dancing in my headlamp like sparks of white fire. I crawled into the tent, snuggled up against Remi for warmth, and fell asleep.

Three hours later, the camp stirred to life again. I got up and dragged my creaky bones out of the tent. Though grumpy and sore, I couldn't feel too sorry for myself. Some blockaders had worked clear through the night, and continued working, zombie-eyed, well into the following day.

I had heard that people were needed in the camps higher up the mountain, so I decided to hike there. One veteran blockader said I should try to eventually reach an idyllic grove of ancient trees called Ridge Camp, at the very top of the mountain, where a smattering of treesits had been erected. "They need tree climbers up there," she said.

Remi had to get back home, so I helped him pack up the tent. I gave him a kiss goodbye and shouldered my heavy pack, crammed with camping gear and a week's worth of food. Before climbing into the car, Remi took a green wool toque from his head and placed it atop mine. "I have a feeling you're gonna need it up there," he said.

I hiked all day in an eternal rain, along logging roads studded with large rocks, past our newly erected double-tripod blockade, past the hideous charnel grounds of clear-cut hillsides, past the ruins of past blockades, past a pair of protesters' cars that had been smashed up by someone (either loggers or police, I never found out) and left there to rot. I didn't see another person for most of the day. I felt like I was walking through the ruins of one type of apocalypse or another.

I tried to imagine what would replace those clear-cut hillsides: thousands of almost identical trees, rising in unison like stalks of corn—a landscape of creepily unentangled life. If you squinted, this new forest would look similar to the old forests, but when you peered closely, you would discover that it was made up of only a few fast-growing species—pines, spruces, Douglas firs—all evenly spaced and similar sized. The understory, which should be teeming with life, would be dead, brown, and quiet. The canopy, too, would be largely free of moss and lichens. A few weeks earlier, I'd watched a YouTube video in which a longtime Fairy Creek blockader named Will O'Connell looks out over a sea of conifers planted where an old-growth forest had once stood, as if gazing into Fairy Creek's future. "It's just *trees*," he says. "There's nothing more than that."

It's just trees. I pondered this phrase as I trudged along the winding gray logging road. For decades, governments throughout the West had been clear-cutting so-called "moribund" old-growth forests, with the support of experts in scientific forestry, who argued that, contrary to appearances, clear-cutting was actually *good* for the environment because newly planted trees would sprout up quickly and absorb more carbon than the comparatively torpid ancients. It was believed that those "vibrant" new forests could later be cut down and subsequently replanted again and again, locking up more and more carbon, in the form of roof beams and bookcases and dinner tables, for decades. It looked like that rarest of things: a win-win solution. The timber companies made huge profits, loggers got decent-paying jobs, consumers got plenty of lumber, and the planet would grow a bit cooler.

The problem with this plan, from an environmental perspective, is that a forest is not the same thing as a tree farm. For one thing, newly planted trees are far more vulnerable to pests, fire, and drought than intact forests. And even if every newly planted tree survived and grew to maturity, the very act of logging would still release massive amounts of carbon. This is because most of where a forest stores its carbon, over the long term, is in the complex ecology of fungi, microbes, and minerals in the soil. When a forest is clear-cut, the soil is disturbed, and that carbon gets released. When those newly felled trees are brought to market, typically about half of them will get converted not into roof beams and dinner tables, but instead into ephemeral products—newspapers, firewood, even toilet paper—that then quickly gets converted back into CO_2. Moreover, the newly planted trees, being similarly sized, densely clustered, and nonbiodiverse, are unusually vulnerable to pest outbreaks, which, as I'd seen in California, can transform a healthy-looking landscape of green trees into a gray expanse of dead wood in a matter of months. The net result, studies have found, is that logging actually releases more carbon than it captures, even when you account for all of the new trees that have been planted. This is no small amount of carbon either; it is estimated that the logging industry in British Columbia alone is responsible for releasing as much atmospheric carbon as the nation's tar sands oil industry. (This is yet another way that our pipeline protest and the Fairy Creek blockade felt like uncanny twins.)

The distinction between a true forest *ecosystem* and *just trees* had been on my mind of late, because the logging industry's simplistic logic appeared to be spreading. Over the past year, I had watched in growing bewilderment as celebrities and multinational corporations and then entire nations acquired a sudden, feverish infatuation with tree planting as a moonshot solution to climate change. The craze began when the journal *Science* published a high-profile paper suggesting that if you add up all the slivers and swaths of unused land on earth, there was room for more than two billion acres of new forest, an area roughly the size of China. In the press, one of the paper's coauthors went on to call tree planting "by far—by thousands of times—the cheapest climate change solution." After reading this study, the billionaire tech founder Marc Benioff helped launch an ambitious new campaign to plant a trillion trees worldwide. A rash of large corporations (including Shell Oil) and national governments rushed to pledge their support. Canada vowed to plant two billion new trees. The US promised to plant more than fifty billion. China, not to be outdone, pledged to plant seventy billion. The rapid and widespread adoption of this initiative, writes the climate reporter Lisa Friedman, can largely be explained by the fact that it was "practically sacrifice-free." It wouldn't require companies or countries to transition away from mining and burning fossil fuels or to invest in renewable energy or to curb their consumption. And it wouldn't even require them to commit to not cutting down those trees at a future date, if they needed some more timber (or cash). It was a bewitchingly elegant solution. As the environmental journalist Jeff Goodell rightly notes, "Who doesn't love trees?"*

However, woefully little thought was given to basic questions like where those trees should be planted, how to keep them alive, and whether they could grow into stable ecosystems. The only way for new forests to successfully slow down climate change is for them to continue growing for decades (or, ideally, centuries). But building a brand-new old-growth forest is a considerably harder task than simply sticking seedlings in the soil. And so, the trillion-tree initiatives inevitably fell into the same traps as the logging industry.

---

*The American president who made this pledge, Donald Trump, though an avowed enemy of the climate movement, is, surprisingly, a great lover of trees. Before becoming president, he would sometimes cruise around in the back of a limo looking for nice trees growing in people's backyards, which he would then buy from the owner, uproot, and ship to one of his golf courses. "Money can't buy happiness," he writes in his book *Trump: Think Like a Billionaire*, "but it sure as hell can buy some great trees."

In numerous places around the world (Turkey, Brazil, India), vast rows of newly planted trees quickly died off due to neglect. Some well-meaning efforts were misguided from the start: Trees planted in the wrong ecosystems did more harm than good, sucking up precious groundwater and killing off carbon-sequestering grasses. In our lust for simple, sacrifice-free solutions, we were quite literally missing the forest for the trees.

And then, of course, there is the problem of wildfire. As the atmosphere warms, more forests will burn, and as they burn, they will release more climate-warming compounds, creating a vicious circle. This transformation will be seen first among tree plantations, because they lack the natural conditions—deep moss, thick trunks, diverse species—that help protect ancient forests from wildfires. A study performed by the US Department of Agriculture forecasts that by the year 2070, American forests will on the whole become a "significant" source, rather than a sink, of atmospheric carbon. Canada's forests have *already* made that horrifying switch. The Amazon rainforest, too, is now likely a net carbon source, and it is feared that the Congo Basin might soon follow suit. It's all a bit surreal to consider. In the words of the climate analyst Barry Saxifrage, we have effectively transformed many of our forests from a "carbon bank" into a "carbon bomb." And each year that passes, the bomb grows a bit larger.

The only way to defuse that bomb is to find a way to keep the world's forests alive for centuries to come. But how? The environmental journalist Fred Pearce tackles this thorny question in a monumental, globe-spanning work of reportage called *A Trillion Trees*. In it, he concludes that it *is* in fact possible to address the climate crisis through cultivating a trillion trees. However, he believes this must be achieved not through mass tree-planting campaigns, but rather through fostering the growth of forest *ecosystems*. First, he suggests that governments (especially in wealthy nations) need to radically reduce their carbon emissions and protect their remaining old-growth forests from clear-cutting. (These points are so obvious that he scarcely pauses to mention them.) Next, we should allow unforested lands—farms, urban lots, and so on—to naturally regenerate, which would establish a diverse mix of species tailored to the local ecology, rather than a handful of commercially advantageous species. The hard part will be managing to keep these new forests alive.

To this end, Pearce ultimately suggests that we should give local Indigenous communities—whom he calls "forest people"—the authority and the financial support to steward both the ancient woodlands and the new ones. This does not mean creating more national parks (which Pearce derides as "fortress conservation"), but rather a kind of *inhabited wilderness* where a limited amount of harvesting would be allowed, based on what the ecosystem can bear. One benefit of this system is that traditional Indigenous practices like the felling of smaller trees and the periodic burning off of underbrush have been found to improve forest biodiversity and increase carbon storage over the long term. More importantly, Pearce points out, if a group of people relies on the health of a forest for their very survival, they are going to care for it as no one else will. "We are relearning what we should never have forgotten," he writes. "That forest people—whether Indigenous Amazonians or Nepalese hill dwellers, Kenyan farmers or Mexican peasants, Native Americans or West African sawyers—are the best custodians and conservators of existing forests and the best at giving new forests room to grow."

When I finished reading Pearce's book, my first reaction was to think, *Well, yes, that's a nice idea, but it will never work.* Then I paused and reflected on why that might be. Why is it so hard for us to imagine a forest as a living, thriving home for humans—a state of affairs that has held true on most of the planet for most of humanity's existence? Moreover, why is it apparently so easy for us to think of trees as (in Benioff's words) a "scalable technology" that can be manipulated to solve the climate crisis, sparing us from any further sacrifice? Shouldn't it be precisely the other way around?

I arrived at a place called Heli Camp a few hours before dusk, so drenched with rain that my fingers had begun to prune. The encampment was built on a cliff overlooking a valley filled with dense fog. A cluster of people sat beside a campfire, underneath a plastic rain tarp. In a tidy kitchen area, a scrawny, witchy character was cooking up a big pot of veggie stew and brewing a smaller pot of tea made from locally foraged red belt mushrooms. I gratefully nestled myself among the protesters gathered around the warm fire.

This site was named Heli Camp because helicopters filled with loggers regularly landed here. Every day, the protesters hid among the fallen logs near the edge of the remaining forest. When the loggers began to rev their chainsaws, some of the protesters would pop up and announce their presence, which would halt the logging until the police could arrest them and haul them away. They called this tactic "playing cops and loggers." As with much of Fairy Creek—the treehouses, the goofy nicknames, the blockades resembling elaborate play forts—this tactic involved an element of juvenilia. It was as if the games of childhood had all been a preparation for this nonviolent (or rather, asymmetrically violent) battle.

Monkey was there, having just finished a long day of installing new treesits. Firestarter was there, too, along with four other people I hadn't met yet. Minutes later, a group of three more protesters, having spent the entire day hidden among the fallen trees, returned to the camp as well, dripping wet, freezing cold, and surprisingly cheerful. The helicopters had apparently been unable to land that day. A slim blond woman from Belgium cupped her hands and called out across the blank valley: "Thank you, fog!"

Sipping my mushroom tea, I squinted through the woodsmoke and studied the faces around the campfire. While the pipeline protest had mostly drawn older professionals (engineers, professors, lawyers, nurses), the people here skewed younger, wilder, and more androgynous. Many of them had the look of full-time blockaders: unwashed, battle-scarred, almost feral. The vibe at the camp was at once cozy and crunchy—not unlike that of a small liberal arts college in, say, Oregon.

I began to pick up on certain linguistic quirks among the land defenders. They often spoke of following the guidance of "the Elders." (By this, they did not mean their own elders, but rather Indigenous leaders like Elder Bill and a Tla'amin organizer known as Grandma Losah, who had dedicated themselves to the movement.) They talked about "Creator." They spoke of tobacco as "sacred medicine," but of alcohol as poison. The most fervent among them tried to shun colonial language altogether. They called Fairy Creek by its Pacheedaht name, Ada'itsx, they called North America "Turtle Island," and they called British Columbia "so-called British Columbia." With my eyes closed, I could have almost been fooled into thinking I was listening to a group of Lakota Sioux land defenders at Standing Rock, rather than a group of mostly white Canadians.

Alongside the white blockaders' (sincere, if somewhat self-flagellating) desire to atone for the crimes of colonialism, I detected something else: a growing hunger for a more human-friendly environmental philosophy—a hunger I myself had long felt. Traveling with Stephen Tamatea King in New Zealand, I had seen firsthand how a love of wilderness can all too easily mutate into a hatred of humans. I shared the Fairy Creekers sense that the rhetoric of old-school environmentalism—caring "only about the trees," as they often said—was worn out, even harmful. However, I had lingering questions about what kind of philosophy they hoped to replace it with. People here spoke of fostering a "reindigenized" worldview, in which humans are brought back into "right relation" with the rest of nature; many of them seemed to agree with Elder Bill Jones when he declared, "We are actually not defending the old-growth trees as much as we are defending our values. And our values are given to us by our Great Mother." The catch, it seemed to me, was that those values, and these lands, were entirely foreign to the vast majority of the people who had traveled here from all over the world. The irreconcilability of this fact produced a quiet tension that I could sense just beneath the surface of the movement, like the slow grinding of a tectonic fault.

Around the campfire that afternoon, I watched a woman from Utah named Sunflower initiate a long, anxious conversation about the proper role of white land defenders here at Fairy Creek. During the height of the blockade a few months ago, the presence of Indigenous leadership had been strong, she said, but many of those organizers had since left, for one reason or another. Sunflower was concerned that settlers had subsequently taken over—had "colonized"—the blockade. There seemed to be a growing sentiment that perhaps it was time for the non-Indigenous land defenders to all leave Fairy Creek, allowing Indigenous people to reclaim the movement.

After about an hour of respectful back-and-forth, the solution the group agreed upon was that white blockaders needed to take a big step back, especially in matters of decision-making and media attention, allowing Indigenous people to come to the forefront.

Then a man named Chiyokten, who, as best I could tell, was the only Indigenous person present at that discussion, spoke up. A longhaired, deep-voiced man in his fifties, Chiyokten was a craftsman, storyteller, and organizer from the W̱SÁNEĆ Nation—a Coast Salish people whose territory lay just south of here. Around camp, he was revered for his calm leadership, his deep ethnobotanical knowledge, and his unflinching composure in the face of police brutality.

"Well, look," Chiyokten said. "Many Indigenous people are just trying to survive. They've had their traditional culture beaten out of them, they've had it raped out of them, they've had their lands stolen. You can't expect them to come here and do this work, fighting a system that they did not create, and solving problems that they did not make. It's white people who primarily have to do that work."

Everyone around the campfire agreed with this as well.

+

The Fairy Creek blockade, with its strange but potent emulsion of environmental and decolonial politics, has a much longer history than most people know. In some sense, it began all the way back in the 1980s, when, a few hundred miles north of where I now sat, the Haida Nation, with help from sympathetic settlers, managed to save their old-growth forests from being clear-cut by marching arm in arm down logging roads. In the 1990s, another blockade manned by a mix of First Nations people and non-Indigenous environmentalists sprang up in Clayoquot Sound, not far from Fairy Creek, in what became known as the War in the Woods. (A record-breaking 856 people were ultimately arrested there, a distinction it held until the rise of Fairy Creek.) Elsewhere in Canada, First Nations had been at the forefront of nearly every recent blockade against new oil and gas pipelines and, with the help of mainstream environmental groups, had often battled heavy industry to a standstill in court. "Indigenous peoples have for some years been the most powerful force in environmental protection," writes the journalist Arno Kopecky. "No other group even comes close."

At first glance, Fairy Creek looked like the logical end point of all these battles: the long-dreamed-of day when the causes of environmentalism and Indigenous sovereignty, united in common purpose, finally begin winning land back for First Nations and establishing a more holistic ecological consciousness. Up close, however, it became clear that Fairy Creek was nearly the exact inverse of what I had supposed. The blockade, I was learning, marked the historical moment when that long-standing alliance began to split apart, revealing a subtle fissure that lay at its core.

Amid all of the victories of the past few decades, it had been easy to overlook the fact that environmentalists and First Nations, though allied, had never quite been philosophically aligned. Environmentalists, raised with the gospel of the Green Revelation, tended to believe that wild lands should be set aside as parks and wilderness preserves, managed by federal or provincial authorities, where they can remain pristine. First Nations, by contrast, tended to argue for a model of hands-on stewardship—which allows for careful hunting, harvesting, selective logging, and the burning off of undergrowth on wild lands—under the guidance of their own elders. In the words of Kathryn Teneese, the chair of the Ktunaxa Nation, "We may be walking in the same direction, but we're not holding hands."

Around the turn of the millennium, the forces of capitalism found a way to drive a wedge into that narrow fissure. Timber companies began signing deals to share a portion of their earnings with First Nations, usually around 1 percent of the raw lumber's value. Tribal authorities also began purchasing stakes in pipelines and oil wells on their own land. The result was, ironically, that just as environmentalists started dedicating themselves to the cause of supporting Indigenous sovereignty, the forces of industrial extraction began swaying Indigenous communities away from the environmentalist cause. Increasingly, First Nations people could be heard referring to environmentalists, rather than industrialists, as unwelcome foreign invaders.

This tension, I was learning, had grown particularly rancorous at Fairy Creek. From what I could tell, the overwhelming majority of the Pacheedaht Nation, a band of about three hundred people, were either quietly agnostic or openly opposed to the blockade. In fact, the elected council of the Pacheedaht, along with the neighboring Ditidaht and Huu-ay-aht Nations, had officially asked the protesters to go home. Huu-ay-aht chief Robert Dennis told a reporter that when he saw white environmentalists on his ancestral land, protesting against the wishes of his own people, what he heard was: "You Indians don't have the ability to carry yourselves, so we're going to fight for you and we're going to protect the old-growth whether you like it or not."

When I raised this point to people at Fairy Creek, they tended to respond that the elected tribal councils are a corrupt colonial by-product, put in place by the repressive law known as the Indian Act, all of which was designed, in the words of Elder Bill, to "obliterate relationships to land and families." The legitimate authority on these matters, they said, was the band's hereditary leadership. But this, too, was problematic, since the hereditary leader of the Pacheedaht, Frank Jones, had *also* asked the Fairy Creekers to leave. When I raised *that* point, they retorted that Frank Jones was not the true hereditary leader; the proper hereditary leader, according to Elder Bill, was a young man named Victor Peter, who was in fact in support of the blockade.

The government of Canada proudly touts its efforts to gain the consent of First Nations communities before it grants logging permits on their ancestral lands. But, as Elder Bill and others pointed out, had the Pacheedaht *really* been given much of a choice in the matter? They now heavily relied on the income from three local sawmills, including one tooled specifically, and exclusively, to process old-growth cedar. The elected council had also signed a contract with the government stipulating they would receive a cut of the profit from the logging of their forests *only* so long as they agreed not to support any acts that "frustrate, delay, stop or otherwise physically impede" the logging. "Colonial systems put us in a position that there is no choice," explained a T'Sou-ke and W̱SÁNEĆ organizer named x^w is x^w čaa. The Pacheedaht were economically and culturally exploited for centuries; finally, when *only* a small percent of the province's old-growth ecosystems remained, then—and only then—were they presented by the government of Canada with the chance to make some money by liquidating their last ancient trees. As Kopecky has quipped, "You could call that consent, or you could call it a hostage situation."

For the past two days, I'd been noticing other, subtler fault lines within the movement. As I'd seen at Heli Camp, some white people no longer knew how best to support the Indigenous cause without risking "colonizing" it, which forced them to continually wonder whether the only ethical action was simply to return home, leaving the forest vulnerable to loggers. Others, I was told, suffered from the opposite problem. Their zeal seemed to spring from some vague, unspoken desire to magically *become* Indigenous, or at least to try that identity on for a little while. I had been picking up on this ever since arriving at Fairy Creek, in the way certain white people here spoke and sang and banged on drums. The night before, while constructing the blockade, I'd observed that before the protesters chainsawed down a tree, they would sprinkle a pinch of tobacco at its base and shout, "Thank you, tree!" The gesture had struck me as hollow and hurried, a childish pantomime of a tradition they didn't fully understand—a form of what the historian Philip J. Deloria calls "playing Indian." These acts of appropriation irked many Indigenous protesters. "They want to have what we have," Grandma Losah later told me. "But what we have is what they tried to kill!"

To the average Canadian distractedly flipping through social media, Fairy Creek looked like a once-in-a-generation uprising, made up of a united front of both First Nations and settlers. Up close, though, what I found was far stranger. Here was a group of mostly white people fighting on behalf of Indigenous people, while Indigenous people were begging those white people to go home. Meanwhile, other Indigenous people, like Elder Bill and Chiyokten, were begging them to stay. To my mind, the movement should have quickly collapsed under the weight of these obvious contradictions. And yet somehow it had grown into the most powerful environmental uprising in a generation.

Clearly, some other force, some other logic, was at play.

Around sunset, Chiyokten stood up from the campfire and walked to the cliff's edge. With his back to us, he began chanting words I couldn't understand, set to a soft, lilting, melancholy tune, while clinking a metal cup with a spoon.

Settling back down beside the campfire, Chiyokten recalled how, come spring, there is a distinct moment when the frogs begin their croaky chorusing, which, in turn, is believed to rouse the medicine plants from their winter slumber. The message of that frog song, he said, is "Wake up, wake up, my relatives. Your relatives need your medicine." He added that before harvesting wild medicine, his grandmother would always explain her intention to the plants she hoped to gather. She would say, *I would only take part of your family to help my family*, and then she'd wait quietly until she felt she had gained their permission. "That's the sacred relation brought down to only a few words," he explained.

Chiyokten added that, among his elders, ancient cedars were often portrayed as the "ancestors" of humans, demanding respect and restraint precisely as one's grandparents do. This ethic of filial respect is deeply embedded in the language many Indigenous peoples use for trees. The Kwakwaka'wakw, for example, refer to cedars as "grandmother." The Haida call them "elder sister." The Arikara refer to a particular old cedar as "mother." In Amazonia, the Kali'na people refer to the ceiba trees as "father." Robin Wall Kimmerer, a member of the Citizen Potawatomi Nation, notes that in her language, it is impossible to refer to a maple tree as "it," only as "he" or "she." "We use the same words to address the living world as we use for our family. Because they are our family," she writes.

I began to understand why, for people like Chiyokten and Elder Bill, there was a clear difference between traditional forms of timber harvesting and the clear-cutting that the Pacheedaht elected council wanted to carry out. "To allow non-Indigenous people on your lands with machines to saw our precious ancestors down? *One hundred of them in one day?*" Chiyokten said. "It is insane to think that you're being respectful to the ways of our ancestors."

I got up and walked to the precise spot where Chiyokten had just been standing on the cliff's edge. Below me was a tundra-like expanse of white fog, and beneath that, I knew, pulsed a vast, venous tangle of living beings. And yet, unlike Chiyokten, I felt no deep kinship with any of it. Instead, what I perceived, quite acutely, was a profound absence in myself.

+

The journalist Brooke Jarvis has written movingly about growing up with a condition called anosmia—the inability to smell. The human nose, Jarvis writes, possesses a kind of evolutionary superpower that most of us take for granted: It allows us to perceive a far-off forest fire, to know when food is ripe or spoiled, even to sense when there is a predator nearby. "If you weren't used to it," she remarks, "it would seem like witchcraft." The odd thing, Jarvis notes, is that she had no idea that her sense of smell was missing until, in her early teens, her sister walked in to find her cuddling her skunk-sprayed dog, and "the pieces began to fall into place." Years later, that same sister came home just in time to stop Jarvis from lighting a match in a cabin filled with propane, saving her life.

Talking with Chiyokten there at Heli Camp, it occurred to me that those of us who grew up without a sense of relationality—the bone-deep knowledge that all living beings are fundamentally interdependent—are suffering from a kind of ecological, or one might say spiritual, anosmia. The absence of relationality from our culture is so total that most of the time we don't even know what we are missing. But, when we start paying attention, we can perceive signs of its absence all around us. One sees it in the suburban commuter, speeding by with glazed eyes in an air-conditioned automobile to an air-conditioned office; one sees it in the urbanite, dwelling high in a steel tower, stepping over supine bodies on their way to work; one sees it in the college student, subsisting on instant noodles fried in palm oil grown in the ashes of razed rainforests; one sees it in our farmers, riding automated machines, harvesting rows of huge, mutated fruits sprayed with poison and pollinated with drones; and, most of all, one sees it in the land itself—ecosystem after ecosystem, all over the planet, growing ever more homogenized and embrittled.

On its surface, relationality might sound like little more than a grade school ecology lesson dressed up in sanctimonious language. However, Indigenous philosophers argue that those of us raised in colonialized cultures tend to only ever skim the surface of this profound truth. The kinship of all living beings is not just a lofty ideal spouted by politicians on Earth Day, nor is it some psychedelic revelation that melts away with the dawn. It is what the anthropologist Bronislaw Malinowski called a "binding force ... based upon mutual dependence." It is as heavy and eternal as gravity.

For years, I had been mulling over Umeek's concise definition of the Indigenous worldview: "It's relationships." The key point, I realized, is that it does not suffice to merely *understand* that the world is composed of relationships. Those bonds must be actively *honored*, just as one honors one's connection to one's own family members. I find this worldview—what the theologian Horace Bushnell rather poetically calls "the brotherhood of other beings"—beautiful in theory, but as Bushnell himself admitted, it seems incredibly daunting to put into practice. How would a life lived under that moral standard actually work? How, for example, can you be said to *truly* revere a medicine plant you're about to pluck? How can you respect a tree you're about to chop down? If you believe a deer is your brother or a salmon your sister, how can you bring yourself to slit its throat and eat its flesh?

Eventually, by talking with people like Umeek and Chiyokten, I came to see that I was thinking about this question not in the wrong terms (after all, I, too, had grown up with concepts like "respect" and "reciprocity"), but in the wrong *shape*, so to speak. In the colonial worldview, our cosmology is segregationist: Bright lines are drawn to separate the good from the evil, life from death, men from women, humans from nonhumans, nature from culture, heaven from earth, wastelands from wonderlands. Within this absolutist framework, we cannot ever *truly* bring ourselves to recognize the fact that plants and animals are fundamentally akin to us—that they are living, breathing, self-willed beings—because then the simple act of eating would constitute murder, and the only ethical action left to us would be to starve to death. Hence, we relegate them to the other side of that bright line, with the inanimate, the mechanistic, and the dead.

Within the Native worldview, explains the Cherokee philosopher Brian Burkhart, those bright lines begin to dissolve. Instead, Indigenous wisdom traditions tend to extend a vibrant thread *between* things, like shining strands of spider silk. "A great deal of care is required at each step not to unbalance or undo the delicate interrelations," he writes. Within this worldview, harvesting one's plant and animal kin is not considered immoral, *even though it results in their death*, so long as it is carried out in a way that respects that plant or animal, as well as the larger web of relationality. To rupture that tapestry through disrespect, however, is seen as a grave, even suicidal, error. For example, children are often taught that if a certain tree is cut down without proper gestures of respect—a pinch of tobacco, an offering of food, a whispered prayer—the spirit of that tree will exact its revenge upon the person who cut it down. My favorite example of this belief, which one finds cropping up in Indigenous cultures all over the world, is a tale from Colombia describing an old woman known as the "mother of Lupuna" with fiery eyes, hair made from leaves, and a face carved from wood, who has the power to make loggers fall ill for the crime of defiling the sacred ceiba tree.

When I first ran across the claim that a deep sense of relationality is common to all Indigenous cultures, I was initially somewhat skeptical. How, I wondered, could it possibly be true that most or even all of the world's various autochthonous cultures are characterized by a shared set of ethical and even metaphysical values? But thinking about Chiyokten's grandmother speaking to the medicine plants, I began to realize that the answer is quite simple. Living close to the land—without the cushion of agricultural surplus, industrial technology, and synthetic medicine—destroys the delusions of segregationist thinking. One must either be kith or be killed.

Perhaps the hardest point for us outsiders to grasp is that in the Indigenous worldview, relationships tend to be considered ontologically primary, meaning that the relationships between things are *as real as the things themselves*. This notion, trippy though it may sound, makes perfect sense when one considers one's own body. Ask yourself: If some malevolent god were to magically reduce you to a pile of atoms, would that pile of matter still be recognizably you? It would not. The body is a particular set of relationships—a Byzantine organization of countless reciprocal alliances—between various living structures. What is the earth if not one vast, celestial body made up of a nearly infinite number of such relationships? And what is the task of living wisely on this earth, if not learning to respect those shimmering, vital, all-but-imperceptible bonds?

+

That night up at Heli Camp, the rain fell hard and steady. It fell as I ate my dinner and washed my bowl, it fell as I set up my tent, and it fell as I crawled inside and pulled my wet pack in after me, arranging it beside me in the place where Remi usually sleeps. In time, it fell so hard, for so long, that it began to drip through the nylon rainfly, and then it fell on me, one drop at a time, in a slow, torturous patter, eventually soaking all the way through my sleeping bag.

I awoke the following morning, shivering and sore, with my sleeping bag sticking coldly to my skin. I slithered free from that horrid chrysalis and stepped outside to find a new, blue sky. I stood for the better part of an hour in the sun, luxuriating in its warmth, with ribbons of steam rising off my damp clothes like incense smoke. Nearby, Chiyokten was standing on the edge of the cliff once again, his back to me, his hands raised in front of his face, for a long time. Later, over breakfast, I asked if he had been performing some kind of ritual. "Oh, no, I was just taking a time lapse," he said, laughing. He held out his phone so I could watch a video he'd taken of fog washing across the valley.

After breakfast, I departed for Ridge Camp. Hauling my wet pack on raw shoulders, I followed the logging road until it dead-ended into a dirt path, which led up a thickly wooded hillside. Blockaders had marked the trail with yellow flagging tape, and in the steepest parts, they had even installed sections of climbing rope to use as a handrail. Nevertheless, I managed to lose the trail at least twice, and I fell down numerous times as the damp, loose soil slipped away beneath my feet. There was something sepulchrous about that stretch of forest, even in the bright daylight, and I was glad to escape it.

Finally, I crested a ridge, then I dropped down into the Fairy Creek watershed.

I made my way downhill using huge, exposed tree roots like the rungs on a ladder. It was, as I had been promised it would be, a wondrous place. The trees here were larger and spaced farther apart, which aired out the gloom. Ancient cedars, both living and dead, presided over a quiet anarchy of moss and ferns. In the dim green light, chanterelle mushrooms glowed softly, like ripe apricots.

As I neared Ridge Camp, I passed a yellow cedar that was larger than all the others. Its ten-foot-wide trunk resembled the hypertrophied, hard-flexed thigh of some Brobdingnagian bodybuilder. I later learned it was estimated to be more than a thousand years old. A hand-carved sign leaning against its trunk read "Titania"—a reference, I assumed, either to Shakespeare's queen of the fairies or to the Titans, those doomed children of the gods of the sky and earth. In either case, it was a fitting name.

I sat at its base in silence, staring up at it, for perhaps twenty minutes, which felt like a long while. But, I thought, what is twenty minutes to a being who has witnessed the passage of a millennium? It occurred to me that if this tree could have perceived us humans, we would have seemed distinctly fairylike: ethereal, mischievous little sprites flitting past.

I hurried on through the grove, the trees growing larger as I went. I spotted some wooden platforms in the tops of a few old cedars, but I didn't see anyone in them. Worried that the camp had been abandoned, I scuttled along the trail—past a row of empty tents, some water jugs, and a charming little wooden swing—until I spotted a campfire beneath a rain tarp. Around the fire sat four pale, soggy, solemn-looking individuals wreathed in brown smoke, like hermits in an old Dutch oil painting.

We introduced ourselves.

On the far side of the fire sat two skeletally thin men with long beards, one dark and the other blond. The dark-haired man I'll call Crow. The blond man was called Elvin. Both smoked a prodigious number of hand-rolled cigarettes. And both were fond of recounting their puckish exploits in past blockades. Crow described how he had lived in a tree for three straight months, while Elvin recalled chaining himself to a machine called a feller buncher and covering himself with red paint so that the loggers would momentarily be fooled into thinking he had been maimed.

Beside them sat a pair of protesters who arrived at Ridge Camp mere hours before I did: a young woman with purple hair and a nose ring named Bone Dog and a rotund, gray-haired man named Smiley.

The mood in the cook tent was a bit grim; above the fire hung a sodden mass of clothes that gave off a thick, sour steam but never seemed to fully dry, and the smoke from the cigarettes joined the woodsmoke to form a dense, eye-watering haze. Crow and Elvin began grousing about how they both had giardia, an intestinal parasite that leads to explosive diarrhea. "The problem is that the mice run through the latrine, then they run all over the kitchen and get our shit everywhere," Crow said.

While I began tidying up the kitchen area, Smiley and Bone Dog tried on climbing harnesses. All around the camp, treesits had been installed, which needed to be occupied each night, in case police performed an early-morning raid, and new treesitters needed to continually be trained so that the people who had been there longer, like Elvin and Crow, could take a break and sleep on the ground now and then. Each subsequent wave of new arrivals was taught by the one preceding it—a worryingly informal way of passing along life-and-death knowledge.

"Do you know how to use one of these?" Elvin asked me, holding up a mechanical rappel device known as a GRIGRI, which a previous treesitter had left behind at the camp. The GRIGRI provides a safe, almost foolproof way to descend from a tree, but no one knew how it worked, so they had been using an old-fashioned, less-safe device, called a figure 8, instead.

It was clear that I finally had something of substance to contribute to the blockade. I happily threw myself into the task. As a stream of new arrivals appeared at Ridge Camp in the following days, I conducted a twice-daily clinic in technical tree climbing. I thought about Ben Atkinson, and Markus Nguali, and Tim Kovar, and Steen Christensen, and Anthony Ambrose, and Wendy Baxter, and Emerald, and Cauliflower, and all of the other people I'd climbed trees alongside and learned from over the years. It felt satisfying to pass along the meager skills I'd amassed, and to know they would be put to good use.

After finishing the first class, I ascended a rope and ducked into one of the treesits to take a look. It was just a flat piece of plywood surrounded on all sides by tarps, about sixty feet off the ground. Sitting with my bare feet dangling off the edge, I had a giant's view of the forest below. At that moment, in that dusky light, I felt a sharp love for the place, and an equally sharp horror at the thought of it being razed.

I decided to spend the night up there. I hauled up a sleeping bag and sleeping pad, made myself reasonably comfortable, and then tied a rope around myself to keep from falling off the platform in my sleep, like Odysseus lashing himself to the mast of his ship. For a long while, I struggled to fall asleep, as my austere little nest waved about in the dark night wind. Once again, I experienced the comforting, tenuous, childlike sensation of being cradled in the arms of a being much larger than myself. Before drifting off, without a hint of irony, I whispered: *Thank you, tree.*

+

In the morning, I awoke in a terror to the sound of a police helicopter hovering directly overhead. I'd heard that tactical squads would sometimes drop down from these helicopters on ropes, arrest treesitters, and airlift them out, but when I'd made up my mind to sleep up here the night before, the possibility of that happening had felt exceedingly low. It seemed considerably less so, now.

Staring up at the helicopter, I felt a surge of courage and a surge of fear, which swirled against one another like hot and cold fluids.

Would this be it? I wondered. Would I make a stand, or would I flee?

The futures that led from that simple binary decision forked in wildly different directions. I pictured a world in which I remained in the tree, got arrested, lost my residency, and was ousted from my home. But then I pictured the future in which I retreated and, later, was forced to read about the felling of those ancient trees, all so that they could be used to build a new sundeck for the seventh home of some oligarch's son. Both options were unbearable.

An eternal moment passed. My mind emptied. I gazed numbly up at the heavens, as if stricken with holy dread.

Finally, the helicopter lifted up into the sky and floated off. It was apparently only conducting surveillance, planning for some future raid. Nevertheless, it left me shaken. In that moment, I sensed, quite acutely, my limitations—as a person, as a protester, as a symbol. Even if I sacrificed my life for this tree, it wouldn't make much of a difference. I would be just another droplet in an endless fire hose of bloody news.

I also understood, more sharply than ever, the shortcomings of the philosophy that had brought me here in the first place—the same ethos that had galvanized the environmentalist movement more broadly, from John Muir to Julia Butterfly Hill—and why that ethos was beginning to falter. The animating force of environmentalism over the past two centuries, the Green Revelation, had been a bright flash of secular nature reverence, born amid the sooty atmosphere of industrialism. But that reverence, I was realizing, was an oddly uneven thing. It burned with blinding intensity in a small handful of people, but for some reason it remained all too dim in the rest of us. It was powerful enough to impel a man to light himself on fire to raise awareness about climate change, but it wasn't enough to convince his compatriots to abide by even a modest carbon tax. It was a religion of shining martyrs and silent onlookers.

Risking one's life to stop a tree from being cut down or a pipeline from being built is a last-ditch effort. To be sure, it is better than no effort at all. But the intervention comes much too late. The treesitter is, as Thoreau famously remarked, hacking at the branches of the problem, rather than striking at the root. The basic problem lies in how we relate to one another, and how we relate to the world. If anything lasting was going to come out of Fairy Creek, I realized, it wasn't going to take place up here in the branches. The real transformation was unfolding back down on the ground, in makeshift kitchens and around campfires, where minds long calcified around the narrow logic of capitalism and colonialism were slowly, quietly being opened to something far more radical.

+

I ended up spending the better part of a week at Ridge Camp. New protesters drifted in and drifted out: a woman named Sand Dune, a man named Ground Squirrel, a dog named Cowboy. One guy slept beside the fire using a chunk of wood as his pillow; another helped wire up a small satellite dish so we could access the internet in an emergency.

The place steadily grew on me. Whereas Heli Camp had felt like a besieged military outpost, Ridge felt like a back-to-the-land commune in its first, hopeful days. Most of the day was simply spent cooking: We would get up, kindle a fire, and wait for water to boil for coffee. By the time the coffee was finished, it was time to boil water to make oatmeal, and by the time that was finished, it was time to boil dishwater, and so on. There was always wood to be chopped, dishes to be washed, and other small chores to be done. In our free time, we went off on little hikes to nearby peaks to meditate, we drank cool, sweet water with cupped hands right from the creek, and we hunted wild mushrooms to fry up for dinner. At night, we huddled around the fire, people read aloud from books, and we held long, rambling conversations, of the kind I hadn't had in ages. One especially cold and lovely morning, a land defender named Otter looked up at the snow-dusted trees and said, "We are so lucky to get to be here." The blockaders often sang a song whose lyrics ran, simply: *Thank you, thank you thank you, thank you thank you* . . .

I began to see that these quiet interludes were as crucial to the success of Fairy Creek as the moments of spectacular conflict. Our days were passed according to human rhythms, surrounded by non-human life. I was often reminded of the tree villages that sprang up to block highways in England in the 1990s, which were designed as an intentional rebuke to mainstream society: communitarian, queer friendly, anti-racist, and largely devoid of advanced technology and capitalist profit making. "We must have looked like lunatics, dressed in gorgeous rags, Lost Boys running around our beautiful, borrowed Neverland," recalls Olivia Laing, who spent a summer living in one of these tree villages. "It sounds hedonistic, and it was, but it also had a tangible effect on the world. The road was canceled, the trees were saved."

The ultimate goal of Fairy Creek, I was realizing, was not to secure a ban on old-growth logging or even to stop climate change. The blockaders generally understood that devising ways to save more trees or store more carbon would not solve the wider problem some have come to call the "polycrisis." Banning old-growth logging would not remove the microplastics from our brains and the forever chemicals from our blood, it would not stop fishing trawlers from raking the ocean clean, it would not halt the steady withering of both biodiversity and cultural diversity worldwide, it would not save the poor from dying of hunger or the rich from gorging themselves sick, and it would not alleviate the ceaseless pressure placed on Indigenous communities to commodify their kin.

In the space afforded by those slow, uncluttered days, one could feel one's mind uncramping. The world, we know, shapes us, just as it can sculpt a sequoia into either a giant or a dwarf. However, one of the miraculous things about being a human, rather than a tree, is that we have the power to seek out alternate worlds. In this case, it meant going outdoors, to places where nothing is bought or sold, where wild foods are gathered, where people use technologies rather than the other way around, where people relate to plants and leave room for animals—and animisms—to flourish. Most importantly, it meant getting to learn from people wiser than oneself, like Chiyokten, Grandma Losah, and Elder Bill. Once one has found that world, one can attempt to help it grow.

The blockade was not quite as utopian as I am making it sound. By design (or rather, by its very lack of design) it was all a bit chaotic, at times even fractious. There were plenty of fault lines within the movement, most notably between the old-school environmentalists and the new-school decolonial indigenists. There were people beating drums and "playing Indian" alongside people telling them to cool it. There were elderly New Agers passing around battered copies of *The Celestine Prophecy* and bespectacled theory-spouting Marxists and paranoid anarchists who'd thrown away their cell phones and tattooed-faced hellions who simply delighted in starting trouble. There were people—a great many people—who showed up naively looking for adventure, and would soon return to their day jobs wearing this experience draped loosely around their soul, like a colorful shawl from a far-off land.

By and large, however, the people I met at Fairy Creek were ones who, having heard Elder Bill's call to "stand with me to protect our forests from destruction and colonialism," traveled from all over the world bearing a sincere desire to help. They were trying to decolonize their thinking, and decolonize the world, as best they knew how. They spoke of rebuilding systems around the Indigenous values of restraint, reciprocity, and redistribution. They sought to dissolve oppressive racial hierarchies and gender binaries. They dreamed of a world in which no one gets rich by poisoning the air and land and water. A world fed with local foods and powered by renewable energy. A world where public land is "rematriated" to First Nations, and a world where those same First Nations are so strong in their traditions and secure in their finances that they would never dream of clear-cutting their relatives. A world where doing the right thing—ecologically, ethically, spiritually—isn't always so damn hard. A world brought back into "right relation" with the earth.

It was while sitting around that campfire, discussing these colossal questions with people who truly believed that another world is possible, and who were busy working in whatever small way they could to bring it into being, that I finally felt I'd reached the glowing heart of Fairy Creek, which had gathered so many people, mothlike, from all over the world.

+

What, I'd often found myself wondering, is the fatal flaw in the modern worldview? What destroyed our understanding that life is a delicate web of relationships? What is it that impels us to steadily chew up landscapes and brutalize other living beings? I had a rough outline of this thing in my mind, but each time I tried to put a name to it, the word eluded me. Was the problem extractivism? Industrialism? Colonialism? Capitalism? Each of these answers seemed to isolate a part of the problem, but none seemed to encompass it in its entirety.

It took me a long time to find a term both capacious and specific enough to capture the phenomenon I was struggling to describe. I came across it while reading a dry and somewhat obscure tome entitled *History of Nature Management* by the prolific Russian geographer L. G. Bondarev, which I was forced to digitally translate into English. (The story of how I ran across that book while night swimming through the ocean of academic archives is far too tortuous to recount.) While describing land-management practices in the Middle Ages, Bondarev includes a passage about how a "wave" of deforestation and "internal colonization" swept eastward across Europe, as woodlands were converted into farmlands and cities—a phenomenon he calls the Great Uprooting.

The Great Uprooting took place more or less organically. Around the eighth century, due to the spread of a handful of new technologies and techniques—most notably, a practice known as triennial rotation, which involved raising three, rather than two, crops per year on a single field—agricultural yields began to grow. This led to a swelling population, which led to the growth of larger towns and cities, which then led to the need for yet more agricultural land. The clearing of land was a backbreaking task, which involved felling a forest, burning the debris, and then ripping the remaining tree roots from the earth. This work was largely carried out by peasants, but the wealth that ultimately flowed from it was channeled upward to the nobles through taxation and to the priesthood through tithing, increasing their hunger for yet more land. Some historians estimate that by the ninth century, the Catholic Church alone had acquired as much as one-third of *all* of the land in Europe. Everywhere the influence of the church spread, it sought to stamp out a belief in nature spirits and other vestiges of the relational worldview. Sometimes this campaign was waged through brute force, as when the bishop Wigbert of Merseburg reportedly "uprooted" a Slavic holy forest that "the local inhabitants honoured as a god." More often, though, animism was crushed by quieter means: at once smothered by edicts (which imposed fines for "heathenship") and choked by a miasma of shame.*

---

*Like Bondarev, I am oversimplifying this process somewhat for the sake of clarity. According to Richard C. Hoffmann's authoritative *An Environmental History of Medieval Europe*, the progression of the Great Uprooting was somewhat messier and less linear than Bondarev makes it sound. For one thing, many of the new settlements in the medieval era were established on the site of land that had previously been cleared under Roman rule and later fell back into a wild or semi-wild state. One such place, I was interested to learn, was Germany's Hambach Forest, which had once been "densely populated" with farms and towns but which, once abandoned, became gradually reforested. Centuries later, that same forest would be fiercely defended by treesitters, who often referred to it, somewhat fancifully, as "one of the few remaining old-growth forests in Germany."

The Great Uprooting, in other words, took place in two places simultaneously: in the soil and in the soul. One sees its fruits in the philosophy of later thinkers like the Renaissance-era theologian Francis Bacon, considered by many to be the father of modern science. "He," writes the intellectual historian Will Durant, "is the voice of all those Europeans who have changed a continent from a forest into a treasure-land of art and science, and have made their little peninsula the center of the world.... Everything is possible to man. Time is young; give us some little centuries, and we shall control and remake all things."

In running across Bondarev's felicitous phrase, I felt I had finally found a name for a social phenomenon that has swept across the planet, from Paris to Papua: first, diverse ecosystems give way to farms growing huge amounts of some shelf-stable grain (be it barley in Sumer, rice in China, or corn in Mexico); farmers gradually become an agricultural workforce, and grain becomes a source of wealth; markets form; wealth circulates and accumulates; and finally a small but steadily growing cohort emerges that grows rich off that surplus, cut off from the rhythms of the land.

Many people around the world have been violently coerced into adopting this new way of life; to foster the market economy and the growth of empires, people were torn from lands and lands were torn from people in a thousand painful ways. But for others, the Great Uprooting was slow, subtle, and largely voluntary. People chose it because they were (gradually, and only ever partially) relieved of the agonies of seasonal famine and child mortality, of going hunting and being hunted, of hypothermia and heatstroke, of all those bothersome ethical checks on selfish behavior and runaway wealth accumulation. To them, *leaving* the forest must have looked like freedom. It was all too easy to overlook what they were trading away—namely, that ineffable thing the philosopher Jean-Luc Nancy calls the "sacred entanglement between ... man and animal, plant, thunder, rock."

The Great Uprooting is not a one-off historical event that occurred in the distant past, like the Black Death. It is an organic process that is occurring right now in every nation on earth, whether it is the Korowai being lured from the forest into farmwork, the children of farmers moving off into cities and factories, or the steady outflow of manual workers into more intangible forms of labor like the "information economy." An exactly parallel process of uprooting has taken place in the realm of human cultures: Across the centuries, the powers of empire and imperial religion have steadily trimmed away one rootlet after another—replacing local languages with lingua franca, animist spirits with divine monism, wild lore with hard science—causing us to lose our grip on the beings around us and the places in which we live.

Recall how the Korowai, when they first encountered white people, were amazed to learn that we laleo subsist almost entirely off food we do not personally harvest. Our food, in their eyes, is "just there." This now strikes me as a tremendously keen insight. After all, it is worth pausing to consider how strange it is, historically speaking, for people to take food for granted the way that we so often do. By contrast, Indigenous people traditionally displayed a level of gratitude for food that is almost impossible to overstate. Native peoples often refer to the species that are most central to their survival—whether it is salmon among the Salish, wild rice among the Menominee, or corn among the Hopi—as "sacred providers" of life itself. The Korowai have forged an intimate relationship with their staple crop, the sago palm: During sago grub feasts, people sing songs calling for both children and sago trees to "grow well," and when a person dies, a sago tree is felled in their honor, so that the two bodies might (symbolically) "decompose together."

William Cronon, in describing the workings of the meatpacking industry, beautifully captures the bizarre psychological toll it takes on us when an animal (or, I might add, even a plant) is "severed" from its ecological context and transmuted from a *being* into a *product*: "Its ties to the earth receded, and in forgetting the animal's life one also forgot the grasses and the prairie skies and the departed bison herds of a landscape that seemed more and more remote in space and time." In every monetary transaction, hidden away behind a veil of abstraction, lies an unseen realm of bodies intermingling, of the quiet miracles of seasonal rainstorms and nitrogen-fixing bacteria, of labor and care and innovation as well as pollution and degradation and cruelty. When we peer down at a shrink-wrapped package of raw chuck or a bag of potato chips, that complex world is collapsed into a simple equation of nutrition, tastiness, and price.

One especially pernicious facet of the Great Uprooting is that the further we drift from the web of life, the more we begin to fear and distrust it. The only time most of us begin to care deeply about the species that feed us (and the wider ecology that feeds them) is in times of crisis—when an especially dry year pulls the avocados from our shelves, when a virus spreads through our chickens, or, worse, when an outbreak of some tiny fungus causes crops to fail, leaving millions to starve. A person who is deeply rooted to their local ecology would see these crises as what they are: a sign that something has gone awry in the relational web of life. But we in uprooted cultures see each new collapse of the food web as little more than a logistical obstacle to be overcome. And so we implement yet-harsher efforts at control, which further severs our food both from us and from its native ecology. Consider the evolutionary trajectory from wild-hunted venison to farmed chicken to canned pork to gas station meat-sticks to hydrolized bovine collagen smoothies, and, now, wholly synthetic meat, grown in petri dishes—the flesh of "animals" that have never touched soil, tasted water, or breathed a lungful of air. As much as we like to talk about "caring for our natural environment," what we ultimately crave, it seems, is *to be emancipated from ecology itself.*

This long, strange arc of cultural evolution—away from entanglement, toward abstraction—has reached its apotheosis in the current caste of tech overlords, who, locked away in their fortresslike homes with their private chefs, confess to wondering, apparently in all sincerity, whether the world is a digital simulation, which is just a roundabout way of asking whether other people and other living things are *really* real, and, if not, whether they can begin to shed the last vestige of their ethical obligations. I am certain that if one of those strange, pale men were to be left alone in a forest for a week with no food, such delusions would quickly evaporate. If the delusions persisted, the person would not. The earth eats people, but it eats solipsists first.

Most people at Fairy Creek, having already freed themselves from this delusion, understood that the uprooted worldview must be repaired on a fundamental level. Indeed, this understanding has been growing in many parts of the West since at least the time of Aldo Leopold, who, in the 1940s, called upon his fellow man to transform from a "conqueror of the land-community" to a "plain member and citizen of it." Every year, it becomes yet clearer that people, especially those in positions of power, need to relearn the traditional values of relationality and restraint. If we don't, a force wholly outside our control—a fierce grandmotherly spirit with a face of wood, hair of leaves, and eyes of flame—will remind us the hard way.

+

At the end of that week, a storm blew in—what meteorologists were calling an "atmospheric river"—which pounded our encampment. We spent one entire afternoon attempting to fortify the tarps of our cook area to withstand the storm, only to discover, in the morning light, that half of the tarps had collapsed and the entire area was now flooded. We stood amid the rack and ruin, feeling utterly defeated. More rain was forecast to come, and then, soon, heavy snowfall. It was becoming dangerous to remain up there without the proper gear. In any case, the likelihood of loggers moving in, in late October, this high on the mountain, seemed low. It was generally agreed that Ridge Camp should be closed down for the winter, to be reopened if and when it was deemed necessary.

I packed up my things, as well as some of the communal gear, hefted my leaden pack, and spent a long, dreary day hiking down along the logging roads on the far side of the mountain. The rain-fed rivers were all swollen like grubs, white-skinned, yellow in their bellies. I passed through one encampment after another, where people were on edge, readying themselves for the next round of police raids.

Exhausted, I finally made my way back to the Roadside encampment. There, I spotted Elder Bill Jones moving slowly down the logging road, using a wooden walking stick with an eagle carved into the handle. He was heading off to strategize with a half dozen other Indigenous leaders about the future of the blockade. A hale man in his early eighties, he was compactly built, with a head of titanium-white hair pulled back in a ponytail and a pair of hooded eyes that appeared at once calm and roguish. He radiated a fathomless patience, a broad outlook, and an unshowy confidence. It was immediately plain why the movement had coalesced around him, like so much space dust gathered around the cool density of an ancient star.

I later caught up with Elder Bill by phone, and we spoke for more than three hours. He described the winding course of his life: his "chaotic" upbringing on the reserve, his years of confinement in a residential school, his decades working off and on in the local logging industry (the sight of piles of slaughtered ancient trees brought him to tears on at least one occasion, he said), the dark spell of time when he descended into addiction, and then his recovery, aided, in part, by spending more time in the forest and reconnecting with his traditions. He recalled that when he was a child, his grandfather had told him, "You don't go up to the forest to cut it down, sonny. You go up there to be quiet." Our remaining ancient forests, he believed, were sacred sites, which should be set aside for prayer, meditation, and the traditional harvesting of materials like cedar bark, not industrial wealth extraction.

To Elder Bill, and to the thousands of land defenders whom he had inspired, the clear-cutting of Fairy Creek was not just an ecological crime. It was a form of profound uprooting. The blockade was made up of a small number of people like Elder Bill and Chiyokten, who were fighting desperately to retain their cultural roots, and a large number of people like me, who had little or no sense of rootedness at all, but who wanted one. What was beautiful about Fairy Creek (and not all of it was beautiful) was that they had managed to create a little world where both of those groups could begin to feel more connected, to the land and to one another, through real action and real sacrifice in the real world.

+

The very first thing a plant does, when it is still a sleepy little seedling, long before it sends up the thin stem that will one day sprout leaves and gather food, is to produce a rootlet so that it can find water and anchor its position in the soil. This first tiny root is known in biology as a "radicle." That word stems from the Latin *radix*. In a wonderful linguistic convergence, that root word also gives us the word "radical." Before it acquired a political connotation, it had another now obsolete usage, meaning something like "fundamental" or "core"—as when a doctor in a play from 1611 remarks that a dead body is deprived "the radicall abilitie of Nature." To be radical, in other words, is to get down to the very root of a problem.[*]

While talking with Elder Bill, I found myself thinking about

---

[*] The great lexicographer Samuel Johnson once remarked on this oddly arborescent quality of language, how one word will over time sprout many meanings, or as he put it, "branches out into parallel ramifications." Often, words can be traced back to other, older languages, which branched apart from yet-older languages, and on and on, into the mists of antiquity. Stepping back further, it becomes clear that every word is a tiny branchlet on a single tree of human language, rooted at some unspeakably distant point in our existence as (radically) conversant animals.

both his rootedness and his radicalness, and how these two kindred qualities supported one another. Places seemed to have immense importance to him—perhaps the right word is that they seemed to *hold* him—and it was this love of place that pushed him to radical action, despite the severe consequences it might bring. For example, I noticed he had the habit of situating every story in a particular location—not just a town or region, but a particular bridge over a particular creek—and he would often grind the conversation to a halt until I pretended to know *which* bridge over *which* creek he was talking about. Years earlier, I had noticed that Charlie Castro, the Miwok-Paiute man I'd met while climbing sequoias, told stories this way too; he seemed to be just as interested in *where* something happened as what had happened. For example, while recounting how his grandmother had been hunted by the Mariposa Battalion, he told the story like this: "Up by Half Dome, there's a trail that goes up, what they call Snow Creek Trail, goes all the way up to Tenaya Lake, goes up into Tuolumne Meadows, heads all the way to the east toward Tioga Pass, goes down through Bloody Canyon, and then down toward Lee Vining, that country. Anyway, my grandma and her sister were hidden in this place called the Indian Caves, pretty close to Half Dome. It still exists, a huge cave. That's where they hid." This form of place-based thinking, argues Brian Burkhart, typifies the Indigenous worldview, unlike the thinking of colonial cultures, which tends to put greater emphasis on abstract ideas, starkly moralized character traits, and tidy story arcs. The colonial mindset, he points out, while ruinous to local ecosystems, proved uniquely adept at foreign conquest. "Part of the capacity to dominate the land as well as Indigenous people," he writes, "arises from a reconfiguration of history and time as floating free from the land."

What does it mean to have deep roots in a place? One key component, Burkhart argues, is precisely the kind of "localized" thinking that Elder Bill and Charlie Castro embody—what he calls "being-from-the-land and knowing-from-the-land." However, that is just one aspect of rootedness. A deeper sense of rootedness—what Burkhart calls "being-in-kinship"—requires fostering a connection to the community of other living beings that make up that place. Just staying in one place, or even loving that place, does not guarantee one will form a deep-rooted relationship with it. As many rich old families in the American South show, you can live on a single plot of land for eight generations—or, in some parts of Europe, eighty generations—without ever developing a sense of loving, binding reciprocity with the ecology of that place and its diverse inhabitants.

To be rooted means to have an awareness of the lives around us, to understand the intimate patterns and routines of those lives, and then to establish deep relationships with those lives over the long term. The care that flows from this outlook differs starkly from the hands-off reverence of the Green Revelation or the heavy-handed manipulations of the Green Revolution, both of which operate from outside those relational networks. The deep-rooted person shapes the world like a gospel singer leading a round of song, her voice mingled amid the multitude, while the unrooted person tries to conduct it, silent and aloof, from a podium.

A deep-rooted worldview begins to sprout, more or less automatically, when you start paying close attention to the world. Elder Bill says that his grandfather often instructed him to go into the forest and just "sit on a log and don't think." The great Oglala leader Luther Standing Bear similarly recalled that, while growing up in the 1860s, he was taught first to "sit motionless and watch the swallow, the tiny ants, or perhaps some small animal at its work" for hours at a time. This difference in upbringing, he believed, is where the "white mind" and the "Indian mind" first begin to diverge. Native children, he writes, raised largely outdoors, "are alert to their surroundings; their senses are not narrowed to observing only one another, and they cannot spend hours seeing nothing, hearing nothing, and thinking nothing in particular." This is the starting point of nearly all Indigenous wisdom traditions on earth: a clear head and sharp senses. Very often, to deepen this clarity into epiphanic insight, cultures have created elaborate rituals, usually through the use of song, fasting, sweat lodges, or plant medicine. In those moments of transcendence, says the Arikara scholar Michael Yellow Bird, the line between self and other begins to palpably dissolve, allowing a "conversation" to open up between humans and nonhumans. Once one learns to listen to these myriad voices—animal spirits, plant spirits, the spirits of dead ancestors, and even the spirits of stones and waters and stars—one can begin gleaning their wisdom and weaving it into one's worldview. The result is a set of beliefs, practices, and ethics that "flow," as the Chippewa scholar Stephen Wall writes, "from the land itself."*

The most common way that deep-rooted cultures make sense of wild voices is by personifying them. However, this act of anthropomorphism does not occur in the cartoonishly simplistic way that outsiders often imagine it does. Spirits (a rather flimsy word for a complex concept) are both kindred and alien. Umeek, attempting to shed the Eurocentric baggage that the word "spirit" carries, prefers to use the word "powers" instead. "There are many kinds of powers in the spiritual realm, some beneficial, some healing, some hurtful,

---

* It is striking how many Native creation myths contain the theme of humans being either shaped from the soil (clay, especially), plants, or parts of animals like feathers. Of course, this belief exists in the Christian tradition as well; in the book of Genesis, God is said to have shaped Adam from dust and then "breathed life" into his nostrils. The main difference—and it is an important one—is that unlike Native traditions, Christians no longer know where that act was meant to have taken place; in Burkhart's words, the Garden of Eden, like so many of our foundational myths, "floats free from the land." It is supremely ironic, then, though also fitting, that Columbus went looking for it, and never found it, here in the Americas.

some painful, and some even destructive to the point of causing death," he writes. These powers, he insists, are "the dominant powers of creation"—something less like mischievous ghosts than what scientists might call *ecological forces*, the complex flows of energy and self-organization through the web of life: the luminous shower of photons from the sun, the awesome heaving of wind and water, the force that through the green fuse drives the flower. Seen in this light, I can *almost* glimpse how, to people who have known them for millennia, the spirits of the wild are both invisible and (vaguely) intelligible.

Thoreau, revealing an openness to other ways of thought all too rare among men of his time, once came close to this realization on a canoe trip through Maine. One night, he awoke and was astonished to find a ring of phosphorescent fungi glowing inside a dead log. In that moment, he felt a rush of "pagan" awe. "I let science slide, and rejoiced in that light as if it had been a fellow creature," he writes. "I believed that the woods were not tenantless, but choke-full of honest spirits ... not an empty chamber, in which chemistry was left to work alone, but an inhabited house,—and for a few moments I enjoyed fellowship with them." The next morning, Thoreau told his Native guide about this encounter, and was informed that the Penobscot have a word for the light that dwells in the fungus: *Artoosoqu'*. "Nature must have made a thousand revelations to them which are still secrets to us," he marveled.

The hardest thing for many settlers to understand about rootedness is that it does not come quickly or easily. It is not a religion one can convert to in a moment of baptismal catharsis. Nor is it a form of enlightenment that arrives, as Zen sages say, in the instant between when a cup strikes the floor and when it explodes into shards. Rootedness *grows*. It deepens over the course of a lifetime, or, ideally, many lifetimes; the kind of place-based wisdom that the early explorers found when they landed here in North America was passed down across millennia, evolving with each telling. This is why Robin Wall Kimmerer refers to Indigenous societies as *old-growth cultures*. "Just as old-growth forests are richly complex, so too were the old-growth cultures that arose at their feet," she writes.

"Old-growth cultures" is a wonderfully apt phrase, in part because it highlights the fact that, though they retain their traditions and respect their history, Indigenous cultures are not frozen in time; the *old* is always balanced out by the *growth*. One curious thing I've noticed while reading Native philosophy is that, unlike many of the Earth First!–style prophets of wilderness preservation I grew up reading in the 1990s, virtually no Indigenous thinker I've run across advises that the solution to our ecological conundrum is simply to return to a Stone Age lifestyle. Albert Marshall, a Mi'kmaw elder, has coined a useful term, "Two-Eyed Seeing," for the side-by-side use of traditional ecological knowledge and cutting-edge science. Old-growth cultures seem to be marked by what might likewise be called Ten-Armed Being: a simultaneous balancing of many forms of subsistence—foraging and farming, fierce competition and mutual aid, advanced technology and ancient traditions—all tethered to specific ecosystems.

Talking with Elder Bill, I was suddenly struck by the fact that in all the years I'd spent thinking about arborescence, I had somehow overlooked a fundamental aspect (no, *the* fundamental aspect) of the wisdom of trees: the value of strong roots. In order to grow up, one must first grow *down*, building a deep relationship to local ecosystems and to other living beings. "Every human being needs to have multiple roots," wrote the philosopher Simone Weil. "It is necessary for him to draw well-nigh the whole of his moral, intellectual, and spiritual life by way of the environment of which he forms a natural part." Then again, it is relatively easy (for Weil, and for me) to recognize our culture's lack of rootedness. Actually remedying that absence is considerably less straightforward. Indeed, at times it can seem as hopeless as coaxing new life from stony ground. However, Elder Bill reassured me that a capacity for rootedness resides within everyone. "You will grow into that when you're ready," he said.

Setting down deeper, stronger roots will look different for each of us. For Elder Bill and Grandma Losah and Chiyokten, it has meant spending more time in the forest, keeping their ancestral traditions alive and fighting the steady creep of colonial capitalism. For Steen Christensen, it has meant working closely with the Hoopa Valley Tribe to reforest their land with native species. For my cousin Gia Gray, it has meant researching her genealogy and tending to the apricot tree in her backyard. For Ben Atkinson, it has meant climbing trees, walking barefoot, swimming naked—getting to know the earth, in other words, with his body as well as his brain. For Tim Takaro, it has meant getting arrested and sent to jail to stop the toxic creep of the carbon economy. For Remi, it has meant learning to grow and gather his own food. For me—perhaps the least rooted person I know—it has meant doing my best to stay put, to slow down, to learn my local ecology, and to follow the radical teachings of people like Umeek. As many of these efforts show, the attempt to regrow one's roots cannot simply be a private endeavor, like learning a new language or breaking a bad habit; it must be done collectively, and it will need to be carried out with a great deal of care. As Elder Bill points out, everyone has the capacity, and even the duty, to establish deeper roots. However, we should also never forget that some people have at least a ten-thousand-year head start.

In the decades to come, as climate chaos sends millions of people fleeing from their homes, the question of rootedness will become only more pressing—and more fraught. Of late, I've noticed that the language of rootedness has been co-opted by many of the world's bigots and bullies, who wield it like a cudgel against migrants and other minorities. Indeed, as Hannah Arendt points out in *The Origins of Totalitarianism*, one of the hallmarks of Nazism was the fundamental "rootlessness" of twentieth-century Germans—their withering traditions, loosening social ties, and evaporating sense of place. It was this very rootlessness, Arendt argues, that led Germans to project their anxieties onto their victims, whom they often recast as invasive pests. "Nationalism," she writes, "became the precious cement for binding together a centralized state and an atomized society." History has shown that there are few things more dangerous than large numbers of small-minded men feigning, and rabidly pursuing, the sense of strength and security that naturally flows from a rooted existence. Rootedness is, by definition, deeply entwined with the lives of others. Ethnonationalism, by contrast, is nothing more than blood and soil—which is to say, mythos and muck.

When I picture a state of deep-rootedness, I recall a trip I took more than a decade ago to an archipelago in northern British Columbia called Gwaii Haanas ("the isles of beauty"), which is home to the Haida people. On the island of Athlii Gwaii, Remi and I spent one dreamlike morning hiking barefoot through a palatial old-growth forest. A shin-deep layer of moss covered everything: the ground, the rocks, even the branches of the trees. It was as if the whole earth had sprouted a winter coat of thick green fur. The shattered, bleached trunks of old cedars stood like ruined columns. Fallen trees lay everywhere, dissolving to dirt, and from them sprang rows of new saplings. One tree, a Sitka spruce, was said to be more than nine hundred years old. Standing at its base, I wrapped my arms around it, measuring its size against my own. It would have taken seven more people to encircle it entirely. I felt like a child—which, to the tree, I very much was.

I later learned that the trees there on Athlii Gwaii were allowed to grow so old because of sacrifices made by the Haida people over many millennia. Some of the older cedars bore long vertical scars on their trunks from where, centuries earlier, Haida weavers had stripped away their bark, careful to leave enough so the tree could survive. Others had been set aside to make into totem poles by carvers thinking many centuries ahead. Each of those ancient trees represented an unbroken chain of care. They are still standing today due to the work of the Haida park rangers, known as watchmen, who patrol the forest. They stand thanks to the bravery of Haida blockaders who, in 1985, prevented this island from being clear-cut. They stand thanks to the ancestors of those blockaders, who managed to survive the ravages of smallpox, missionaries, and colonialism. And they stand because of the careful ministrations of every preceding generation of Haida people, dating back to the very birth of the forest.

The oral literature of the Haida maintains that their ancestors were here on these islands long before the first trees even arrived. To outsiders, this may sound like a mythic, rather than a historical, truth. But, I was amazed to learn, it isn't. The archaeological record suggests that humans first migrated to the islands more than thirteen thousand years ago, around the end of the last ice age, when the land was still a shrub-strewn tundra. Ancestors of the Haida people may well have watched the very first cedars sprout up from the soil, and they have been tending to them ever since. This level of rootedness is a civilizational feat on par with any of the great wonders of the world—greater, even, because instead of being carved from dead stone, this one remains alive. I can't help but ask myself: What is my culture creating today that will still be around in the year 15000? Some nuclear waste will still be fizzing somewhere beneath the earth, and a few mutated genes will be floating around, but by then every skyscraper we've built will have toppled, every bridge fallen back into the sea. Barring some miracle, every last trace of the Great Uprooting will likely be covered over by layers of deep soil.

It is important to remind ourselves that the Haida did not achieve this incredible feat by virtue of some otherworldly quality that the rest of us lack. They are not living embodiments of ecological purity, trapped in a timeless past. They are not—to borrow the poet Harmony Holiday's perfect phrase—"monsters of innocence." But they are grounded. They know their history; they know their lands; they know their waters; they know their relations. They know their ancient traditions, and they know how to innovate upon those traditions. They have been growing with the land for millennia, and they will likely find a way to continue doing so long into the future. The question is whether the rest of us are smart enough to listen to what they have been trying to tell us for centuries.

In 1966, Chief Skidegate, the leader of the Haida people, proclaimed:

> People are like trees, and groups of people are like the forests. While the forests are composed of many different kinds of trees, these trees intertwine their roots so strongly that it is impossible for the strongest winds which blow on our islands to uproot the forest.... In the same way the people of our Islands, composed of members of nations and races from all over the world, are beginning to intertwine their roots so ably that no troubles will affect them. Just as one tree standing alone would soon be destroyed by the first strong wind which came along, so it is impossible for any person, any family, or any community to stand alone against the troubles of this world.

+

Five years after the blockade first began, a small encampment of protesters remains at Fairy Creek, but their ranks have steadily dwindled; out of the thousands who once gathered there, only a skeleton crew of little more than a dozen remain, mostly just to keep an eye on the forest and raise the alarm should the loggers try to quietly move into the watershed area once more. The news coverage has dried up, and the public's fickle gaze has moved on. Many old trees have been cut down in the surrounding area, and they continue to fall throughout the province.

Today, it is common to hear former blockaders at Fairy Creek remark that they lost in their battle against the timber industry, because they failed to secure their ultimate goal of a province-wide (or better yet, a nationwide) ban on clear-cutting old growth. However, being so close to the fight, it is easy for them to overlook the victories they helped secure. The logging of the ancient trees all around Ridge Camp and down into Fairy Creek has been halted. Large swaths of old growth have been placed under a rolling deferral order, which the Pacheedaht elected council, in a remarkable turn, supported. Best of all, in 2023, the federal and provincial government signed a new, billion-dollar program to protect more than two million acres of forested land in BC, by placing it under the control of First Nations and paying them to keep the trees standing.

I had come to Fairy Creek in part because I wanted to know why they were winning and our pipeline protest was not. In the end, the answer was quite simple: They succeeded because people wanted to be there. Their blockade felt both radical and hopeful in ways that our treehouse blockade did not. We both stood against something, but they stood *for* something as well. And then, of course, there were the trees themselves: All those arboreal sisters and mothers and grandmothers, looming over us raucous toddlers of nature, silently urging us to emulate their restraint, their reciprocity, and most of all, their rootedness—to the land and to one another.

One evening at Ridge Camp, Elvin, Bone Dog, and I hiked out to a nearby logging road, which provided a sweeping vista of the valley below and the mountains beyond, in order to watch the sunset. Elvin explained to me that this was where the very first blockade had been set up, back in the summer of 2020. A gargantuan crosswise slice of an old-growth cedar—the very same one that started the protest—stood there in the middle of the road. I took a photograph of it. Across it, someone had painted the words "Still here"—a hauntingly poetic phrase, suggesting both the Indigenous people who never ceded this land and the blockade itself, which refused to be crushed. I sat on a sun-bleached stump and looked out into the hazy distance. The sky was the color of an illumined eyelid. Parts of the nearby mountains were furred over with dense forest, while others were marred with a mange of fresh clear-cuts and the cicatrices of logging roads. It was so ugly and so beautiful, all at once.

Elvin tilted his head back and let out a howl, which rang across the pink-lit valley.

A long silence followed.

He said that back in August, when the blockade was at its height, he would howl down below to the next camp over, which would prompt the blockaders there to start howling, too, and then the next camp, and the next. Sometimes, he added with a laugh, people's dogs would join in as well. This image stirred something deep in me. In those moments, I imagined, if one listened hard enough, one would have also heard the chirp of frogs and the chitter of squirrels, the inscrutable mutterings of ravens and, perhaps, farther off in the distance, the soft, liquid croon of wolves, shy in their dark hollows. And yet-fainter still: the roar of rivers, the hush of trees, the osseous crackle of soil, the high, loud silence of stars. All across the land, this dusk chorus would rise, and soon the empty valley would be filled to spilling over with the voices of so many kindred strangers.

+

It is common, in these surreal times, when the summer sun bleeds at noon and the light seems to be dimming upon all our collective hopes, to hear people talk about the end of the world. But as the Aboriginal scholar Tyson Yunkaporta has argued, it is a dangerous delusion to view the coming disasters as a single apocalypse. The apocalypse will be multiple, local, and asynchronous. Many will die, but others will likely find a way to survive. To reduce this planetary rash of mass death and agony, over the course of centuries, down to a neat binary between eschaton and the status quo is not just dishonest; it's cowardly. It erases our responsibility and quiets our conscience: Either the world will end (in which case I don't have to get off my ass and do something!) or it won't (in which case, I don't have to get off my ass and do something!).

In *The Uninhabitable Earth*, the journalist David Wallace-Wells manages to clarify the nature of the climate crisis by reducing it to a clear, tree-shaped choice: Do we want to warm the planet by an average of one degree centigrade, two degrees centigrade, three degrees centigrade, or four degrees centigrade over the preindustrial norm? Above four degrees of warming is so nightmarish, Wallace-Wells writes, it is barely worth contemplating. At that temperature, "New York City would be hotter than present-day Bahrain, one of the planet's hottest spots." We have now passed the 1.5-degree threshold, and we continue to build out the infrastructure that will lock us into yet more warming. It is estimated that if we use up all of our known fossil fuel reserves, the resulting emissions could push the climate to an unthinkable eight degrees above average. At that level of warming, Wallace-Wells writes, "humans at the equator and in the tropics would not be able to move around without dying; hardly any land on the planet would be capable of efficiently producing any of the food we now eat . . . and what are today literally unprecedented and intolerable droughts and heat waves would be the quotidian condition of whatever human life was able to endure."

One, two, three, four, five, six, seven, eight: Each of those little-sounding numbers represents a potential future we can travel down, a potential branch in our collective timeline. The world of zero degrees would have been far more livable than that of one degree, but the world of two degrees will be yet worse; the world of three degrees will be hellish, but the world of four degrees will be more hellish still. We have countless choices to make, and each one matters.

One way to rid oneself of both a paralyzing sense of doom and a debilitating sense of apathy, in other words, is to apply tree thinking to our understanding of time itself. How one envisions time, it turns out, has a profound effect on how one sees the world and how one lives in it. Many Native cultures conceive of time not as a straight line but as either a circle or a spiral looping through the cycles of the seasons and the long arcs of human birth and death. The Potawatomi philosopher Kyle Powys Whyte notes that his people think in *deep time*, understanding that "we're just operating in what must be a smidgen of all of the time that ever existed." Thinking on this sequoiac timescale helps put things in perspective, easing "the panic that whatever is happening right now is completely unprecedented." The Apache philosopher Viola F. Cordova notes that her people see time as participatory and entangled, rather than abstract and distant. "Since we are participants in a process of motion and change, we know that we can affect the future," she writes. "If we chop down all the trees, we will live in a world without trees. . . . There is no glorious 'future' out 'there' waiting for us to arrive. We build the future through our present actions."

Over the decade it has taken me to write this book—a mere ten rings on the trunk of a tree, forty seasons, a hundred new gray hairs at my temples, a thousand pages sprouted and shed—trees have molded my brain in myriad ways, large and small. Thinking in trees has helped me see myself as kin to other species. It has allowed me to ponder how the actions of our ancestors have shaped the gnarls of the present, and to consider how my actions might shape someone's life a hundred years hence. Most recently, it has revealed to me—a perpetual wanderer, born of wanderers—the necessity, the beautiful necessity, of setting down deeper roots, and listening to those whose roots run deeper still.

The easiest way to begin thinking like a tree, I've learned, is to recognize how not to think. Thomas Aquinas famously put forward a doctrine of divine simplicity, believing that God, being the simplest of all things, also sat highest on the ladder of nature. Throughout history, this reductive, hierarchical, totalizing view of the universe has led to the devastation of both local ecologies and local belief systems. By contrast, notes Cordova, old-growth cultures are stubbornly branchy. Rather than seeking out one ironclad truth that dominates all others, they make room for diverse views, understanding that they sprang from diverse ecosystems. "The challenge to find a way to live on the earth without wrecking it is so great, that we cannot afford to limit ourselves to only one way of thinking," she writes. Scholars have called this worldview a "unified plurality": many ways of being, all rooted to one earth.

In perilous times, it is tempting to eschew branchiness in favor of an easy reductiveness and a sneaky segregationism. If a person loves wilderness, then he gives up on trying to build greener cities; if he loves cities, then he scorns the woods. If he loves his own race, or his own gender, or his own cause, then he is willing to trample all others. A narrow mind finds itself obsessed with the false promise of purity; it scorns half measures and small victories, it makes the perfect the enemy of the good, and it makes the evil the twin of the imperfect. Though reductive thinking can sometimes feel wonderfully sharp, the end result is a shrinking of the soul and a contraction of the realm of the possible.

An arborescent mind, by contrast, branches, prunes, gnarls. It is open to many needs, many theories, many allegiances. It meshes with others, sharing their wisdom. Then, awake to its own shadowy tendencies, it pares away falsities and failed techniques. It focuses not on how things are, but on how they grow. And it understands that growth, lest it become wasteful and destructive, must always be balanced with sacrifice; it prunes even as it branches, it bends even as it gnarls. Over time, an arborescent mind gives shape to an arborescent life: we begin setting down deeper roots, cultivating greater patience, forging stronger bonds to others. My one hope for this book is that it might help sprout a new little forest of such arborescent beings, united in a long, slow, wild state of coflourishing, across various lands and across time. As Julia Butterfly Hill once told me, "We are ancestors of the future, and we need to start living that way."

Whenever I find myself falling prey to pessimism, fearing that the wild green thing George Eliot once called "the growing good of the world" is withering to dust, I look to the saviors of trees—a peaceful but unruly mob of wise elders, fiery youths, fussy scientists, dreamy artists, feral anarchists, esoteric thinkers, daring inventors, and quiet gardeners, all dedicated to the task of helping beings wholly unlike themselves. The work they perform requires self-sacrifice, but it is not thankless. For their labors, they are given back sage counsel, plain but potent words, passed from one arborescent life-form to another: Branch wildly. Prune carefully. Widen your sense of kinship. Deepen your sense of time. Know history's gnarls. Embrace otherness. Send down deep roots. Live with dikost. Die with grace.

Grow, so that the earth might continue to grow.

EPILOGUE: SOIL

WHILE RUNNING my little tree-climbing clinic among the ancient trees up at Ridge Camp, there was only one person I never managed to get up into the branches: the man we all called Smiley. Each day, he tried valiantly to learn, but he never made it more than a few inches off the ground. Nevertheless, he remained undaunted. He vowed to go home, start doing some pull-ups, and then return to Fairy Creek. "I'll be back soon enough," he said.

Among the land defenders up there on the mountain, Smiley stood out. At a glance, he looked more like a fishmonger than a blockader: a stout man in his sixties, his long gray hair messily contained by a red watch cap, bundled against the cold in a thick, purple, hand-knitted wool sweater. I caught glimpses of his life in casual conversation. Born Gerald Kearney, he first worked as a lawyer, then he shed his suit and bought a head shop called Petite Amsterdam, then he sold that so he could move out to the seashore and live aboard a sailboat with his cat, Moogins. He liked to say he was now "homeless on a yacht." Around camp he shared tales of living on the sea, told rude jokes, and tried to recruit new members to the Green Party.

A few days after he arrived, Smiley left for home. That morning we had awoken to find the air filled with cold white fog. Beams of molten light angled through the trees. We all stood around outside the kitchen tent, taking photos and shouting in wonder; if we stood just right, we discovered, the sunbeams struck the back of our heads and burst into coronas of golden spines. Smiley paused to admire the atmospheric light show with the rest of us, then he gave a few quick hugs goodbye and headed off. The trail he was planning to follow that day was somewhat treacherous, so one of us offered to hike with him, but he politely refused, assuring us he would go slow and be careful.

We never saw Smiley again. Nor, to my knowledge, did anyone else. We still don't know precisely what happened to him.

In the loose weave of the Fairy Creek community, people frequently slipped away unnoticed, so alarms were not raised until a week later, when someone posted on Facebook that Smiley had never returned to reclaim his sailboat or his cat. By that point, I was safely back home. I called the local police repeatedly, giving them every detail I could recall about that morning, in hopes it would sharpen their search parameters. A day or two later, the police and some specially trained dogs hiked between the two camps looking for him, but they found no clues.

As of this writing, Smiley's body has never been found. It is almost certainly still up there on the mountain, being slowly absorbed by the old trees and deep moss.

+

In the years that followed, I often found myself thinking about Smiley's death. I was haunted by his sudden disappearance and saddened by the thought that his surviving family members had no grave to visit. The rituals of burial and mourning are designed to give us closure. But his life remained forever open, unfinished, a story without an end.

I later returned to Ridge Camp with some other land defenders, and together we spent a day hiking through the watershed, hoping to find some clue of what had happened to him. It quickly became apparent, however, that it was a lost cause. The land was thick with plant life, and there was so much land to cover.

I began to think about death, and soil, and trees, and how those things intermingle. Around this time, I became fascinated by the rise of what are called woodland cemeteries, where bodies are placed beneath trees rather than traditional gravestones. Some of the people who reserved plots in these forests told me they saw it as a way of being reborn as a tree; others told me it was a way of protecting a patch of wilderness in perpetuity. I immediately saw the appeal. I ran the math and figured out that if every cemetery in the United States were covered in woodlands instead of mown lawns, those forests would cover roughly one million acres, an area larger than Yosemite.

After talking it through with my family, I decided that I, too, want my body to be laid to rest in a forest. I liked the idea that my atoms will be gathered into the dark heft of a tree and reside there for a century or ten, in a state of swaying stillness. But a cynical voice in my head worried this was all just a lot of wishful thinking with no basis in science—metempsychosis by another name. Where, I wondered, do we actually go, biologically speaking, when we die?

The scientific answer to this question turns out to be more complicated—and more wondrous—than I'd imagined. The earth beneath our feet, I quickly learned, is much more than just a big pile of dirt. Soil is, in some sense, both a being and a bardo: It is a living multiplicity that takes us in, breaks us down, and then regenerates us in new forms. In *Grounded*, the scientist Alisa Bryce relays the astonishing fact that "there are more microbes in a single teaspoon of soil than there are people on the planet." Without those microbes, without that invisible superabundance of life, the dead would continually pile up, eventually squeezing out the realm of the living.

Soil is created when lichens latch on to hard stone; soon after, they begin oozing out acids and extending their hyphae into its cracks, breaking the rock down into smaller and smaller pieces. This slow chewing of stone—what scientists call biochemical weathering—releases a flush of nutrients, some of which the lichen absorbs. (This process is aided by what's known as biomechanical weathering, which is, in effect, the earth chewing itself.) Eventually, a thin layer of soil forms; plants, fungi, and microbes spring up in that layer of dirt; and then they die and are broken down in turn. Each death contributes a tiny share of soil back to the earth, fostering more life, and more death.

After I finished reading her book, I wrote to Bryce to ask: Assuming a person is buried beneath a tree, approximately how much of that person's atoms will actually get sucked up by the tree's roots?

Her response delicately let the air out of this neopagan fantasy of mine. "At a guess, I don't think too much of a person would end up as a tree," she wrote back. She suspected that, since "the soil ecosystem has to do the work of decomposition," most of a person's atoms would simply end up "bound to the soil."

In other words, even if your body is laid to rest beneath a tree, you will not really be reborn as a tree.

You will be reborn as a forest.

+

Thinking about my body returning to the soil forces me to confront one of the deepest, if simplest, questions in all of environmental philosophy: Why should we care about what happens to the earth once we're gone?

The most common answer I hear is that people want to leave behind a habitable planet for their children and grandchildren. But Remi and I don't have children, and neither do many of our friends. In this we are far from alone; the birth rate in nearly every industrialized nation has begun to decline, and it is projected to plunge further in the decades to come, swelling the ranks of the childless. Surely this does not liberate us from any wider responsibility to the future. That is one form of liberation—the moral free fall of pure nihilism—I would not wish upon anyone, least of all myself.

Trees help us outgrow this grim philosophy, both by widening our sense of compassion and by transforming our understanding of time itself. When one walks into an ancient forest, the long slow passage of time becomes tangible, vitally *present*. The beauty of the place knits us, emotionally and ethically, to both the past and the future. The geologist Marcia Bjornerud refers to this quality as *timefulness*: "the habit of seeing things not merely as they are now, but also recognizing how they evolved—and will continue to evolve—over time." We can suppress this sense of timefulness, just as we can stifle our sense of relationality, but we are ultimately only starving ourselves.

Once, while staying in a mountain hut, I struck up a conversation with a social worker who often counseled patients at the very end of their lives. I asked her what their biggest concern is, when death was mere moments away. She said that most people just want to know that their families are taken care of, and they hope they are remembered as having been a good person. I was startled by this response. What it suggests is that, in the end, a dying person cares less about what they are losing (which is, essentially, everything), and more about what they are leaving behind for others. Life—its messy, stubborn persistence—consoles us, even in death. As the author Barbara Ehrenreich writes, "It is one thing to die into a dead world and, metaphorically speaking, leave one's bones to bleach on a desert lit only by a dying star. It is another thing to die into the actual world, which seethes with life, with agency other than our own, and, at the very least, with endless possibility."

For us to live fully, we must care about the fate of those who will outlive us, just as those in the past cared for us. Otherwise, the ecology of time itself is severed, and we find ourselves utterly alone—truly dead.

+

Up at Ridge Camp, when the land defenders sang protest songs around the fire, I could never quite bring myself to join in; I felt too self-conscious, too acidly analytical. But there was one song they sang that I eventually grew to love. I still catch myself humming its melody from time to time.

The lyrics went something like this:

Here we stand
by the river
through the wind,
the rain, and snow.
When the wind blows
our branches may quiver.
We will sway
but we will stay.
And one day
when we fall—
we will rot
and crumble.
But we'll know
we have given our all.
To feed
the seeds of tomorrow.

AUTHOR'S NOTE

REGARD THIS book, like all of my work, as a living thing, which still has room to grow. If you have any comments, suggestions, questions, or feedback for future editions, please email me at robertmoor.intrees@gmail.com.

A brief note of thanks: First and last, I owe the existence of this book to Remi Morawski, my co-climber of life's strange tree. I also owe an incalculable debt to my brilliant editor, Jon Cox, whom I've known nearly as long as my husband, and with whom I argue nearly as often. Additional thanks are owed to: my family, especially my dad, who cheerfully braved my genealogical interrogation, and who has never questioned my strange career choice; my perspicacious editors, Megan Hogan, Evangeline Stanford, Daniel Crewe, and Amanda Betts; my friend and sage legal counsel, Conrad Rippy; my valiant agent, Bonnie Nadell; my botanical fact-checkers, Lise Nehring and Andrew Hipp; Tim Kovar and Peter Jenkins for teaching me to climb tall trees; the editorial team at *The New Yorker* for their work on parts of the bonsai chapter, especially Daniel Zalewski; and Jon Karp, who saw a grand future for *In Trees* when it was just a frail sprout. I owe a great deal to the friends who helped shape draft after draft of this book: Ferris Jabr, Sandy Allen, Andrew Marantz, Rebecca Giggs, Will Hunt, Lance Richardson, Holly Haworth, Ben Goldfarb, Brandon Keim, Rahawa Haile, John Vaillant, Arno Kopecky, Peter Wood, and Zach St. George. Thanks to Carolyn Levin and Maxime Faille for their prudent legal advice. Lastly, I am grateful to all the thinkers and scholars I cite in these pages, as well as the ones I didn't have space to mention: Giovanna Calvino, Adrian Bejan, Katie Holten, Andrea Bowers, John Quigley, Yuri Mazurov, Sebastien Boret, Serge Aroles, Barbara Hawkins, Oskar Franklin, Mark Holton, Sue Darlington, Aaron Ellison, Albertina Nugteren, Steven Thair, Diane Haddad, Judy Rose Weaver, Rosamund Hogan, Roger Underwood, Russell Leong, David Geary, Daegan Miller, Alistair Tones, Lynne Feeley, Greg Rothman, Patrick Young, Paul Rogers, Nancy Folbre, Beth Campbell, George Dyson, Susan Morrow, Matthew Hall, Jim Ace, Paul Bensemann, Kent Bar-Shov, Fredrik Hjelm, Catriona Kelly, Kevin D. Hunt, Steven Mintz, Michelle D. Elleray, Tsim D. Schneider, Benjamin R. Jordan, Benedikt Meyer, Rosmarie Zeller, Ariane Huber, Hamid Dabashi, Martin Surbeck, Nayanjot Lahiri, Zanna Clay, Suzanne Simard, Matthew Beatty, Barbara Fruth, Graeme Berlyn, Giorgio Ascoli, Nikolaus Amrhein, Vivek Venkataraman, Irene Taylor, Michael J. Sheridan, Jacqueline Jones-Peace, Denise Su, Holly Dugan, Darren Speece, Cleve Hicks, Rui Diogo, Nate Stephenson, Frank Sievers, Pete Nelson, Dorothy Kennedy, Derek Bousé, Peter Bassett, Gelya Frank, James Andrew Cowell, Daniel Clément, Kathy Strain, Nancy Turner, David Neale, Jared Farmer, Kyle Smith, Sumana Roy, Lisa Samuelson, Patrick House, Michael Lambert, Ankit Bhardwaj, Justin Smith-Ruiu, Robert Foley, Philippe Charland, Tania Cordes, Will Bryan, Joseph Gazing Wolf, Vitali Bartash, Pam Crabtree, Jen Muranetz, Jenny Odell, Kwame Anthony Appiah, and Ruth Plenty Sweetgrass-She Kills-De La Cruz.

ABOUT THE AUTHOR

Hailed by critics as a "philosopher on foot," Robert Moor is a bestselling author living in Halfmoon Bay, British Columbia. His first book, *On Trails*, garnered the National Outdoor Book Award, the Pacific Northwest Book Award, and the William Saroyan International Prize. His writing has appeared in *The New Yorker*, *The Atlantic*, *Harper's*, *New York*, *Outside*, *Emergence*, and *n+1*, among other publications.